Producing Queer Youth

"Berliner challenges existing truisms about digital media and youth empowerment with a thoughtful examination of anti-bullying rhetoric, the logic of public service announcements and public health messaging more generally, and the discourses of neoliberal resilience that undercut possibilities for solidarity and subversion in social movements. Rather than approach youth media without examining the biases of ageism and classicism, Berliner encourages readers—from her position as an experienced educator—to consider the media practices of queer youth on their own terms."—Elizabeth Losh, *William and Mary, USA*

Producing Queer Youth challenges popular ideas about online media culture as a platform for empowerment, cultural transformation, and social progress. Based on over three years of participatory action research with queer teen media-makers and textual analysis of hundreds of youth-produced videos and popular media campaigns, the book unsettles assumptions that having a "voice" and gaining visibility and recognition necessarily equate to securing rights and resources. Instead, Berliner offers a nuanced picture of openings that emerge for youth media producers as they negotiate the structures of funding and publicity and manage their identities with digital self-representations. Examining youth media practices within broader communication history and critical media pedagogy, she forwards an approach to media production that re-centers the process of making as the site of potential learning and social connection. Ultimately, she reframes digital media participation as a struggle for—rather than, in itself, evidence of—power.

Lauren S. Berliner is Assistant Professor in the School of Interdisciplinary Arts and Sciences at the University of Washington Bothell, USA.

Routledge Research in Gender, Sexuality, and Media

Edited by Mary Celeste Kearney, University of Notre Dame

The *Routledge Research in Gender, Sexuality, and Media* series aims to publish original research in the areas of feminist and queer media studies, with a particular but not exclusive focus on gender and sexuality. In doing so, this series brings to the market cutting-edge critical work that refreshes, reshapes, and redirects scholarship in these related fields while contributing to a better global understanding of how gender and sexual politics operate within historical and current mediascapes.

Queercore
Queer Punk Media Subculture
Curran Nault

Lifestyle Media in American Culture
Gender, Class, and the Politics of Ordinariness
Maureen E. Ryan

Emergent Feminisms
Complicating a Postfeminist Media Culture
Edited by Jessalynn Keller and Maureen Ryan

Producing Queer Youth
The Paradox of Digital Media Empowerment
Lauren S. Berliner

Producing Queer Youth
The Paradox of Digital Media Empowerment

Lauren S. Berliner

NEW YORK AND LONDON

First published 2018
by Routledge
711 Third Avenue, New York, NY 10017

and by Routledge
2 Park Square, Milton Park, Abingdon, Oxon OX14 4RN

Routledge is an imprint of the Taylor & Francis Group, an informa business

© 2018 Taylor & Francis

The right of Lauren S. Berliner to be identified as author of this work has been asserted by her in accordance with sections 77 and 78 of the Copyright, Designs and Patents Act 1988.

All rights reserved. No part of this book may be reprinted or reproduced or utilised in any form or by any electronic, mechanical, or other means, now known or hereafter invented, including photocopying and recording, or in any information storage or retrieval system, without permission in writing from the publishers.

Trademark notice: Product or corporate names may be trademarks or registered trademarks, and are used only for identification and explanation without intent to infringe.

Library of Congress Cataloging in Publication Data
A catalog record for this book has been requested

ISBN: 978-0-415-79084-0 (hbk)
ISBN: 978-1-315-21281-4 (ebk)

Typeset in Sabon
by Out of House Publishing

Printed in the United Kingdom
by Henry Ling Limited

In Memory of
Miriam Berliner
and
Gloria Israel

Contents

List of Figures	viii
Acknowledgments	ix
Introduction	1
1 The Problem with *Youth Voices*	22
2 "Look at Me, I'm Doing Fine!": The Conundrum of Legibility, Visibility, and Identity Management in Queer Viral Videos	54
3 Vernacular Voices: Business Gets Personal in Public Service Announcements	85
4 "I Can't Talk When I'm Supposed to Say Something": Negotiating Expression in a Queer-Youth-Produced Anti-Bullying Video	118
Conclusion: Out of the Closet and into the Tweets	138
Index	155

Figures

i.1	Google Trends comparison of terms in news media	11
i.2	A comparison of Google Trends search terms between January 2008 and January 2013	12
1.1	Image from Canadian Women's Creative Foundation *Girls' Voice Contest*	23
2.1	Jamey Rodemeyer's *It Gets Better Project* video, May 4, 2011	55
2.2	Dan Savage and Terry Miller's inaugural *It Gets Better Project* video, 2010	57
2.3, 2.4, and 2.5	Posters associated with "ReTeaching Gender and Sexuality" promotional materials	74
2.6	Still from "SupaFriends: The Fight for Acceptance" (Global Action Project), St. Clair et al., 2013, YouTube video still	76
3.1	Yul Brynner addresses smokers in a 1985 American Cancer Society public service announcement (PSA)	86
3.2	Pam Laffin in "I Can't Breathe," Massachusetts Department of Public Health, 1999	94
3.3	Dr. John Clarke raps about how to prevent H1N1 in "H1N1 Rap by Dr. Clarke," 2009, YouTube video still	101
3.4	Sascha Sternecker in "I am…" 2011, YouTube video still	106
3.5	Sascha Sternecker threatens her scale with a hammer in "goodbye, scale!" 2011, YouTube video still	108
C.1	Elementary students produce an anti-bullying music video in the *South Park* episode, "Butterballs", 2012	139
C.2	"Who Do U Think U R?" Cypress Ranch High School Anti-Bully Lip Dub, YouTube video still	140

Acknowledgments

One night in the summer of 1997 I slipped out of my parents' house and stole away to an unmarked storefront in the middle of a strip mall in White Plains, New York, with my childhood friend Ilan Weissman in the passenger seat. Ilan was taking me to my first meeting at The Loft, a group for queer and questioning teens. There I would meet Tey Meadow, who would become a lifelong friend and colleague, and an eclectic cadre of teens crammed into a room the size of a storage closet. We had very little in common other than zip codes and the rainbow ribbons we strategically concealed from most people but had, on rare occasions, displayed on our backpacks and water bottles, like passports to a queer nation. We were too young for the bars, and just starting to date. This was our only space to connect with others.

These days, queer teens can find one another other in less than a minute and with very little fanfare, assuming they have a reliable internet connection and a device. Clearly the options for locating other queer teens look different than they did before Web 2.0. But the purpose—connecting—remains the same. This book takes up the challenges and opportunities that digital media offer queer youth, with the intent of helping to identify where and how meaning can be made. There are countless people who made that possible for me, and I am sincerely grateful.

The creativity and spirit of the youth at the Hillcrest Youth Center, the volunteers, and Sophia Arredondo, the HYC's former program coordinator, formed the heart of this book. I honor their trust in me and am grateful to have had the opportunity to share so much time together. The text cannot possibly capture the enormous place they hold in my heart. My sincere thanks to Diana Fisher and the Collective Voices Foundation for funding and supporting the media workshop, and for the many friends who provided us with cameras, books, guest workshops, and their acting talents.

I am especially indebted to Christian Anderson, Toby Beauchamp, Jaimie Baron, Dan Berger, Debra Berliner, Arianna Ochoa Camacho, micha cárdenas, Erin Cory, Johanna Crane, Ben Gardner, Jennifer Hsu, x *Acknowledgments*

Nora Kenworthy, Ron Krabill, Kate Levitt, Stephanie Ann Martin, Carl McKinney, Reece Peck, Pooja Rangan, Josh Rosenau, Pawan Singh, Emily Thuma, and Kara Wentworth, for not only nourishing the project on multiple levels, but also providing the comfort, guidance, and strength that made it feel possible to write a book.

Other colleagues and friends who have read sections, thought about the project, and offered input and inspiration for the manuscript at various stages include: Amaranth Borsuk, Marisa Brandt, Nancy Chang, S. Charusheela, Jonathan Cohn, Shannon Cram, Negin Dahya, Sarah Dowling, Jody Early, Emily Fuller, Kristin Gustafson, Susan Harewood, Kate Hoffman, Nia Lam, Maggie Levantovskya, Lauren Lichty, Kelli Moore, Katrina Pederson, Susan Pearlman, Kyla Schuller, Sid Jordan, Monika Sengul-Jones, Jed Murr, Andy Rice, Eric Stewart, Wadiya Udell, Amoshaun Toft, Kalindi Vora, Michaela Walsh, Isra Ali, Allyson Field, Alka Kurian, Dolissa Medina, Janelle Silva, Jade Power-Sotomayor, Thea Quiray Tagle, Crispin Thurlow, Miriam Bartha, Julie Shayne, and Camille Walsh.

At the University of Washington Bothell, I am especially lucky to share in community with a remarkable group of individuals who inspire me in the fight and in the classroom. I am grateful for the camaraderie and wisdom of too many colleagues to name—in particular, my collaborators in Media and Communication Studies and in Cultural Studies, Jennifer Bean and Eric Ames in Cinema and Media Studies, and Ralina Joseph and LeiLani Nishime in the Commmunication Department at UW Seattle. I would also like to recognize the role my remarkable students at UW Bothell have played in stretching my thinking. The students in the Cultural Studies graduate program have been especially impactful. I am also very grateful to my Dean, Bruce Burgett, for ongoing, enthusiastic support.

The book began as a dissertation in the Department of Communication at UC San Diego, where I was lucky to benefit from the wisdom and encouragement of many friends and mentors. Lisa Cartwright and Brian Goldfarb were exceptionally committed advisors, convincing me that it could be possible to craft an interdisciplinary, praxis-oriented scholarly identity that seeks to strengthen the contiguity between academia and the world that contains it. Brian has continued to offer me guidance throughout the book project, and his friendship and unmatched enthusiasm for the work are a constant source of strength. Since my early graduate school days Zeinabu irene Davis has motivated me to place practice at the center of my work, and has been a valuable sounding-board and collaborator. Nitin Govil first introduced me to pathways for applied media studies research and has offered me tremendous practical advice along with stunning insight. Having had Shelley Streeby and Roddey Reid as committee members is also reflected in the work—I deeply appreciate their rigorous and thoughtful approaches to Cultural Studies. I also wish

Acknowledgments xi

to thank Chandra Mukerji for facilitating the writing group that helped me to find my scholarly voice, David Serlin for helping me to develop my scholarly spirit, and Patrick Anderson for leading me towards theory that shaped my understanding of performance in everyday life. I am also grateful for the feedback I have received from colleagues at various talks and conference presentations, particularly Alex Juhasz, Katie Morrissey, Liz Losh, Leah Shafer, Sam Ford, Henry Jenkins, and Mary L. Gray.

The editorial team at Routledge is magnificent. It is a gift to have people read your work not just for the clarity of the prose, but for the strength of the political intervention and purpose.

Felisa Salvago-Keyes has overseen the manuscript since its inception, and has been patient and supportive throughout. Christina Kowalski was also immensely helpful. I was provided with very meticulous and useful feedback by my anonymous reviewers and thank the editors for securing them. I am also lucky to have worked with the Routledge Research in Gender, Sexuality, and Media series editor Mary Celeste Kearney, whose scholarship has inspired me since I first encountered it early on in graduate school, leading me to believe that studying the politics and nuances of youth media production could reveal broader truths about social organization and power. And Catherine Dunn deserves a medal for close reading and copy-editing. I am also grateful to Laurie Predergast for indexing and Dara Cerv for a book cover that I hope people will judge the contents by.

The world needs to watch for rising academic star Meshell Sturgis, who was instrumental in the production of the book with invaluable research assistance. This project benefited from her intellectual curiosity, insights, and fantastic organization. Jessie Dixon also offered excellent research assistance early in the manuscript development.

The Helen Riaboff Whiteley Center provided me an idyllic setting for gathering my ideas and feeling the stillness that was necessary to write. I am appreciative of the University of Washington Bothell for supporting my multiple visits, which were essential for the completion of the book.

I could also not have written this without the support, guidance, and love of several friends and childcare providers who made it possible to birth and develop both a new human and a book at the same time, among them Mirjana Milosavljevic Balevski, Melissa Braxton, Elissa Josse, Alice Pederson, and Katie Zimmerman. My family has also been important in this endeavor—David and Donna Berliner, Debra Berliner, Josh Rosenau, Rob Berliner, and Miles and Ollie.

My incredible partner, Minda Martin, deserves all of my gratitude for sustaining and invigorating me, as does our child, Lucien, who delights and distracts me in wonderful and creative ways each day. They both help me to pick up the work—and put it down, too.

As the dedication reads, this is for my grandmothers, Miriam Berliner and Gloria Israel. They taught me everything I know about how to open

xii *Acknowledgments*

myself to the unexpected, simultaneously manage multiple tasks, and to love with all I have. A few months before I submitted the final manuscript, they both passed away within a week of each other. I know that they would be so proud to see this in print.

Introduction

The fall of 2010 marked a moment of crisis in which the United States was beset with anxieties surrounding queer youth suicide. For a period of months, it seemed as though every week another teen suicide was announced in the news media, with at least ten reported in September alone (Badash 2010).

> Billy Lucas (15) Indiana; Cody J. Barker (17) Wisconsin; Seth Walsh (13) California; Tyler Clementi (18) New Jersey; Asher Brown (13) Texas; Harrison Chase Brown (15) Colorado; Raymond Chase (19) Rhode Island; Felix Sacco (17) Massachusetts; Caleb Nolt (14) Indiana; Zach Harrington (19) Arkansas.
>
> (David Badash, "Breaking: ELEVENTH September Anti-Gay Hate-Related Teen Suicide" [The New Civil Rights Movement, 2010])

The widespread coverage of the deaths brought attention to public health and education research studies that showed that queer young people are more likely to experience suicidal ideation compared to the general young population (The Trevor Project 2017).[1] The apparent increase in the rate of queer teen suicides was quickly linked to the teens' common experience of having been harassed by their peers (Crary 2010; O'Connor 2011).[2] Indeed, *bullying* was continually cited as a key motivating factor in the suicides, discursively linking a perceived crisis of queer teen suicides to an epidemic of teen-on-teen harassment.[3]

The crisis in bullying-related queer youth suicide not only captivated the attention of national media outlets, but also elicited national governmental concern. On October 1, 2010, Secretary of Education Arne Duncan released a statement calling for action (Duncan 2010):

> These unnecessary tragedies come on the heels of at least three other young people taking their own lives because the trauma of being bullied and harassed for their actual or perceived sexual orientation was too much to bear. This is a moment where every one of

2 Introduction

us—parents, teachers, students, elected officials, and all people of conscience—needs to stand up and speak out against intolerance in all its forms.

(Arne Duncan, "Statement by U.S. Secretary of Education Arne Duncan on the Recent Deaths of Two Young Men" [US Department of Education, 2010])

The list of names quickly became a rallying call for youth advocates, educators, legislators, celebrities, academics, and community organizers, who scrambled to make sense of the suicides and find tools and methods to support the well-being of queer youth (Dallara 2010; Lim et al. 2010; Calmes 2011; Friedman 2010; State of Michigan 2011; Berkman Klein Center 2012).[4] It was during the week of this national call to action that self-produced online video emerged as a primary tool for establishing contact with and channels of support for queer youth.

It began with the *It Gets Better Project*, launched by columnist Dan Savage and his partner Terry Miller. The campaign used YouTube as a space for posting and circulating short, testimonial-style videos intended to deliver messages of hope to struggling young people. The project's immediate and remarkable popularity not only garnered mainstream media attention, it inspired thousands of user-produced videos. While adults (many of them public figures and celebrities) were the primary contributors of early campaign videos, soon many queer youth were posting too. The growing involvement of teens in the campaign, paired with the predominance of adult testimonials, prompted many educators and youth advocates to encourage more young people to contribute to the anti-bullying discourse through the production of their own online videos (GSA Network 2010; Give a Damn 2017).[5]

Next, there was an explosion of online video projects aimed at engaging queer youth as producers. In community centers and schools, and through national contests sponsored by government, nonprofit organizations, and corporations, queer youth were encouraged to create and circulate personal, message-oriented videos. Many of these organized video projects specifically called on young people to produce videos in the style of public service announcements (PSAs), a form designed to encourage attitudinal and behavioral change on the part of its audience.

Youth-produced anti-gay-bullying PSAs soon peppered the digital video landscape, buttressed by a discourse around youth digital media empowerment. Philanthropic organizations and foundations have been putting money into these PSA projects since the beginning of the 2000s, especially ones that encourage young people to produce them. Ease of access to digital video and the internet, combined with the increased affordability of media production technologies, has helped this kind of PSA project become the central technique for addressing the concerns of queer youth. Such projects engaged young people in a praxis-oriented approach that seemingly made good on the legacy of media activism and self-representation that has been fostered for decades by scholars and educators seeking to center self-produced media as a tool for producing agency and power. But, looking closely, it emerged that self-produced video was not the panacea it seemed.

Critical Media Production

Digital participatory media is often positioned in the popular imagination as a catalyst for social progress. It gets credited with the potential to not only transform individual lives but also the world as we know it. By now we are all familiar with claims that social media can help forge powerful networks of people, amplify marginalized voices, and provide a platform for visibility and self-actualization.

YouTube, in particular, has been celebrated as a platform that seemingly gives everyday users the opportunity to circumnavigate the formal barriers of institutional spaces and the constraints of mass communications with self-generated and self-directed videos, or what Manuel Castells (2013) has referred to as "mass self-communication." With relatively low barriers to participation, opportunities for informal mentorship, and strong support for collaboration, networked self-produced media sites, particularly YouTube, are seen by many educators and activists as model platforms for facilitating interaction among those with shared affinities (Jenkins, Ito, and boyd 2016). Through the act of producing and circulating videos, everyday users engage in what Peters and Seier describe as a "self-staging" of identities, in which producers can reflect on how they perform in the world (Peters and Seier 2009). Within educational and advocacy contexts, participation in digital media production is often framed as an antidote to the social and economic disparities faced by young people and a method for incorporating them into a healthy social life. Such discourses suggest that enabling and encouraging young people to produce and circulate digital video will lead to an improvement in their circumstances, or that their sense of self will improve. These claims are particularly salient in relation to millennial youth, especially those presumed to be disenfranchised and "at-risk." But how true are they?

Producing Queer Youth provides a critical appraisal of popular conceptions of empowerment by examining concrete accounts of the affordances and limits of networked media culture as a platform for cultural transformation and social progress. It offers a complex picture of the uneven formations of agency arising from social forces and institutions that situate participants differently from each other with respect to media culture. Unlike many mainstream accounts of youth media and empowerment, I consider the differences in race, social class, and other dimensions of identity that play a crucial role in how individual queer young people situate themselves within media practices.

4 Introduction

Contrasting with prominent discourses that describe this generation of young people as *digital natives* who express themselves most naturally through their media use, or who are empowered through new media to participate in areas of civic and social life previously closed off to them, I point to new approaches to youth media production that pay greater attention to the complexities of finding a voice, visibility, and power.

This book challenges the perception that when young people are enabled and encouraged to produce and circulate digital video, their circumstances, or their sense of self, necessarily improve. I interrogate discourses that naturalize the connection between digital media use and power while I seek to locate where social difference matters for young people in their experiences with media technologies. An important foundation of my argument is the critique of the model of the self-actualizing, self-empowered youth that is precipitated through empowerment discourse. I suggest that this ideology is transferred and perpetuated through institutions that are poised to aid and educate youth. I seek to show that when educational and funding institutions create opportunities for youth media production, institutional priorities inevitably commandeer youth expression in ways that are projected as representative of the agency of young subjects.

My concern is that well-intentioned institutions and individuals that fund, teach, and encourage media production may collectively put forward a model of empowerment that does not fully address the needs and rights of the minority groups they support, and which may overlook other opportunities for meaningful engagement. As digital technologies for multiple forms of media production and circulation become ever more accessible and a mainstay of everyday life, it is increasingly important to hold to the light the lessons we have learned from critical studies of media. Indeed, the idea that participatory media production is inherently empowering did not emerge with digital video—rather, it has deep roots in cultural studies and media studies traditions. It should not be surprising, then, that participation in these campaigns would be widely considered beneficial to the people involved. As Sarah Banet-Weiser (2011) and Leslie Regan Shade (2011) instruct in their analyses of girls' media production practices, it is critical to foreground the disciplinary logics that work to contain young producers and their creative expression using digital media production technologies.

For over two decades significant scholarly research has been conducted into the educational benefits for youth when various forms of digital media production activities are integrated into the pedagogical and community spaces they inhabit. While in the area of development, human rights, and critical pedagogy there is a long history of the critique of the idea that someone or something external (whether that be a teacher or a technology) can help to give voice or power to a group or an individual, in the study of digital media pedagogy the relationship between youth media production and power is often naturalized. This is, I argue, because it assumes a relationship to a tradition of *media praxis*, where participation is treated as a democratic decentering of mass media power (Juhasz 2016).[6] This book seeks to bring the cultural study of media praxis into the realm of digital media studies while contributing to our understanding of what empowerment means in the age of digital video pedagogy.

While much of the research and scholarship pertaining to youth digital media use has emphasized learning, rarely has a critical pedagogy framework been applied (Freire 2014).[7] The emphasis has instead been primarily on skills-building, training, access to necessary technologies, and participation. Following media scholar Julian Sefton-Green (2006, 279–306), this project shares the view that studying forms of media culture can help us to understand wider notions of learning beyond education or school systems.

I am primarily interested in examining queer youth digital media production in relationship to access to power (real and imagined). At the core of this discussion are questions concerning young people's access to digital technologies and how their socioeconomic and cultural identities may affect the possibility of their empowerment. I offer a critique of the ways in which attempts to promote digital media access and media literacy describe participation in generic terms that do not fully address which subjects are best able to participate and which are not. In a similar fashion, educational and funding institutions are treated as neutral factors in youth digital media pedagogy. Bringing the specific context of sexual and gender identity into the overall investigation of digital media pedagogy, I identify several ways that real opportunities for queer youth may, in fact, be foreclosed by the power dynamics inherent in adult-authored video assignments. In doing so, I show how institutions that fund, teach, and encourage this kind of production are fully implicated in a model of empowerment that distracts from the needs and rights of queer youth.

In this book, I consider pedagogy to be the connective tissue between the personal and interpersonal experiences of queer youth, advocacy and educational institutions, culture, and social structures. *Critical pedagogy* as an approach helps me to identify some of the forms of education that occur both inside and outside classrooms and where learning and culture coincide (Goldfarb 2002).[8] Feminist approaches to critical pedagogy are particularly useful in my examination of digital media production and youth empowerment because a central tenet of this approach is to investigate assumptions about *empowerment* and *voice*. These concepts are often taken for granted in the broader literature and discourse around youth and digital media production. By bringing a feminist critical pedagogy-influenced approach to bear on my examination of how digital media use has been imagined as the antidote to queer bullying and suicidal ideation, I seek to problematize the understanding of youth digital

6 Introduction

media production and media participation as inherently empowering. I draw on feminist critical pedagogy critiques of efforts to elicit *authentic youth voices* as a method of empowerment. These approaches help us to think about the ways that discourses on student voice in fact may *limit* young people. If empowerment is the ability to have one's voice heard, how does this affect queer youth, who may not necessarily experience power through visibility and other forms of expression of their sexual identities?

Many contemporary educators, scholars, and policymakers agree that fluency in new media technologies now functions as a key component of young people's identity formation. Concerning what has been called the *digital divide*, or the *participation gap*, since the 1990s, tremendous focus has been placed on the question of how to close what was believed to be a divide between those who have regular access to information and communication media technologies and those who do not. Areas of inquiry in education and media studies have tended to center around whether or not young people have the *access* to technologies necessary to fully participate in production activities. Jean Burgess (2006, 201–14) has historicized this shift, noting that anxiety over a *digital divide* "has shifted to concerns around social inclusion and the unevenness of access to 'voice' in the global mediascape."

Scholars of youth media such as Sonia Livingstone (2002) have argued that media content creation is a key component to media literacy that is "crucial to the democratic agenda," positioning everyday media producers "not merely as consumers but also citizens." Yet these approaches treat learning, social connection, and civic and social empowerment as the expected outcome of participation once access and the conditions for critical reflection are provided. I seek to add complexity to our understanding of how empowerment functions in youth digital media production, emphasizing the structural demands of what is produced. I argue that youth participation in media production projects must always be understood in terms of both the social and institutional context from which they originate and broader trends in content production across professional and nonprofessional spheres.

One of my aims is to consider how the pedagogical approaches of youth media programs result from a chain of negotiations that lead from funders to community organizations, or from educational institutions to educators and students—who each recast production projects in various ways. Another objective is to examine individual- and community-produced online videos in the context of broader media campaigns. This project is concerned with how those technologies got there in the first place and asks, "What do the funders and media pedagogues who promote production imagine as its social value? What is expected of the producers, and how might that have an impact on what they produce? Finally, and perhaps most importantly, what is it that these young

Introduction 7

producers understand they are making and what is its impact on their lives in the short and long term?"

Another goal of the project is to explicate continuities between the history of broadcast advertising (which is responsible for advancing the public service announcement genre) and self-produced video, showing the entanglements between social issues of marketing and media praxis. Extending our knowledge of the PSA as a normalizing technology to the realm of user-generated content, might we come to understand how factors such as *messaging* and *publicity* relate to the expression and action that is encouraged in young producers? How does an ethos of participation, voice, and visibility interact with the vocational and pro-fessionalizing motivations that often undergird participation?

Part of my argument in this book is that self-produced anti-gay-bullying PSAs create archetypal narratives of bullying that exclude the heteroge-neous lived experiences of queer youth. The project also contributes to queer studies research that aims to critique the homogenizing forces of neoliberalism. I claim that participation in anti-bullying discourse allows queer youth to leverage themselves as visible—both in their identities *and* as successful media-makers; but professionalism colludes with a neoliberal marketplace where certain kinds of identities are permitted visibility and others are not. In this way, the prerogatives of image man-agement and professionalization mingle with a politics of queer visi-bility and a rapid movement towards what Lisa Duggan (2003) has called *homonormativity*—the liberalization of social and legal attitudes towards homosexuality since the early 1990s (Warner 1999; Eng 2010; Puar 2007; Barnhurst 2007). Kevin Barnhurst explains the stakes:

> A simple acknowledgement that difference is inescapable is the first step toward understanding what is at stake in queer visibility. That acknowledgement is also the first step toward knowing what to do about queer visibility. The necessary action is to reject the question of visibility, to set it aside, and to choose something other than focusing on queer difference.
>
> (Kevin Barnhurst, *Media Queered: Visibility and its Discontents* [New York: Peter Lang, 2007], 18)

For Barnhurst (2007, 13) visibility without personal innuendo is just another form of media popularity, rather than a radical political act. My study calls attention to the self-produced anti-gay-bullying PSA as an instance where the sexual politics of neoliberalism are refracted through youth media practice; where a politics of identity-based visibility gets conflated with expression and *giving voice*, and technologies of self-production blur with technologies of (self-)promotion and publicity.

While much scholarship since the late 1980s has discussed the ways in which neoliberalism promotes individualized responsibility for social

8 Introduction

well-being through consumption practices, I draw attention to the ways in which digital media production is now also imagined as a site of self-production and self-care. As Nikolas Rose (1999, 243) argues in his critique of the engrained notions of self-actualization and self-discovery that have pervaded Western thinking and social life, "the autonomous self, freed from the burden of the past can say, 'I'm OK, *and* you're OK.'" Rose argues that the collective emphasis on self-protection and individual behavioral adjustment that is symptomatic of neoliberalism distracts people from the realities of their oppression with the hopes of achieving a perfect state of contentment and autonomy. I pivot from Rose to argue that the well-being of young producers is often imagined to be achieved and sustained both through their production and their consumption of media messages that ascribe a teleological and prescriptive self-oriented narrative that enfolds them in the positivist discourse to which Rose refers.

Methods and Approach

Producing Queer Youth puts pressure on the intersections of a politics of queer visibility and the valuation of queer youth video production as an inherently emancipatory practice. The book examines what we, as scholars, educators, parents, and youth advocates, may be missing when we promote digital media campaigns and other social media use to young people as a route for expression, connection, and problem-solving. This project interrogates the strong imbrication between a politics of visibility, forms of publicity, and personal expression as a route to empowerment. I am critically concerned with the notion of *empowerment*, which is so often leveraged in the promotion of media production work with marginalized people. The widespread enthusiasm for youth media production projects as a tool of empowerment obliges us to evaluate the value of such an approach. Thus, the book turns a critical eye towards the common utilization of digital media production as identity work, community-building, and as part of an ongoing effort to garner resources for queer youth.

As Mary Celeste Kearney (2011) has argued, research on production and technology necessarily entails close attention to both text and practices. *Producing Queer Youth* examines what values undergird the media empowerment approach as it seeks to identify factors that motivate young people to produce media in the first place by looking at how and why they make what they make.

I foreground three manifestations of this approach. First, I examine historically situated assumptions about the so-called *millennial* generation's comfort and ability to have meaningful interactions with and through digital technologies. Second, I historicize the self-produced PSA as a particular modality that is strongly imbricated in a history of broadcast media as a tool for reproducing social norms. Finally, I turn to the youth media production context to examine the practices and choices that are involved in the execution of these kinds of media campaigns.

My approach draws on my experiences with queer youth media producers in a media production workshop that I designed and facilitated at a San Diego community center called the Hillcrest Youth Center (HYC) over a period of two and a half years (2010–2013). This component of the research is critical for understanding how particular young people engaged with media production technologies and initiatives within the context of a queer community center. Unlike the majority of media ethnographies which focus on a given audience's reception of particular media and its presumed effects, this approach "radically de-centers media" as the focus of study (Gray 2009, 26). Studying the process of production enables us to see social divisions that emerged through production and which I believe are indicative of larger social arrangements that made some young people more prepared to participate (behind or in front of the camera) by virtue of their background. These dynamics are rendered invisible in the circulating video, and thereby feed the dominant pedagogical discourse that PSA production is uniformly empowering for youth. My in-situ approach enables me to detail how adult expectations for youth to produce media content that carries particular expressive and thematic objectives may ultimately mask resource needs and homogenize representations of the queer youth population.

For this portion of the research I used participatory action research methods. This means that I worked collaboratively with the community to identify issues of concern and to determine strategies for effecting change (Lewin 1946; McIntyre 2000a, 2000b). As action researcher Geoffrey Mills explains, the method is about "incorporating into the daily teaching routine a *reflective stance*—reflecting on one's teaching in order to improve or enhance it." Participatory action research nicely complements critical pedagogy's focus on dialogical methods of learning. It is participatory and democratic, socially responsive and takes place in context. It is inherently a reflexive method, which has been described as helping "teacher researchers examine the everyday, taken-for-granted ways in which they carry out professional practice" (Mills 2010). In this case, I would extend the notion of "professional practice" beyond my teaching and mentoring in the community space to the network of resources and guidelines with which the teens and I interacted in our work together.

Action research enables me to approach the undertaking of collaborative production from a critical and a practical perspective simultaneously. I see this book as one method for determining meaningful uses of digital media production in queer youth community contexts. My overarching goal is to examine how media production pedagogy has been operationalized in attempts to support queer youth while

10   *Introduction*

suggesting new approaches. In a sense, action research is not simply my chosen methodological approach for the one chapter in which it was clearly utilized—the action research approach undergirds the entire purpose of the project. As a scholar–practitioner, teacher, and activist who has worked with young media-makers for over a decade, I have experienced networked media's opportunities and challenges firsthand. This book reflects a deep engagement with and commitment to surfacing those attendant challenges.

A Note on Language

Taking cues from Mary L. Gray and Susan Driver, I am less interested in theorizing about queer identity than in examining the co-production of technologies and identities (Gray 2009; Driver 2007). For the majority of the book I refer to *queer youth*, the preferred term in queer studies literature at the time of my writing. It is generally considered by scholars of gender and sexuality to be a more inclusive term that rejects strict gender and sexual identity categories in favor of a spectrum of identity. The term also carries important sociopolitical connotations, evoking the efforts of anti-assimilationist activist groups like *Queer Nation* (Kalin 1990, 21–23). As Siobhan Somerville (2014) explains, "to 'queer' becomes a way to denaturalize categories such as 'lesbian' and 'gay' (not to mention 'straight' and 'heterosexual') revealing them as socially and historically constructed identities that have often worked to establish and police the line between the 'normal' and the 'abnormal.'" In contrast, LGBT, the term most often used by the mainstream news media and anti-bullying campaigns, has been set aside by many scholars, educators, and activists in favor of more inclusive nomenclature that resists the associated identity politics. I could have opted to use LGBTQIA (Lesbian, Gay, Bisexual, Transgender, Queer, Questioning, Intersex, Asexual, and Ally), which is increasingly preferred by youth advocates and many young people themselves (Schulman 2013).[9]

For the reader who comes to this book familiar with queer politics and queer studies, it will perhaps seem odd that in some places I choose to use *LGBT youth* as opposed to *queer youth* or another, perhaps even more contemporary, categorical term that attempts to refine the taxonomies of sexual identity.[10] When I use the phrase *LGBT youth*, I do it for two reasons that I believe further illuminate important threads of the overall argument I am making about youth and media production.

The first reason is simple: it was the term that the community at the Hillcrest Youth Center used to represent themselves and others during the period that this study was conducted. Some of the young people at the center were quick to point out that my use of the term *queer* marked me as someone from outside of their community, and, as one teen put it, from "another generation." To them, *queer* was a word that adults in the broader community used, and they did not identify with it. I soon began to feel as if my using the term *queer* was an expression of my aspiration for a shared politics more than the product of true exchange. To use the term *queer youth* in this book, therefore, would be to map my own discursive framework onto theirs.[11] However, when I moved to Seattle from San Diego soon afterwards, I was surprised to find that the youth in my new city espoused a much more radical lexicon and variance when it came to representing both gender and sexuality. This differing use of language reflects the political tenor of each city's community.

The second reason is more complex. I should begin by noting that *LGBT youth* was not the dominant term used by the teens when I began working with them in 2010; it increased in use in tandem with the proliferation of mainstream news coverage of issues concerning the community.[12] In mainstream coverage of the debates in the United States over same-sex marriage, the repeal of the United States military's "Don't Ask, Don't Tell" policy, and the highly publicized suicides of teens who were presumed to be gay—among other issues—*LGBT* was the dominant terminology used in reporting. A Google Trends (2013) analysis of news headlines during the period from 2008 to 2013 makes evident this claim. As the following chart indicates, the use of *LGBT* increased in news media usage and the term *queer* remained low. As it turns out, one of the news headlines associated with a major increase in the use of the term is related to an announcement of celebrity video contributions to the *It Gets Better Project* (Donnelly 2010).[13]

As the trends report indicates, search terms that included the word *queer* were most often linked to words relating to culture, such as theory, and the titles of television shows. On the other hand, *LGBT* was most often searched for in relation to terms linked to sociopolitical alignments. Terms like "community," "center," "rights," "pride," and "youth" appeared most often. It should not be surprising, then, that a youth center advocating for the rights and inclusion of youth would want to align themselves with broader discourses.

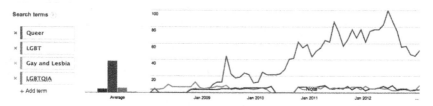

Figure i.1 Google Trends comparison of terms in news media

12 Introduction

queer folk	100	
queer as folk	100	
queer eye	55	
queer click	10	
queer theory	10	
queer free	10	
queer me now	10	
queer definition	5	
queer lyrics	5	
what is queer	5	
lgbt center	100	
lgbt community	50	
lgbt rights	50	
gltb	35	
lgbt pride	35	
lgbt youth	30	
what is lgbt	30	
lgbt nyc	30	
lgbt health	20	
lgbt people	20	

Figure i.2 A comparison of Google Trends search terms between January 2008 and January 2013

In her research with rural youth in the early 2000s, Mary L. Gray noticed a similar trend in language use, which, she explains, is linked to the politics of queer visibility and rights. For Gray, the young people's use of the term *LGBT community* spoke "to the power of nationally mass-mediated conversations to manifest an 'imagined community' of lesbian, gay, bisexual, and transgender people whether L, G, B, and T-identifying people are present or not" (Gray 2009, 27). These references, she explains, represent their striving towards a "coherent and tangible 'LGBT community.'"

Introduction 13

The social-service parlance of "LGBT" has become commonplace in the politics of visibility and indexes how deeply steeped some of these youth are in that political culture. So the pervasive use of "LGBT" as a phrase among youth commuting to social-service agencies like urban-based youth groups is not surprising.

(Mary L. Gray, Out in the Country: Youth, Media, and Queer Visibility in Rural America [New York: New York University Press, 2009], 27)

Drawing on Gray, I would propose that the young people with whom I worked also used the terminology strategically, intentionally aligning themselves with the identities in the eye of news headlines and national debates. My choice to retain the phrase *LGBT youth* in certain places, therefore, is a reminder to the reader of the teens' situatedness in the intertwining discourses of the news media, the law, social services, education, youth advocacy, and community centers. In my use of the term *LGBT youth*, I seek to point towards possible occurrences of what postcolonial theorist Gayatri Spivak has termed *strategic essentialism*, in which members of a minority group intentionally align themselves with each other along the lines of (often reductive) hegemonic discourse with the objective of securing rights and resources. For Spivak it is possible to participate in maintaining counter-hegemonic self-identification (Chakraborty 2010).[14] This was true for the PSA producers in my case study, who produced media that recapitulates essentializing discourses, but who were otherwise crucially concerned with difference and resistance.

Chapter One, "The Problem with *Youth Voices*," examines scholarly and pedagogical approaches that treat youth participation in digital media production and circulation as inherently empowering. The objective is to disentangle the threads that tie together media and empowerment and to expose areas where young people's needs might be overlooked when they are brought into that fray. I begin by discussing prevailing discourses that posit youth as more equipped and comfortable with digital media than other generations. I then examine the ways in which scholars of digital media have engaged with these discourses, advancing media production projects as if they were inherently empowering. In particular, I focus on the way these discourses equate media participation with the mobilization of *youth voices*. I challenge this framework by examining what it means to have a "voice" in media. Critiques from feminist critical pedagogy, documentary studies, and visual anthropology challenge assumptions that for young people, having a voice, visibility, and recognition is necessarily equivalent to gaining rights and resources.

14 Introduction

Chapter Two, "'Look at Me, I'm Doing Fine!' The Conundrum of Legibility, Visibility, and Identity Management in Queer Viral Videos," presents online video as central to the emergence of the discourse of queer youth empowerment. In this chapter I examine the uptake of media production as a response to the phenomenon of anti-gay-bullying in order to argue that the phenomenon and the approach are co-constitutive. I describe how the *It Gets Better Project* viral video campaign has precipitated a discourse of anti-bullying that posits viral video as a tool for addressing the needs of queer youth, as well as a technique for circumnavigating the legal and logistical barriers that have historically prevented adults from being able to provide direct support. I discuss how the success of user-generated video campaigns is contingent on the *spreadability* of videos, which is believed to be achievable when producers follow the dominant stylistic and messaging conventions that are consistent with the campaigns that they contribute to.[15]

These normative practices have limiting effects, as they promote particular representations of queer young lives and experiences of bullying. These representations are inherently normalizing and risk further marginalizing young people who do not fit the picture. This chapter expands the discussion to examine the ways in which the campaign has been used by public figures, educators, and young people alike to enact what I call a performance of "conspicuous concern" for queer youth. I contend that the viral video approach, championed for the expressive and connective opportunities it appears to provide for struggling young queer people, is limited in its potential to address the complexities of their lives. The aim of this chapter is to illustrate the constraints of the viral video approach in order to make a case that viral video production might be best thought of as a tool for specific forms of publicity and image management rather than as a technique for mobilizing the most potentially high-impact sets of human and financial resources.

As a counterpoint, I draw attention to the ephemeral and personal archive of queer youth media images in order to show how media empowerment can take place beyond the mainstream approach. Through an analysis of dozens of online videos uploaded and circulated by queer youth since 2010, I identify a variety of narrative templates that share formal and expressive similarities. These videos resist formula, and perform and circulate marginal positions, narratives, and experiences. They appear to emerge from local publics that have existing audiences and knowledge embedded in the production process, and rarely circulate outside of their geographical sites of origin. Taken together, they realize a world in which many other possibilities and ways of being queer emerge, and the multiplicity of narratives, coalitions, symbolic representations, and mimetic re-imaginings they create can help form the basis for transformative social change.

Introduction 15

Chapter Three, "Vernacular Voices: Business Gets Personal in Public Service Announcements," critiques the ways in which youth-produced online videos and PSAs are presented as novel forms of youth expression and self-advocacy. I do this by emphasizing continuity between youth-produced videos and those created by advertising agencies and advocacy organizations in traditional broadcast public service campaigns. Comparing PSAs across time periods makes evident the fact that although the producers and distribution strategies have changed, the messaging tactics have not. I trace the development of a mode of appeal that is presented as coming from inside an identity group to others as insider individuals. I suggest that this mode, which I call the *vernacular voice*, is integral to the PSA's history. It emerged as a form in tandem with deregulation and the rise of a neoliberal model of individualism that characterizes the cause-related advertising and charity tactics that have been adopted to promote the causes of LGBTQ youth. I argue that, like traditional broadcast public service advertising, contemporary user-generated PSAs homogenize complex social issues into singular experiences and easily digestible messages. I use this discussion to argue that queer-youth-produced anti-bullying PSA videos must be understood as social norming strategies more than solely as forms of expression and connection.

Chapter Four, "'I Can't Talk When I'm Supposed to Say Something': Negotiating Expression in a Queer-Youth-Produced Anti-Bullying Video," brings into play the questions and concerns of the previous chapters through an action research case study with queer youth producers. In this chapter I provide a narrative account of my experience as an instructor in a video production workshop at a San Diego youth community center, where, at the height of the anti-gay-bullying public campaigns, I was charged with the task of leading youth in the production of a PSA for online distribution. Through a detailed analysis of the production choices made by the group, I illustrate how the process of producing the PSA laid bare some of the limitations of this model of video production and of the PSA form in particular. I show how seemingly entwined pedagogical priorities—encouraging young people to express themselves and motivating them to participate in production—are often at odds with each other. Examining the different objectives of the participants emphasizes the ways in which, for them, *participation* is simultaneously structured by *expressive* and *vocational* drives. I argue that while the production process opened up opportunities to identify the needs of the youth involved, on its own the video could neither represent nor mobilize the necessary support for them. Moreover, the project emphasized the difficulty, perhaps even the impossibility, of making bullying visible.

This chapter traces the misalignments of adult assumptions against the diverse ways in which teens already use digital technologies to produce

16 *Introduction*

and reflect on their identities and experiences, allowing us to re-imagine what media empowerment might mean for queer teens. A close examination of the empowerment discourses that underwrite PSA production also elucidates the constructive uses of the PSA as a pedagogical exercise, allowing us to recuperate an otherwise problematic mainstay of media pedagogy and social action.

The concluding chapter, "Out of the Closet and Into the Tweets," considers the promise and peril of participatory media projects in queer community contexts and offers an alternative approach to the popular PSA genre examined in earlier chapters. Developing my findings from the action research case study, I outline best practices in media production pedagogy that emphasize the production process over the final video product as the site of connection, intersubjectivity, and mutual understanding.

Contemporary media empowerment discourse has led to trends in youth video production pedagogy that have enmeshed young people's identities and experiences with institutional goals to educate and professionalize them. My challenge to this approach grows out of an interest in developing an attentive form of pedagogy that engages youth in a reflexive dialog with their roles as media producers and the social and institutional contexts in which they operate. I advocate for an alternative approach to media pedagogy that places more emphasis on the contexts and dynamics of media production as a meaningful site of expression than on the ultimate video productions. Indeed, the goals of this research reach beyond the book, and will only be actualized when the findings of this project are communicated within communities of practice. The ultimate objective of the project, then, is to propose an approach to media production that re-centers the *process* of production as the site of potential learning and connection while reframing the digital videos as the site of performance and intention, as opposed to the evidence of power.

Notes

1 A 2016 study by the Center for Disease Control and Prevention found that lesbian, gay, bisexual, transgender, and questioning youth are up to four times more likely to attempt suicide than their heterosexual peers. A 2009 study by the Family Acceptance Project looked at the relationship between family relationships and suicide attempts of lesbian, gay, and bisexual-identified teens and found that those who came from highly rejecting families were eight times more likely to attempt suicide than those who came from families with low levels of rejection.

2 These are just two examples of headlines linking queer suicide and bullying.

3 I refer to this as a "perceived crisis" because there is not sufficient data to suggest that at present more teens identifying as or perceived to be queer

commit suicide than in prior decades. The lack of comparative data has to do with the fact that it is difficult to know how many of the teens that committed suicide in the past actually identified as queer, as until the mid-1990s, comparatively few young people publicly identified themselves as queer and there has been no reliable method for gathering that kind of sensitive population data. To boot, the heightened media awareness around the suicides in 2010 perhaps enhanced perceptions that more suicides were occurring in greater numbers. With this in mind, it may be more useful to think of LGBTQ teen suicide as an *ongoing* problem that must be urgently addressed.

4 Several queer studies scholars collectively published these responses to the suicides. The White House held an anti-bullying conference. Several states (such as New Jersey and Michigan) adopted anti-bullying legislation. The pop star Lady Gaga launched her anti-bullying foundation Born This Way, in partnership with Harvard's Berkman Center for Internet and Society, with grants from major funders like the John D. and Catherine T. MacArthur Foundation. The launch of the foundation was announced at an inauguration that featured Lady Gaga, esteemed faculty members, the President of Harvard University, media mogul Oprah Winfrey, writer Deepak Chopra, and United States Secretary of Health and Human Services Kathleen Sebelius. This list barely scratches the surface of the widespread international response to the suicides.

5 The *Make It Better Project*, www.makeitbetterproject.org (site discontinued), initiated a week after the *It Gets Better Project*, described its purpose as "filling in the gaps—and the action" of the "it gets better" narrative with personal stories from young people about what they do to "make it better," in the context of helping to change circumstances for LGBTQ youth in their schools. Another project that emerged at this time was the singer Cyndi Lauper's *Give a Damn* project, sponsored by her organization the True Colors Fund. See "A Brief History of Give a Damn," Give a Damn, accessed December 6, 2016, www.wegiveadamn.org/.

6 *Media praxis* refers to the merging of media, practice, and politics. It entails a project of self- and world-changing through interactions with media. The concept of praxis originated with Marx but was popularized by British Cultural Studies, which brought it into the realm of media production and consumption.

7 Here, I am defining critical pedagogy as co-intentional education that insists on transforming the world. As Paolo Freire, the foremost theorist/practitioner of critical pedagogy, explains, it entails teachers and students as "co-intent on reality," where both are subjects "not only in the task of unveiling that reality, and thereby coming to know it critically, but in the task of re-creating that knowledge. As they attain this knowledge of reality through common reflection and action, they discover themselves as permanent re-creators. In this way, the presence of the oppressed in the struggle for their liberation will be what it should be: not pseudo-participation, but committed involvement."

8 For an excellent discussion of pedagogy beyond schools, see Brian Goldfarb, *Visual Pedagogy*.

9 In this article, cultural studies scholar J. Jack Halberstam argues, "In the next 10 or 20 years, the various categories heaped under the umbrella of L.G.B.T. will become quite quotidian."

18 *Introduction*

10 I also switch between using the terms "anti-bullying" and "anti-gay-bullying" to refer to bullying discourse. My vacillation is meant to mirror the somewhat interchangeable usage of these two related terms in popular discourse. Chapter One further explicates my rationale for this lack of distinction.

11 It is worth noting that in 2012 there was a change of adult leadership at the youth center that resulted in an increased politicization of the group of teens. Many new activities and discussion groups were organized to familiarize the youth with expansive and inclusive terminology as well as queer history and politics. Activism was encouraged, and as the youth center became a more politicized space, the term *queer* began to be used by some of the youth.

12 When I began working at the HYC in early 2010, I heard many of the youth refer to themselves and others (regardless of gender) as *gay*, which I found to be curiously anachronistic. I had assumed their usage to be a conscious re-appropriation of the word; perhaps an ironic reclaiming of the liberationist history or an intentional diffusing of the more derogatory usage of the word (as in the insult "that's so gay!"). I was wrong. As these teens informed me, their use of *gay* instead of *queer*, *LGBT*, *LGBTQ*, or *LGBTQIA* was their response to terms they felt were either too academic or convoluted jargon, used by adults to refer to them. *Gay* struck them as an inclusive and accessible umbrella term that could encapsulate a spectrum of sexualities and gender. For these youth, who by and large appeared not to be familiar with queer history, *gay* was the term they used within their families and that they heard in their communities. They described it as organic and unadulterated, and a common denominator. As 18-year-old Molly explained, "it's just that I'm gay, you know? I'm not LGBT, I'm gay, he's gay, you're gay." Yet by early 2011, the dominant terminology used at the youth center had shifted from *gay* to *LGBT*. The move away from *gay* was due in part to the simple fact that a number of the teens that preferred that term had stopped attending the youth center.

13 The *Los Angeles Times* news headline that Google Trends attributes to the October 2010 peak in the usage of *LGBTQ* reads "Anne Hathaway, Jenny McCarthy among latest to join the 'It Gets Better' campaign to help LGBTQ teens."

14 Gayatri Spivak first coined the term in a 1984 interview. It should be noted that since her introduction of the term, she has moved away from using it, claiming that it has been misused to the point of no longer standing for what she intended it to mean.

15 I borrow the term *spreadability* from Jenkins, Ford, and Green. The authors make a point of distinguishing between "viral" and what they call "spreadable" media. "Spreadability" takes agency into account.

References

Badash, David. 2010. "Breaking: ELEVENTH September Anti-Gay Hate-Related Teen Suicide." The New Civil Rights Movement. Last accessed October 8, 2011. www.thenewcivilrightsmovement.com/breaking-eleventh-september-anti-gay-hate-related-teen-suicide/bigotry-watch/2010/10/11/13606.

Introduction   19

Banet-Weiser, Sarah. 2011. "Branding the Post-Feminist Self: Girls' Video Production and YouTube." In *Mediated Girlhoods: New Explorations of Girls' Media Culture*, edited by Mary Celeste Kearney, 277–94. New York: Peter Lang.

Barnhurst, Kevin G. 2007. *Media Queered: Visibility and Its Discontents*. New York: Peter Lang.

Berkman Klein Center. 2012. "Lady Gaga Testifies at Harvard on Behalf of Born This Way Foundation." Berkman Klein Center for Internet and Society at Harvard University. Last accessed February 29, 2013. https://cyber.harvard.edu/node/95364.

Burgess, Jean. 2006. "Hearing Ordinary Voices: Cultural Studies, Vernacular Creativity and Digital Storytelling." *Continuum:Journal of Media & Cultural Studies* 20 (2):201–14. https://eprints.qut.edu.au/6243/1/6243.pdf.

Calmes, Jackie. 2011. "Obamas Focus on Antibullying Efforts." The New York Times, March 10. www.nytimes.com/2011/03/11/us/politics/11obama.html.

Castells, Manuel, ed. 2013. Communication Power. Oxford: Oxford University Press.

Chakraborty, Mridula Nath. 2010. "Everybody's Afraid of Gayatri Chakravorty Spivak: Reading Interviews with the Public Intellectual and Postcolonial Critic." *Signs* 35 (3):621–45. Doi: 10.1086/649575.

Crary, David. 2010. "Suicide Surge: Schools Confront Anti-Gay Bullying." NBCNews.com. Last accessed October 9, 2011. www.nbcnews.com/id/39593311/#.UV6JNqWkJD8.

Dallara, Angela. 2010. "Media Roundup: The Tragedy of LGBT Teenage Suicide." GLAAD. Last accessed October 1, 2011. www.glaad.org/2010/10/01/media-roundup-the-tragedy-of-lgbt-teenage-suicide.

Donnelly, Matt. 2010. "Anne Hathaway, Jenny McCarthy Among Latest to Join the 'It Gets Better' Campaign to Help LGBTQ Teens." Los Angeles Times, October 4. http://latimesblogs.latimes.com/gossip/2010/10/gay-teen-suicide-it-gets-better-trevor-project.html.

Driver, Susan. 2007. *Queer Girls and Popular Culture: Reading, Resisting, and Creating Media*. New York: Peter Lang.

Duggan, Lisa. 2003. *The Twilight of Equality?* Boston: Beacon Press.

Duncan, Arne. 2010. "Statement by U.S. Secretary of Education Arne Duncan on the Recent Deaths of Two Young Men." US Department of Education. Last accessed October 1, 2012. www.ed.gov/news/press-releases/statement-us-secretary-education-arne-duncan-recent-deaths-two-young-men.

Eng, David L. 2010. *The Feeling of Kinship: Queer Liberalism and the Racialization of Intimacy*. Durham: Duke University Press.

Freire, Paulo, ed. 2014. *Pedagogy of the Oppressed*. New York: Bloomsbury Academic.

Friedman, Matt. 2010. "N.J. Assembly, Senate Pass 'Anti-Bullying Bill of Rights' in Wake of Tyler Clementi's Death." Nj.com. Last accessed November 22, 2011. www.nj.com/news/index.ssf/2010/11/nj_assembly_passes_anti-bullyi.html.

Give A Damn. 2017. "A Brief History of Give a Damn." The True Colors Fund. Last accessed July 19, 2017. www.wegiveadamn.org/.

Goldfarb, Brian. 2002. *Visual Pedagogy: Media Cultures in and Beyond the Classroom*. Durham: Duke University Press.

Google Trends. 2013. Last accessed March 8, 2013. www.google.com/trends/explore#q=Queer%2C%20LGBTQ%2C%20Gay%20and%20Lesbian%2C%20LGBTQIA&geo=US&cmpt=q.

20 *Introduction*

Gray, Mary L. 2009. *Out in the Country: Youth, Media, and Queer Visibility in Rural America*. New York: New York University Press.

GSA Network. 2010. "Youth Suicides Prompt Make It Better Project." GSA Network. Last accessed October 3, 2012. https://gsanetwork.org/news/youth-suicides-prompt-make-it-better-project/100310.

Jenkins, Henry, Mizuko Ito, and danah boyd. 2016. *Participatory Culture in a Networked Era*. Cambridge: Polity Press.

Juhasz, Alexandra. 2016. "What Is Media Praxis?" Media Praxis: Integrating Theory, Practice & Politics. Last accessed December 6, 2016. www.mediapraxis.org/?page_id=8.

Kalin, Tom. 1990. "Slant: Queer Nation." *Artforum* 29 (9):21–23. Last accessed March 6, 2018. www.artforum.com/inprint/issue=199009.

Kearney, Mary Celeste. 2011. *Mediated Girlhoods*. New York: Peter Lang.

Lim, Eng-Beng, Jasbir Puar, Ann Pellegrini, Jack Halberstam, Oluchi Joon Lee, Lynne Joyriche, and Gail Cohee. 2010. "Queer Suicide: An Introduction to the Teach-In." *Social Text Online* 7 (1). Last accessed March 6, 2018. https://socialtextjournal.org/periscope_article/a_suicide_teach-in/.

Livingstone, Sonia. 2002. *Young People and New Media: Childhood and the Changing Media Environment*. London: SAGE Publications Ltd.

Lewin, Kurt. 1946. "Action Research and Minority Problems." *Journal of Social Issues* 2 (4):34–46. Doi: 10.1111/j.1540–4560.1946.tb02295.x.

McIntyre, Alice. 2000a. *Inner City Kids: Adolescents Confront Life and Violence in an Urban Community*. New York: New York University Press.

———. 2000b. "Constructing Meaning about Violence, School, and Community: Participatory Action Research with Urban Youth." *Urban Review* 32 (2):123–54. http://rdcu.be/uruS.

Mills, Geoffrey E., ed. 2010. *Action Research: A Guide for the Teacher Researcher*. London: Pearson Publishing.

O'Connor, Anahad. 2011. "Suicide Draws Attention to Gay Bullying." *The New York Times*, September 21. http://well.blogs.nytimes.com/2011/09/21/suicide-of-gay-teenager-who-urged-hope/.

Peters, Kathrin, and Andrea Seier. 2009. "Home Dance: Mediacy and Aesthetics of the Self on YouTube." In *The YouTube Reader*, edited by Pelle Snickars and Patrick Vonderau, 187–203. Stockholm: National Library of Sweden.

Puar, Jasbir K. 2007. *Terrorist Assemblages: Homonationalism in Queer Times*. Durham: Duke University Press.

Rose, Nikolas, ed. 1999. *Governing the Soul: The Shaping of the Private Self*. London: Free Association Books Publishing.

Schulman, Michael. 2013. "Generation LGBTQIA." *The New York Times*, January 9. www.nytimes.com/2013/01/10/fashion/generation-lgbtqia.html.

Sefton-Green, Julian. 2006. "Chapter 8: Youth, Technology, and Media Cultures." *Review of Research in Education* 30:279–306. www.jstor.org/stable/4129775.

Shade, Leslie Regan. 2011. "Surveilling the Girl via the Third and Networked Screen." In *Mediated Girlhoods: New Explorations of Girls' Media Culture*, edited by Mary Celeste Kearney, 261–76. New York: Peter Lang.

Somerville, Siobhan B. 2014. "Queer." In *Keywords for American Cultural Studies*, edited by Bruce Burgett and Glen Hendler. New York: New York University Press. http://keywords.nyupress.org/american-cultural-studies/essay/queer/.

State of Michigan. 2011. "Snyder signs anti-bully bill." State of Michigan. Last accessed December 6, 2012. www.michigan.gov/snyder/0,4668,7-277-57577-266963--,00.html.

The Trevor Project. 2017. "Facts About Suicide." The Trevor Project. Last accessed March 6, 2018. www.thetrevorproject.org/pages/facts-about-suicide.

Warner, Michael. 1999. *The Trouble with Normal: Sex, Politics, and the Ethics of Queer Life*. Cambridge: Harvard University Press.

1 The Problem with *Youth Voices*

"Hey Girls, Let Your Voice Be Heard! Are you creative, passionate, and wanting to make a difference? This might be your chance to have your voice heard and talents showcased. ... You don't have to have technical skills or any experience. If you care about issues affecting you and other girls in your school or community, you can rock this contest. Think about one of the following topics [having a mentor, dealing with violence, feeling confident, and the media and how you are affected by it or feel about it]. Think about what you want to say and the message you want to send to other girls that might see the video. Then come up with a cool and creative concept for a video."

(Beth Malcolm, "Hey Girls, Let Your Voice Be Heard!"
[Canadian Women's Foundation Blog, 2013])

Does this call for youth-made videos seem familiar? During the course of my research I encountered hundreds of calls like this on posters hanging in libraries and schools and through simple online searches, all advertising competitions encouraging young people to produce videos for circulation. Most of the campaigns were launched by nonprofit organizations that had partnered with major business sponsors and featured topics including public health, national politics, and "issues youth care about" like violence, eating disorders, pressures in school, and recycling.[1] In 2012 alone, at least four national media campaigns were launched that called for youth-produced digital videos on issues faced by queer teens.[2] The solicitations commonly specified that video submissions take the form of a public service announcement or educational video, and, like the call above, aimed to leverage and mobilize "youth voices," particularly those at the margins.[3]

This idea of a youth voice as a unique and distinct entity is pervasive among scholars, educators, and policymakers, as is an emphasis on the empowerment of that youth voice through media self-production. As we shall see, the history of those ideas stretches back decades, and they have shaped education policy, advocacy campaigns, and scholarly

Figure 1.1 Image from Canadian Women's Creative Foundation *Girls' Voice Contest*

communities. Recent scholarship has challenged the notion of a distinct youth voice and the role of media production in empowerment. It is worth unpacking the assumptions and history behind these related concepts before delving into the role of youth media self-production today.

Whether made explicit or not, the programs promoting these campaigns assume a correlation between production and circulation of youth-produced media, their voices, and their empowerment. This assumption drives many media programs and informs adult expectations of how youth should use media technologies in their everyday lives. It has become common sense logic in the field of production-based pedagogy and activism. Even though digital natives discourse has been rigorously eschewed by a formidable cadre of critical media scholars, it still persists in the education system and in activities aimed at supporting youth (boyd 2014; Herring 2008; Vaidhinayathan 2008; Jenkins 2007). The notion of "youth coming to voice" or expressing themselves through media productions aimed at circulation appears to be a mainstay of media pedagogy.

The transformed modes of production and distribution that have accompanied the dissemination of digital and networked media, and the accompanying shifts in access, demand that we ask: what assumptions are implicit in the call to voice, and what outcomes for youth are anticipated?

In order to provide a more robust conception of youth digital media empowerment, we must interrogate essentializing notions of who young people are generationally and, by extension, what they want and need to express about their lives and experiences through media. It is imperative that we disentangle the threads that tie together media and empowerment to expose areas where young people's needs might be overlooked when they are brought into that fray. My aim in this chapter is to problematize the ways in which "youth voice" and "empowerment" are often

24 *The Problem with* Youth Voices

deployed by scholars and educators to promote youth engagement with digital media production in informal and formal educational settings. I seek to complicate notions of empowerment as a viable process and desirable social and pedagogical goal, and emphasize how the burden of feeling a sense of belonging and experiencing power is often placed on youth, who, through digital media production, are expected to produce their own conditions of freedom and develop core educational competencies through their (identity-based) expression and connections with each other and imagined global networks.

While there is certainly evidence of "highly motivated" youth making their voices heard through online civic engagement and participatory politics, in general the connection between media and empowerment is not fully substantiated by the evidence of what actually happens in the lives of the majority of youth at the margins who are encouraged to make media towards expressive or political ends (Jenkins et al. 2016; Allen and Light 2015). More importantly, the adoption of the media empowerment view may in fact obscure the structural conditions that inform what young people produce and why they make the production choices they make. I wish to challenge the assumption that, for youth, having a voice, visibility, and recognition through viral video can be equated to their gaining rights and resources. Even the best-intended media projects may redirect young people away from opportunities to experiment with media form and content in ways that may be more appropriate to their particular sensibilities, affect, concerns, and motivations for communicating through media production. And, what's more, it is increasingly difficult to disentangle youth voice from a web of influential marketizing forces and pressures that may be present in pedagogical contexts.

The Digital Generation?

Looking at texts that have contributed to *digital youth* discourse, I would like to briefly consider the ways in which young people born in the digital age have been discussed in terms of *generation*—a concept that continually undergirds pedagogical assumptions about their distinct relationships to media. I am not arguing against the existence of generation-specific relationships with media. My situated research with youth (discussed in Chapter Four) has led me to believe that young people who have grown up with digital media production technologies tend to have a much more intimate and habitual relationship to producing media. However, generalizations about their relationships to media tend to mask the nuances of these relationships, threatening to obscure opportunities for more meaningful engagement. I am particularly interested in the role of institutional structures in the promotion of digital youth empowerment discourse and their impact on queer and other marginalized youth. The

The Problem with Youth Voices   25

conceptualization of the *digital native* in particular ignores differences in sexual identity and the ways in which freedom, power, and voice may not always be equally available to particular subjects.

The existence of the concepts of *youth* and *media* have long been inextricably linked (Grossberg 1994; Buckingham 2000). In the beginning of the digital era, media scholarship often represented youth engagement with media, and particularly with media production, as inherently empowering. Additionally, as the taxonomy of *millenials* became a catchall to describe young people born in the digital age, cohorts tended to be identified by their relationship to technology.

In 2001, education pundit Marc Prensky introduced the terms "Digital Natives" and "Digital Immigrants" as part of a framework for educators considering how to integrate media into the classroom. Echoing Don Tapscott's *Growing up Digital* (1998), Prensky describes "Digital Natives" as those people who were born into an already-digital world and who are assumed to possess fluency with technology (Prensky 2001). This fluency must be *acquired* by the "Digital Immigrants," who, born before digital technologies, must consciously and continuously work to acculturate and familiarize themselves with new technologies. These terms entered the popular lexicon through John Palfrey and Urs Gasser's bestselling book, *Born Digital*, which helped them spill over into popular discourse[4].

But there are many limitations of framing a "digital generation," and in the last decade many scholars have expressed concern (Buckingham 2008; Herring 2008; Jenkins 2007; Vaidhyanathan 2008). Jenkins takes issue with describing digital skills as part of a "native" sensibility, claiming that it threatens to undermine attention on participation gaps based on access to certain skills and competencies, cultural experiences, and social identities. He writes:

> Talking about youth as digital natives implies that there is a world in which these young people all share a body of knowledge they have all mastered, rather than seeing the online world as unfamiliar and uncertain for all of us.
>
> (Henry Jenkins, "Reconsidering Digital Immigrants..."
> [Confessions of an Aca-Fan, 2007])

The commonly asserted claims that young people possess unique abilities to use technologies and as a result are self-reliant and "in charge" emerges from (adult) media producers and researchers in academic and other institutions who have indeed constructed the millenial generation as such (Herring 2008). For Herring, this age-based generational digital divide that casts young people as having greater access and abilities is a symptom of what she calls "technological exoticism" and a belief in technological determinism that overshadows the contextual factors and

26   *The Problem with* Youth Voices

social motivations that shape youth behaviors and attitudes and the roles of these technologies in their lives. This leads to a presumption of youth having a level playing field and equal access to time, knowledge, skills, and technologies. This stems from biases about ethnicity, nation, gender, and class, and further casts those with less access to digital media technologies as outside of zones of participation, knowledge production, and civic participation (Vaidhyanathan 2008). As danah boyd argues in her 2014 *It's Complicated: The Social Lives of Networked Teens*, equitable access to digital technologies must also be met with new digital literacies to educate youth about the information they receive and produce, and the roles of media technologies (from Wikipedia to algorithms) in shaping messages and their circulation.

These authors have introduced important concepts that can be adapted to the unique experiences of queer youth. Unfortunately, there is still a paucity of work that effectively takes up this call to attend to the particularities and radical variation in the practices of young people of different demographics, regions, classes, etc. It is precisely the filling of this gap that my project aims to achieve. Opportunities to convene resources for the complex needs of the individuals and groups of youth who lend their voices in their production are sometimes overlooked in the attempt to contain the identities and needs of this heterogeneous group.

For queer youth in particular, there is often the need to carefully and cautiously manage certain aspects of their identities for their own safety, and they may choose to reveal or hide their sexual or gender identity depending on the context. Access to easy-to-use digital technologies may make certain kinds of freedom and mobility possible while at the same time presenting other limits to self-presentation and expression.[5] If what is deemed to be empowering about digital media use is that it allows for new forms of participation, collaboration, and connections, we must ask what complexities, challenges, and specific applications exist for those youth for whom identity is highly negotiated.

One significant pedagogical concern in working with queer youth is that encouraging open participation in public discourse regarding their sexuality may leave them vulnerable in unanticipated ways. The rhetoric of freedom encourages an approach to digital media that has serious repercussions for queer people in general, but particularly queer youth (Barnhurst, 2007). According to Barnhurst, the promise of digital freedom is structurally linked with the increased danger of repression when people with marginal identities make their identities public online. He argues:

> The rise of new communication technologies at the end of the millennium may have raised hope for queers, especially the young under the control of heteronormative families and communities but also those under repressive national regimes around the world. The paradox, of course, is that the same persons expecting digital

freedom experience physical attacks and discrimination. The existence of high expectations changes the tenor of the dangers, so that both states exist in simultaneous contrast to each other.

(Kevin G. Barnhurst, *Media / Queered*
[New York: Peter Lang, 2007])

For Barnhurst, the celebratory rhetoric around digital media participation marks particular kinds of freedom and empowerment for queer people, but stands in contrast to the embodied and material realities of their lives. While this is clearly not a paradox specific to queer people, his example emphasizes that mobility and free expression in online spaces do not necessarily translate to offline realities. At the same time, it is important to temper Barnhurst's argument by noting the potential benefits of increased representation. The success of shows like Fox's musical hit *Glee*, which features several "out" queer characters and devotes entire episodes to issues regarding their sexual identities, provides examples that should lead us to a more qualified and nuanced understanding of Barnhurst's critique. As queer studies scholar Larry Gross has argued, representation offers a visualization of what it means to be queer. While it may not always map onto lived experience, queer media icons can offer a sense of a life that exists beyond social structures. Perhaps, in an era where YouTube videos have more viewers than some broadcast television shows, the everyday queer youth video producer can offer a range of life possibilities to others (Gross 2001). We might then ask what types of pedagogical approaches would best benefit sub-groups of youth in exploring how they regulate modes of self-disclosure as they use digital media to engage in public discourse.

It is important to consider the ways in which the negotiation of online identity is part of queer youth's everyday participatory media activity— for them, participating on websites and in social media as open queer people often requires them to practice what David J. Phillips calls "context management and identity management" as a means of self-protection (2002). Managing when and how to reveal their sexual and/or gender identity to match the social context is as necessary online as it is offline. And, as Marwick and boyd have argued, online identity negotiation is intrinsic to youth social media networking in general (2011; 2014). So, while producing digital video may provide new points of connection and community, as well as additional channels for resources, support, and expression for queer youth, it can also be a site of violence, alienation, and (negotiated) anonymity.

From Digital Natives to Participatory Culture

In a move away from the broad-sweeping "digital natives" framework, Henry Jenkins has been prolific in his advocacy for what he calls

28   *The Problem with* Youth Voices

"participatory culture," a model of digital media use that shifts the focus from individual expression and experience to community involvement and processes of learning, connection, and social engagement. In the 2009 Digital Media and Learning (DML) MacArthur report *Confronting the Challenges of Participatory Culture: Media Education for the 21st Century*, Jenkins et al. (2009) posit that participatory culture is directly connected to empowerment, as it offers opportunities, not formerly available to youth, to participate in civic and social life. He describes participatory cultures as having

> relatively low barriers to artistic expression and civic engagement, strong support for creating and sharing creations, and some type of informal mentorship whereby experienced participants pass along knowledge to novices. In a participatory culture, members also believe their contributions matter and feel some degree of social connection with one another (at the least, members care about others' opinions of what they have created).
>
> (Henry Jenkins et al., *Confronting the Challenges of Participatory Culture: Media Education for the 21st Century* [Cambridge: MIT Press, 2009])

For Jenkins, these skills extend from traditional literacy and research, technical, and critical analysis skills learned in the classroom and, therefore, are issues concerning critical pedagogy.[6] Whereas Buckingham sees youth disengaged from political life because political debate has been conducted "almost entirely over their heads," Jenkins et al. see youth becoming active citizens through participation:

> Empowerment comes from making meaningful decisions within a real civic context: we learn the skills of citizenship by becoming political actors and gradually coming to understand the choices we make in political terms. Today's children learn through play the skills they will apply to more serious tasks later. The challenge is how to connect decisions made at local, state or national levels.
>
> (Jenkins et al., *Confronting the Challenges of Participatory Culture: Media Education for the 21st Century*, 13)

Jenkins and his co-authors point out the flaws in what they call a "laissez-faire" approach to digital cultures in which youth are expected to acquire skills without intervention or supervision and use them towards meaningful participation in society (civic participation, community dialogues, etc). These flaws include an underestimation of the gaps in access that exist, an assumption that youth are actively reflective and can articulate what they learn from their participation, and an assumption that they can develop the necessary ethical norms to cope with social environments

The Problem with Youth Voices   29

online. The authors argue for a paradigm shift away from earlier approaches to education and digital technologies that "stressed tools above all else," towards providing contexts for young people to "evaluate their own work and appraise their own actions ... helping them to situate the media they produce within its larger social, cultural and legal context" (Jenkins et al. 2009, 15).

For Jenkins and his co-authors, technological access can only be meaningful for users who have developed the critical skills necessary to use technologies in ways that will enrich their lives. And even when provided with access, young people may not always be actively reflecting on their media experiences or possess "the ethical norms to cope with a complex and diverse social environment online" (Jenkins et al. 2009, 15). Therefore, the authors suggest, any meaningful media education must also include guidance towards developing these faculties. Specifically, they advise that schools and after-school programs should devote more attention to fostering "new media literacies" which they describe as "a set of cultural competencies and social skills that young people need in the new media landscape" (Jenkins et al. 2009, xiii).

The skill sets described in the 2009 MacArthur white paper are reflected in other central media pedagogy texts, most notably the 2007 publication *Core Principles of Media Literacy Education in the United States*, a document that was commissioned by the National Commission for Media Literacy Education and authored by a team of scholars and practitioners, meant to serve as a common ground for the field. Media education scholars Renee Hobbs and Amy Jensen suggest the document is meant to reconcile what they call the "protectionist and empowerment" wings of media literacy, the goal being to not only create informed consumers of mass media and popular culture, but to encourage and enable active democratic citizenship (Hobbs and Jensen 2009). Together, these kinds of texts have helped to articulate a valuable set-list of core competencies that explicitly counter the framework of "digital natives" that assumes all young people to be inherent masters of new media technology. At the same time, the focus of this work runs the risk of being used to forward normative conceptions of competency, especially within the climate of public education in the US which has been increasingly dominated by policies aimed at enforcing educational standards. Though the work of these scholars has been strongly at odds with standards-based education, especially insofar as they embrace Freierian student-centered approaches and advocate for the value of popular culture and vernacular knowledge forms, their guidelines paradoxically mirror the goals of standardized literacy programs. Circulated to educators with the aim of empowering students, these national media literacy guidelines help to institutionalize pedagogy that does little to account for the "diverse social environments" that different students will encounter depending on their distinct backgrounds, interests, and persuasions. Specific positionalities require

30   *The Problem with* Youth Voices

distinct competencies that are acquired through direct experience. The guidelines treat knowledge as a priori rather than situated.

Turning our attention to modalities of instruction, it is worth considering how some principles of critical and feminist pedagogy could help recast approaches to teaching that have been put forward in these digital media education guidelines. The guidelines emphasize the need for adult involvement as an important step in developing forms of youth criticality considered necessary for their empowerment, but do not address the power relations inherent in pedagogy. Carmen Luke and Jennifer Gore have advocated that such dynamics define the classroom, students, and teachers, as "we are inscribed as either student or professor: students take exams, teachers don't; students are graded, teachers grade. Such inscriptions are key in the production of subjectivity, identity and knowledge in pedagogical encounters. In short, we might argue, subjectivity, identity and knowledge *are* the work of schooling" (Luke and Gore 1992).

Brian Goldfarb's research on the role of the visual in the media education of the early 2000s also provides useful insight into the reality that alternative work with new media in education is, and has always been, institutionally situated (Goldfarb 1992). Hence, the viability of the kinds of programs encouraged by these new media literacy and pedagogy advocates is dependent on a network of institutions rather than a commonly assumed trickle-down scenario whereby educational programs outside of schools adopt or re-imagine educational objectives that were initially designed in formal education institutions. Goldfarb suggests that they are instead products of a longer history of intertwining missions to entertain and to educate that has deep roots in the public education system. In this way, "the voice of new youth media is institutionally situated and is thus subject to the same forces of the market as adult media production" (Goldfarb 2002). This is not to say that youth voices are inherently compromised, but that they are indeed bound up in the same social and economic forces as adult media production. I would add that the particular "grassroots" quality of youth digital media production also obscures its location in the established political economic order of traditional media production. Goldfarb refers to these as "market forces," which is appropriate for the circulatory pathways of the anti-gay-bullying viral video PSA or the videos of the *It Gets Better Project*, which has simultaneously driven and expanded a particular kind of media market, one which doesn't generate any kind of visible profit, but which is deeply enmeshed in the funding structures and flows of several institutions.

The rise in popularity of youth digital video production in informal and formal learning contexts and social life has inverted what, in the mid-1980s, media education scholar Len Masterman called the "technicist trap" to describe what he believed a sense of inferiority students were likely to feel when they learned how to use media production tools

The Problem with Youth Voices   31

only to find their productions to be weaker than the commercial media they were used to consuming (Masterman 1985; Hobbs and Jensen 2009). Masterman encouraged media educators to teach students about the relationship between economic constraints that structure the media and culture industries and the way that comes to bear on meaning and representation. Rather than an "inferiority" complex, digital youth producers now find themselves working within an economy of media amateurism that intersects with commercial media, assigning value to work that is explicitly non-professional. Not only are prizes available through the myriad of video contests and youth film festivals, according to Google's video monetization policies on their user-content-driven site YouTube, young producers may receive income from videos they post that receive a minimum number of views.

The judging criteria for online video contests and the production guidelines posted on channels like the *It Gets Better Project* site emphasize that videos are valued for presenting "authentic youth perspectives" and "youth voices" more than for aesthetic production values. Yet what constitutes an "authentic youth voice" in the context of online video is typically overdetermined by the specifications being made by the organizations which are making the calls. Most sites are very specific about video content, length, and style. The expectation is that participants already have access to the skills and technologies needed to film and edit high-quality video. The question of *who* is able to participate is ultimately shaped by who has both access to the necessary technologies and an interest in responding to the guidelines provided by the organization.

Problematizing "Youth Voice" as Inherently Empowering

My goal in this book is to help pivot away from youth media production as a catch-all approach to serving queer youth, and find ways to engage multiple public spheres that relate to diverse modes of citizenship and positionalities. The prevailing discourse on digital media literacy programs and youth-produced media contests emphasizes a connection between youth media production, the mobilization of "youth voice," and empowerment. We have examined the prevalence of digital youth discourse and its impact on expectations of media literacies; we can now more closely examine how that emboldens an uncritical embrace of the notion of voice and empowerment.

While digital youth media empowerment projects now proliferate, their ubiquity may actually be evidence that, on a collective level, we really have no clear idea of how—or even whether—they function. The term *empowerment* is employed so often in descriptions of youth media outcomes that it has lost specificity and power. Also, many of the existing digital youth media production projects and programs in the United States describe their philosophies and pedagogical and philosophical approaches in ways that

32   *The Problem with* Youth Voices

suggest that they aim to contribute to a legacy of progressive learning and, one might argue, feminist critical pedagogy itself, as that is the scholarly area where the notion of *empowerment* and *voice* first emerged.

In the early 1990s, feminist pedagogy scholar Jennifer Gore asked her contemporaries, "what is the vision of empowerment anyway?" (Gore 1992). Here, Gore was addressing what she saw to be an unproblematized use of the term "empowerment" in activities that involved critical approaches to youth learning and identity development. Though she was writing nearly a decade before digital media production technologies would really take hold as pedagogical tools, her provocative questions are useful for making sense of the approach of the empowerment philosophy that is so prominent in digital media pedagogy and the incorporation of digital media into forms of self-expression and promotion.

Gore explains that the meaning of "empowerment is contingent on the specific discourses that construct it." She argues that discourses of critical and feminist pedagogy construct empowerment to more generally presuppose "(1) an agent of empowerment, (2) a notion of power as property, and (3) some kind of vision or desirable state" (Gore 1992, 56). Gore sees this approach as perpetuating a dangerous dichotomy between empowerment and oppression "through a level of abstraction which mystifies the meanings ascribed to either term (empowerment or oppression)" (Gore 1992, 59). She notes that discourses of critical and feminist pedagogy tend to decontextualize empowerment and express concern for youth at "the broad level of societal relations and institutions and ideologies (be they capitalist and/or patriarchal)" rather than focusing on specific contexts and practices. Following Michel Foucault, she suggests that instead of treating power as a possession or a commodity, a thing to be held or exchanged, it is important to look at where it is exercised. To do this, she proposes that more attention be paid to the "microdynamics of the operation of power as it exercised at particular sites." In the context of contemporary critical pedagogy, empowerment is understood as being available through specific contexts and practices that involve digital media production, while it is also believed to have an impact on social relations, institutions, and ideologies. Contemporary media pedagogy that pertains to digital tools tends to conflate both the specific practices and broad ideologies, uncritically grafting notions of empowerment in pedagogy from the prevailing pedagogical perspectives that Gore was critiquing onto current media use. So, rather than building from critiques of empowerment, it appears that contemporary media pedagogy has reproduced earlier, problematic conceptions of youth power in which a simplistic dichotomy between youth power and oppression prevailed.

Mimi Orner offers another useful intervention into the pedagogical limitations of *liberatory* and *emancipatory* educational traditions by using frameworks and concepts derived from feminist appropriations of poststructuralist discourse. Arguing that "calls for 'specific student voice'

The Problem with Youth Voices   33

contain realist and essentialist epistemological positions regarding subjectivity which are neither acknowledged specifically nor developed theoretically," she calls out and challenges the ways in which the student voice is often mobilized in the service of pedagogical and political goals designed and articulated by adults (Orner 1992). Orner's examples point to scenarios in which youth are asked to speak (such as telling personal stories in class or participating in a "talking circle" as part of a democratic classroom), and her argument can clearly be extended to include situations in which they are asked to either articulate or explicitly represent themselves through technologically mediated practices. She claims that while the reasons students are being called upon, and the topics they are being asked to talk about, represent a variety of social, political, and economic commitments as well as a range of research and teaching agendas, calls for young voices all share a "deeply entrenched and less examined" pattern of relating to youth as "Other" (Orner 1992, 76). She expresses deep skepticism about the way in which the student voice has been conceptualized and solicited by people who claim to empower students, and goes as far to suggest that the student voice in itself is "an oppressive construct—one that [I argue] perpetuates domination in the name of liberation" (Orner 1992, 75). Here she echoes an earlier claim by Elizabeth Ellsworth that the "discourse of critical pedagogy is based on rationalist assumptions that give rise to repressive myths" (1989, 297).

As Meryl Alper has argued, "'giving voice to the voiceless' regularly stands in for the idea that the historically disadvantaged, underrepresented, or vulnerable gain opportunities to organize, increase their visibility, and express themselves by leveraging the affordances of information media, and communication technologies" (2017, 2). However, despite the opportunities media production may offer to interrupt dominant discourses about the expectations or assumptions about one's ability, and as Herman Gray has cautioned, representation does not automatically usher in equality; instead, it *presumes* it (2013). Visibility, therefore, can be a particular trap; one that appears to be the result of a struggle for rights, rather than a distraction from the political, legal, and social disempowerment the subjects may experience outside of the image and the necessary actions that must take place to correct power imbalances.

In her discussion of the production of photographs by the "voiceless" children of women working in brothels in India prompted by their Western teacher, featured in the documentary *Born into Brothels*, Pooja Rangan found that the qualities that made particular photographs appropriate for global circulation reveal "a coercive cultural logic [that] underpins the invitation to subjecthood mediating their auto-ethnographic labor" (Rangan 2017, 146). The humanitarian impulse of the adult teachers and the transparency and expression on the part of the child photographers entwines participation and abjection in a market in which the expression of youth at the margins has particular currency.

34   *The Problem with* Youth Voices

Banet-Weiser underscores the normalization of equating visibility with empowerment, claiming that "the increasing imperative to 'put yourself out there' ... is part of a broader context of neoliberal entrepreneurialism, where self-branding is becoming normative" (Banet-Weiser 2015, 189–90; 2012; Berliner and Kenworthy 2017). The move to thinking of the "branded self" is the result of a widening of the "intertextual zone" in which individuals pattern their self-representation with those historically taken up by celebrities and other public figures and empowerment becomes a selling tactic (Marshall 2010). In the case of girls' media, Banet-Weiser has observed that performativity and self-representation dovetail in an uneasy entanglement with "girls" as a demographic that is simultaneously "in crisis and in need of empowerment" and capable of producing their own forms of power through performance, that can gain traction through commodification and marketization (2015, 183). For Alison Hearn, outer-directed expression of the self, which often relies on the visual codes of the mainstream culture industry, is increasingly "subject to the extraction of value" in both broadcast and social media (Hearn 2008, 197). Any single video can simultaneously act as a means of communication with a network of friends and family and an audition tape for a prospective agent (Berliner, 2014).

We might begin to consider the ways in which calls for youth voice through video production may be interpreted as something closer to a *prompt* to perform particular aspects of their identities and demonstrate formal media skills rather than as flexible, open opportunities for expressions of their feelings and needs. Moreover, as media production has become an increasingly popular way for organizations to engage youth in their particular institutional agendas, and prizes and professional opportunities are generally offered as rewards for successful submissions, we must question whether the power lies entirely with the youth producers. As Dussel and Dahya (2017) have noted, since the early 2000s there has been a shift from a "potentially decentralized and horizontal peer-to-peer network to a concentrated ring of transnational corporations" and this is shaped by an impetus to spread media through the rhetoric and codes of the culture industries.

Much critical pedagogy calls for youth voices as a corrective to the lack of power that teachers and mentors imagine that students— and themselves—have in culture at large. Orner claims that many pedagogues seek to *empower* students to find and articulate their silenced or delegitimized voices while aiming for young people of various social, political, and economic groups to come to see how they have been dominated by those with power. She warns that, instead, discourses on student voice in fact *limit* youth, as they are "premised on the assumption of a fully conscious, fully speaking, 'unique, fixed, coherent' self" that "ignore[s] the shifting identities, unconscious processes, pleasures and desires not only of students, but of teachers,

The Problem with Youth Voices   35

administrators, and researchers as well" (Dussel and Dahya 2017, 79). Orner's approach can help us think more critically about how the particular framing and structure of types of youth media empowerment projects may require youth to participate as particular types of subjects. Hauge and Bryson have made a similar claim based on their research with young rural media-makers involved in an international development project in Nicauragua (2015). They observed that female producers "kept their distance" from narratives that were personal to (or about) them and their lived experiences. The authors cite the limitations of liberation discourses that are enacted through pedagogical interventions, and challenge the notion that telling personal stories is equivalent to agency (Hauge and Bryson 2015, 297). Similarly, in her research with black and Muslim girl media producers, Negin Dahya has emphasized the need to consider the context in which digital media are produced to truly understand how voice and representation are "identified, recognized, affirmed, and authenticated." If we think of digital artifacts in terms of "networks and assemblages" that are reflective of their contexts, we can successfully move away from notions of "giving voice" in digital media made by young people in educational settings (Dussel and Dahya 2017, 108).

Online digital video contests, in particular, overtly call *specific* youth voices to the fore. For instance, when a public service announcement (PSA) contest invites queer student activists to tell their stories of how they improved their communities and schools through their activism, the sponsor is essentially asking youth to produce a video in which they represent themselves in terms of particular frames of identity. The PSA prompt has had an especially strong life in recent decades as a way in which commercial as well as nonprofit organizations make claims to doing educational and justice work. PSA videos that are produced as part of assignments or contests are also often used as public relations material and do other forms of legitimatizing work for the organizations that sponsor them.

Orner (1992) advocates for more scrutiny of the way in which "liberatory" educational discourses may actually work *against* the intentions of those who produce them. She argues:

> Liberatory educational discourses call for the transformation of "reality" through a consciousness of one's social position through the articulation of one's voice. Little or no attention is given to the multiple social positions, multiple voices, conscious and unconscious pleasures, tensions, desires, and contradictions which are present in all subjects, in all historical contexts.
>
> (Mimi Orner, "Interrupting the Calls for Student Voice in 'Liberatory' Education: A Feminist Poststructuralist Perspective", in *Feminisms and Critical Pedagogy* [New York: Routledge, 1992], 79)

36   *The Problem with* Youth Voices

The question of *voice* is inextricable from competence in talking and listening and assumes a students' desire to speak or be heard by their educators in the first place.

Without denigrating the intentions motivating the pedagogical approach she criticizes, Orner offers an alternative to thinking about the place and function of power in pedagogy. She aims to re-direct focus away from "questions such as 'Who is powerful?' or 'What are the intentions of those with power?' to questions regarding the processes by which subjects are constituted as effects of power" (Orner 1992, 82). Working with a model of power as circulating through discourse rather than enacted through hierarchy and overt oppression, she shows how pedagogues are implicated in reproducing systems of domination through the discourses and social interactions that they, too, are part of. In a Foucauldian framework, the act of asking students to talk, confess, or share information about themselves and their experiences in the presence of authority figures such as teachers puts a "hidden curriculum" into action, one in which a student's divulgence is automatically subject to disciplinary power (Giroux 1981; Foucault 1977). Orner urges pedagogues to consider the extent to which students monitor themselves as they imagine being seen through the eyes of others, including those who called for their voice in the first place.

One might even argue that the video version of student voice poses the possibility of added injury, as the video file, link, or tape can be used to archive and reproduce the student's response over time, even long after that student has left the educational or community environment in which they were once encouraged to produce. For students seeking control over the storage and circulation of their video files, digital video technologies present an increased challenge compared to analog video technologies. The capacity of video to be distributed presents a concern for young people who choose to reveal sensitive, personal information that might put them at risk, as is the case for those who experience ongoing bullying, or queer youth who may not be open about their sexuality with friends and family and who may be at risk of further alienation or violence as a result of going public. Often, the level of publicness cannot be fully anticipated, as a simple retweet or share of a link can catapult a little-seen media artifact to prominence (Marwick and boyd 2014; 2011; Livingstone 2008; Tufekci 2008; Lange 2007). Orner suggests that educators who are concerned with changing power relations "must continually examine our assumptions about our own positions, those of our students, the meanings and uses of student voice, our power to call for students to speak, and often unexamined power to legitimate and perpetuate unjust relations in the name of student empowerment" (Orner 1992, 77).

Accordingly, I would urge that Orner's proposed reflection on how unjust relations are perpetuated through calls for and uses of student voice also be applied to calls for youth voice through video production

The Problem with Youth Voices   37

(in both formal and informal educational contexts). How might specific requirements, rules or narratives styles suggested by program organizers introduce or reaffirm relations of power? Who has the power to solicit videos and what is their relationship to those who are being called on to produce? What does the youth producer have to gain from producing a video?

The prevailing notion in popular culture that media representation gives *voice* and visibility to young people through production presents a particular challenge for many queer youth, whose security and safety is sometimes predicated on their delicate negotiations of what they can and cannot express about their identities, in which contexts, and to whom. When asked to make public expressions that identify them as queer, some youth expose themselves to possible harassment, alienation, or compromised comfort. Losh and Alexander (2009) have identified the "coming out video" as a lens for observing the management of sexual identity in media culture, at times producing what Alexandra Juhasz (2008) has called a "niche-tube" that flouts the tendency for hegemonic narratives to trend in online media. Yet, we must question what such personal videos actually reveal about sex, sexuality, and sexual identity when they are externally motivated. Furthermore, when media pedagogues encourage queer youth to produce content on universalizing, identity-based themes, they risk overlooking the needs of the individual participants. These needs can be related to health and housing, or legal and emotional concerns, as well as other forms of identity-based discrimination that the youth may be experiencing. Several queer scholars, including Dean Spade, J. Jack Halberstam, and Lisa Duggan, have cautioned against normatizing forces that seem to offer liberation but which instead produce more constraint in terms of the performance of particular versions of queer identity (Spade 2015; Halberstam 2011; Duggan 2003). Although I am focusing here on queer youth in particular, much of my argument pertains to thinking through the ways in which the empowerment model obfuscates the complexities of how power is found and articulated among marginalized youth in general. The question of identity is itself at the center of the problem of youth empowerment that I am foregrounding.

Youth Radio education director and scholar Elisabeth Soep, whose direct involvement in youth digital media production has been formative of her critical writing, is also skeptical of the emphasis on "youth voice" expressed through media production as a "site of free expression and social critique" (Soep 2006, 197). Citing a 2001 study of the youth media field in which Campbell et al. revealed "youth voice" as one of the primary goals that programs claim (alongside professional outcomes, youth development, media literacy, and academic achievement), she calls for more attention to be paid to the actual language that young people use when producing and evaluating their own projects.

38 *The Problem with* Youth Voices

Drawing on the research of Nicole Fleetwood and her own ethnographic field work and interviews in over 20 media production programs, she argues that the discourse of *voice* dominates discussions about youth media literacy in scholarship and practical discourse but is under-examined. Whereas "literacy" is understood by scholars and practitioners to exist in a myriad of forms with multiple applications (e.g., multiliteracies, popular literacy, critical literacy, media literacy), the notion of *voice* is all too often used to support youth media projects without any qualification of what it really means. Based on her experience as a media scholar and producer, she asserts that "youth projects very often describe what they do as a process of 'giving voice' to young people, or helping them to 'find their voice' or highlighting 'silenced voices' by providing teenagers with the skills and access needed to express their stories" (Soep 2006, 198). For Soep, *voice* is too often used as a unitary and monolithic concept that gets employed in ways that are not only reductive, but which border on paternalistic. Citing Janine Marchessault, Soep notes that video in particular holds apparent appeal as a resource for "dispossessed" communities (Soep 2006, 201; Marchessault 1995). Here, she suggests, we should turn to Fleetwood's study of youth video programs for a cautionary reminder that media projects "have a tendency to purse the fantasy of 'authentic' youth experience, which itself often embodies a sensationalized portrayal [of racialized urban youth]" (Soep 2006, 201). She observes:

> Literacy scholars, particularly those interested in multiliteracies as they form through media production, consider an analysis of power to be central to young people's capacity both to make and interpret original media. It is not enough for many of these scholars that young people acquire the technical and aesthetic skills required to create within a given medium; there is often an expectation that they concurrently develop habits of considering implicit messages, assumptions, and biases within their own and others' products, and to understand the social structures and tensions behind systems of media production and consumption.
>
> (Elisabeth Soep, "Beyond Literacy and Voice in Youth Media Production," *McGill Journal of Education* 41 [3]:208)

The investment in having youth filming and circulating "raw" first-person video testimonies tends to stand in place of critical questions about the reification of inequalities within youth media products and processes. Soep argues that production is far more than merely a vehicle for testimony. Noting that video production requires constant collaboration and negotiation of intent, perception, and judgment, she suggests that youth producers must inevitably engage with many kinds of voices in their production and post-production process (Soep 2006, 205). To make

The Problem with Youth Voices   39

a collaborative media project, young people must engage in many forms of literacy, which depend on their ability to enter into different kinds of talk and intersubjective practices that require them to engage with other voices. She argues:

> When we notice the varied voices young people use as they create work, especially at moments calling for judgment or evaluation, we can no longer limit ourselves to a focus on the redeeming value of youth media as a way to honor young people's "true" voices.
>
> (Soep, "Beyond Literacy and Voice in Youth Media Production," 208)

For one, young people often use "reported speech;" they often speak in the name of "we" rather than "I." In this sense, voices are often "crowded" rather than one-dimensional authentic representations of the speaker's perspective. Soep notes the extent to which individual young people "strategically leverage, dramatize, and experiment with varied real and imagined voices, even in a single utterance" (Soep 2006, 199). Youth video testimonies often include what Bakhtin calls "double-voiced" discourse, in which a person "might report someone else's speech as a way to align with a voice of authority, or to mock another speaker, or to dramatize a scene or to convey a sense of empirical reliability, to name just a handful of pragmatic implications of reported speech" (Soep 2006, 202; Bakhtin 2004). She suggests that this speech often enters one's own speech in "concealed and ambiguous ways" (Soep 2006, 205). Hence, youth video-makers may be presenting the opinions and ideas and values of other people through their performances.

Soep's research emphasizes that youth video production is a site of "crowded" speech through which many voices come to the fore. Her work suggests that perhaps what is most valuable about youth media production programs is not that they that bring marginalized voices forward or teach hands-on skills to young people who might not otherwise have access (she notes that these skill sets may not have measurable social and educational value outside of the short-term program), but that they provide opportunities for youth to bring other voices together for their own analysis of power. For researchers and educators involved with such programs, there appears to be an opportunity to leverage the collaborative practice of media production to engage youth in an analysis of power based on their vocalizations of other voices of power with which they imagine themselves in dialogue.

Soep raises an important question: even if media programs have everything in place to elicit voices, do we have the necessary frameworks for interpreting them? As Nick Couldry argues in *Why Voice Matters*, the amplificiation of voices through participatory media tools in itself has not been enough to secure equality in democratic participation; we must

40 *The Problem with* Youth Voices

invest in new "intensities of listening" to the multiplicity of stories that emerge and seek out platforms and tools to leverage existing diversity in the public sphere (Couldry 2010).

Visual anthropologist Richard Chalfen is another useful figure to turn to for approaches to interpreting self-made media that go beyond simply eliciting the voices of makers. His collaborative research with public health researchers Laura Sherman and Michael Rich in the 2000s offers a valuable listening-centered model for self-produced video that clearly develops out of his experience since the late 1960s eliciting ethnographic research subjects' perspectives through their self-made media. Chalfen's early work as a research assistant to Sol Worth and John Adair on the Navajo Film Themselves project (which later became the seminal book *Through Navajo Eyes: An Exploration in Film Communication and Anthropology*) is credited as being one of the first ethnographic projects to put cameras in the hands of the research subjects (Worth and Adair 1997). The research study, designed to examine what the shooting, editing, and content choices made by the Navajo makers might reveal about Navajo culture and visual language more broadly, has been widely acknowledged by anthropologists as having catalyzed a turn in ethnographic practice towards the authority of research subjects, and helped to popularize reflexive research methods that have had wide influence across disciplines and inspired the types of youth-produced media projects that are at the center of my discussion.[7] The Navajo project has also been commonly, and, as anthropologist Faye Ginsburg has argued, mistakenly, taken up as an empowerment project, which even Chalfen and the other Navajo project collaborators have denied was their intention. Chalfen's work with the Video Intervention/Prevention Assessment (VIA) method continues his sustained emphasis, in the solicitation of video narratives, on the shift from *giving voice* to video-makers to *listening* to what they have to say. Yet while the research findings of the Navajo project arguably had little benefit to the Navajo compared with their value to the study of visual communication, Chalfen's more recent work with the VIA method, through which the researchers use audiovisual narratives of illness produced by patients to "reveal how subjects construct personal understandings of their medical conditions," is a more directed effort to improve the health of the research subjects (Chalfen, Sherman, and Rich 2010). In their article "VIA's Visual Voices: The Awareness of a Dedicated Audience for Voices in Patient Video Narratives," Chalfen, Sherman and Rich emphasize the important role of *listening* to voices that have been elicited through digital video production under the auspices of empowerment in order to more thoroughly understand what producers wish to communicate. The authors offer a generous and open approach to interpreting content, yielding a textured interpretation of the video text. They explain:

The frequently heard justification for many projects that supply cameras to young people for their own photography and filmmaking is a simplistic and carelessly delivered cliche—namely, "to give them a voice." This phrase has been widely used, and more often than not, abused. Aside from certain paternalistic and politically awkward features, this noble calling of sharing cameras has seldom been matched by sensitive attention to the reception side of the communication process—namely, "to lend an ear". In truth, careful attention to what is "said" is often a missing component in light of other harmful cliches—namely, "the pictures speak for themselves" or even, "every picture tells a story". Thus the preferential attention to "voice" might not be matched with attentive looking and listening to what first-time image-makers might be saying. In short, we may be seeing "an uncritical celebration of representation" in the context of participatory media.

(Richard Chalfen, Laura Sherman, and Michael Rich, "VIA's Visual Voices," *Visual Studies* 25 [3])

Here the authors underscore the dynamic relationship between video narrative elicitation and making meaning out of what has been produced while they call out the importance of understanding the descriptive and analytic frameworks within which video-makers express themselves. Influenced by Pat Thompson, who has argued that an important principle of both communication and sociolinguistics is that "*what* one says and *how* one says it are significantly structured by knowledge of *who* is being addressed," the researchers conclude that one of the "primary variables" in the elicitation of voice and in the process of understanding the value of using those voices as research comes from anticipating the kinds of audiences to which video producers imagine they speak (Chalfen, Sherman, and Rich 2010). Using the five models of voice that Thompson outlines in *Doing Visual Research with Children and Young People*, the researchers found they were better able to evaluate the different kinds of expression at play: "The Authoritative Voice," in which participants make statements on behalf of people who share their illnesses; "The Critical Voice," in which the speaker challenges policies, practices, or stereotypical portrayals or attitudes; "The Therapeutic Voice," in which the speakers communicate their vulnerabilities in a more confessional mode; "The Consumer Voice," in which they state their needs and preferences related to their lifestyle, and finally, "The Pedagogic Voice," which reflects the ways the speakers have been "schooled" into certain modes of expression. This framework provides a model through which we can begin to ask which kinds of voices are elicited through youth media production projects.

While it may seem that their analysis has limited applications because they are primarily invested in participant media as a research tool, their

42   *The Problem with* Youth Voices

model does the important work of putting *listening* and *interpretation* back at the center of communication by underscoring that empowerment is not possible without meaningful communication. The model itself stands as a critique of the persistent links made between self-produced media, voice, and empowerment. So while the proliferation of communication technologies and increased ease of access for mediated expression may present more opportunities to hear from vulnerable populations, without methods for interpreting what these people are trying to express, or who they are seeking to communicate with, they are not actually communicating to anyone who might be able to help them. The researchers working with the VIA method take it as a given that patient empowerment cannot be gained simply by producing and making public their personal narratives. They recognize production as a component of research into how to support populations of people who have had similar experiences with illness, but never claim that the production of a personal video will lead to the empowerment of the person who has produced it. This aspect of their approach has broad implications, as it suggests that expression in itself will not necessarily change the material conditions of the person who is doing the expressing.

Howard Rheingold has made a similar argument concerning the elicitation of youth voices in the realm of civic engagement. An early proponent of the potential for digital media to catalyze political and civic participation, since the 1980s his research on the value and power of cybercultures has helped to foment scholarly discussion of the relationship between interactions with digital media and personal and civic empowerment. His significant body of scholarship has featured centrally in the development of the sub-field of digital humanities and has been taken up by many educators in the development of media pedagogy thought to enhance students' experience of power through digital media use. In a 2008 essay, "Using Participatory Media and Public Voice to Encourage Civic Engagement," he adds nuance to his earlier accounts of online participation as inherently empowering when he writes that for young people who put their thoughts and ideas online "'having your say' doesn't mean 'being listened to'" (Rheingold 2000a; 2000b; 2008; 2014). Here Rheingold begins to sculpt an approach to youth participation that extends beyond simpler conceptions of "voice" that circulate in empowerment discourse in order to acknowledge that participation doesn't automatically confer on youth a sense that they are being heard and understood. Therefore, our understanding of their sense of power should not be limited to an analysis of what they make public.

Interested in leveraging young people's increased use of media tools for self-expression and connection with peers towards "active citizenship," he suggests that educators must help students to "communicate in their public voices" about issues they care about. The crux of his

The Problem with Youth Voices   43

argument is that young people don't feel they have a voice because they think that, despite their participation and presence in participatory media, no one is listening.[8] Citing a Pew Research study that found that more than 50 percent of today's teens have created as well as consumed digital media, he locates his concern with the 50 percent who are producing, asking how, "rather than blaming young people for their apathy, the finger might instead be pointed at the online and offline structures of opportunity that facilitate, shape and develop young people's participation" (Lenhart and Madden 2005; Rheingold 2008, 98). Rheingold acknowledges that many youth producers are already making their perspectives and feelings known through blogs, vlogs, and social media sites, and many use peer networks to engage with issues of concern. He believes more can be done to encourage young people to put these skills to work towards furthering the goals of democracy, and that this can be achieved by bringing the discussion back to participatory media literacy as a goal for educating youth about using technology to participate actively in the democratic process.

Contributing to the critique of the digital natives generational rhetoric, Rheingold argues that while young people are self-guided when it comes to technology use, they are also in need of guidance, because "although a willingness to learn new media by point-and-click exploration might come naturally to today's student cohort, there's nothing innate about knowing how to apply their skills to the process of democracy" (2008, 99). The solution Rheingold offers is for youth to be taught to develop their voice, which he defines as "the unique style of personal expression that distinguishes one's communications from those of others, can be called upon to help connect young people's energetic involvement in identity-formation with their potential engagement with society as citizens" (Rheingold 2008, 101). He considers his an "activist approach," grounded by the hypothesis that "active use of networked media, collaboration in social cyberspaces, and peer production of digital cultural products has changed the way young people learn and that their natural attraction to participatory media could be used to draw youth into civic engagement" (Rheingold 2008, 115). For educators to encourage youth to develop a "public voice" would mean to aid them in "consciously engaging with an active public rather than broadcasting to a passive audience" (Rheingold 2008, 101).

It is clear that Rheingold imagines youth broadcasts as directly linked to their participation and place within the public sphere, and he is invested in the power of voices that have been trained to participate in debate, advocacy, criticism, persuasion, and politicking. Arguing that "the public voice of individuals, aggregated and in dialogue with the voices of other individuals is the fundamental particle of 'public opinion,'" he proposes that

44   *The Problem with* Youth Voices

learning to use blogs, wikis, digital storytelling, podcasts, and video as media of self-expression within a context of "public voice" should be introduced and evaluated in school curricula, after-school programs, and informal learning communities if today's youth are to become effective citizens in the emerging era of networked publics.

(Howard Rheingold, "Using Participatory Media and Public Voice to Encourage Civic Engagement," in *Civic Life Online: Learning How Digital Media Can Engage Youth*, edited by W. Lance Bennett [Cambridge: MIT Press, 2008], 103)

Rheingold builds on the work of Yochai Benkler, who, in *The Wealth of Networks*, suggests that fundamental changes in media now enable people today to *participate* in conversations rather than being limited to the role of passive receivers of information gleaned from news and opinions produced by designated experts, as well as on that of danah boyd, who, using ethnographic findings as evidence, argues that, for young people, interest in participating in political and civic conversations begins with the immediate issues that concern them. Combining these perspectives, Rheingold posits that, from participating in the blogosphere, youth can be habituated to participating in the public sphere, where he imagines consequential dialogue occurs (Benkler 2006; boyd 2017). For Rheingold, the "power to publish" should be understood by youth as a power to participate. In other words, he imagines the blogosphere as something of a proverbial "gateway drug" to the public sphere. His whole argument rests on a few presumptions that, taken together, advance a position that threatens to diminish different modes and means of youth production by determining what kind of expression and production is most meaningful.

He begins with the premise that all people inherently possess a coherent and singular voice that simply needs to be trained and amplified through education. I argue that this narrow notion of subjectivity and expression sets limits on what kind of expression is possible. In light of longstanding feminist critiques of the Habermasian public sphere that is rooted in nostalgia for the European salon and, thereby, privileges a particular public that is determined along racial, socioeconomic, gendered, and ethnic lines, it seems problematic that Rheingold chooses to uphold it as the ideal state of youth communication (Squires 2002; Karppinen 2008; Igo 2007; Born 2006). Habermas imagined the public sphere as an intentional turn away from identity politics towards an imagined "rational" discourse, so for Rheingold to valorize the public sphere requires that he overlook the fact that certain kinds of perspectives, not least those of youth, are always marked as less rational. Finally, having established pedagogy as the site where youth media production and participation can be made to become more valuable to democratic society, Rheingold fails to account for the way the structures of the classroom and the call

The Problem with Youth Voices   45

for student voice, let alone a "public" student voice, might make certain forms of expression compulsory for a student's academic success. In this way, he runs the risk of ignoring the ways in which students are already using media to make connections that are meaningful to them. In other words, he assumes that because the ways that youth currently express themselves and connect with each other online are not as legible to him as those that fall within his model of how communication can facilitate civic participation, these ways of communicating have less social value.

Recalling Orner's concern that in the space of the classroom there is often a tendency for students to self-monitor and project opinions and perspectives that they imagine their teachers and classmates will approve of, we are left to wonder what added pressures are placed on students when they are asked to not only produce a voice, but to use that voice to connect with others outside of the classroom in particular ways. Asking them outright to monitor and evaluate *what* they say, *how* they say it, and, now, *where* online they say it may prepare them to contribute to civic debates and action efforts that fit within models that have been established and used by adults, but it fails to account for what such a pedagogical move may foreclose. In his desire to make student voices public, and by privileging particular forms of social and civic activity, Rheingold's approach could push other kinds of student voices to the margins. This is of particular concern in my work with queer youth producers, who have said that they sometimes feel excluded from communicating their perspectives and preferences in public, particularly in the classroom. I am concerned that the way participation is being described here vis-à-vis "public voice" drives queer youth first and foremost towards contributing to already-existing debates on topics that are commonly addressed in mainstream political discourse. Queer youth are ostensibly asked to participate within pre-existing frames already established through mainstream debates on popular issues, such as the legality of same-sex marriage, the US military's former "Don't Ask, Don't Tell" policy, and anti-bullying policies. It seems that, for Rheingold, these frames take pedagocial precedence over frames that young people might already be developing to make sense of their feelings and experiences. Institutions and educators who adopt the "public voice" model of youth participation risk tethering youth producers to pre-existing identity-based debates. In my own pedagogical practice I have found that it can be very productive to engage youth producers in such debates as a way to encourage them to begin thinking about their own commitments and concerns, but only when combined with a discussion of other issues in which they are interested.

Furthermore, Rheingold assumes that when young people post comments or content online, they have already chosen to share with anyone and everyone. In this sense, he perceives them as already conceiving of themselves as operating in a singular public sphere, and,

46 *The Problem with* Youth Voices

therefore, perfectly primed for activities like podcasting, blogging, and citizen journalism. Yet as Patricia Lange has observed, many millennial youth who produce online content actively manage their presence and have a very nuanced sense of publicness online (2007). She suggests that, for youth, private and public spheres are not binaries; instead, they are mutually imbricated and constantly in play. Most millennials who produce or participate in online networked publics (such as Facebook) have developed tactical approaches to controlling who their audience is at any given time, while many work to cultivate different online identities and personas that are intentionally distanced from each other in such a way as to work against the possibility of others piecing them together into one coherent profile (Phillips 2002).[9]

Rheingold's suggestion—that both young people and civil society as a whole benefit if young people think of themselves as possessing a public voice—can in one sense be seen as empowering in that it affirms that they can and should participate in political and social life, but what are the risks if performing particular kinds of publicness becomes compulsory through pedagogy? What might students be compelled to reveal or mask in the service of going public for pedagogy or towards the purpose of performing an "active stance" towards a community or institutional goal? In particular it is necessary to question what the risks and stakes are for already-marginalized youth who are in the process of developing their own identities. Rheingold overlooks the fact that identity politics immediately come into play when students are prompted to give voice to issues they care about. For queer youth in particular, some of whom may use participatory media in an effort to understand their own desires and preferences, to what extent might such a pedagogy compel them to make public (or to hide) their sexual identities?

Conclusion

When we assume the existence of normative subjects and practices in any media production environment, we risk missing opportunities to attend to the heterogeneity of the expressive modes of the people with whom we work. I see possibilities within media pedagogy to support the participation of youth from radically diverse positions and identities that exist within multiple public spheres. If we wish to truly model student-centered media pedagogy, we must abandon expectations of how or why young people use media production technologies and instead initiate production by first identifying what types might be most meaningful and useful to them. And if we listen and learn from them about what drives their interest in production, we can design activities that respond flexibly to their goals and which address issues that they want to explore.

A flexible approach to media pedagogy should be predicated on the expectation that some students may not wish to participate in production activities at all. The option for students *not* to produce content is something we must assimilate into our expectations. This is particularly true in non-school contexts, where students and teachers are less likely to be held to standardized sets of requirements and outcomes. In addition to educators, the funders and program administrators who support media production curricula must also expand their expectations to include the possibility that the youth in their programs may have alternative means of empowerment that don't result in visible products.

In this chapter I have advocated for attention to be paid to digital media pedagogy in broad terms, as I believe that funders and policymakers have sometimes masked the complexity of how younger generations' relationships to digital media (which are certainly distinct) are formed. We need to be more attentive to their discrete and perhaps more intimate relationships to digital media and their production goals, as well as the ways in which their identities and their voices are "already plural, incomplete, and inconsistent, broken, and woven through and with different strands" (Dussel and Dahya 2017, 2). We must begin with the premise that identities are relational, and developed and performed through social action, to approach our expectations of youth digital media production in educational contexts (Livingstone and Sefton-Green 2016).

When we take the link between media and empowerment at face value, we may miss troubling issues such as the misdirection of resources and the influence of funding institutions on the choices made by youth in the production process. We also risk overlooking nuanced pedagogical relationships and institutional contexts that shape what young people produce and, more importantly, what they, as producers, learn. Distracted by the allure of a final video product and the empowerment claims made within it, we may fail to assess the outcomes for the youth involved or, worse, we may reinforce existing hierarchies by compelling them to perform their identities in particular ways that we mistakenly perceive as liberatory.

Notes

1 Some examples of online youth-produced PSA campaigns included those held by the organization Mothers Against Drunk Driving, the National Association of Schools of Public Affairs and Administration, and the National Crime Prevention Council.
2 Queer youth-oriented projects include the *Make It Better Project* (www. makeitbetterproject.org/), the *It Gets Better Project* (www.itgetsbetter.org/), and the Anti-Homophobia Youth PSA Competition (www.outinschools.com/content.php/PSA_Tips/24).
3 Since the early 2000s, hundreds of thousands of calls for youth-produced PSAs have been advertised online. A simple search on YouTube in the spring of 2012 for youth-produced PSA contests turned up over 7,000 videos, which of course only represents those that were posted on that particular site and

48   *The Problem with* Youth Voices

not the projects like MakeItBetter.org and ItGetsBetter.org that are hosted on their own websites. To boot, umbrella media organizations like Adobe, Inc. sponsored ListenUp.org, which boasts over 4,000 PSA videos made by young people from across the US.

4 It is worth mentioning that the metaphor equating new media use and belonging did not originate with Prensky. It dates back to the early 1970s, when the emergence of home computers was at the center of prognostications about the potential impact on youth empowerment. In 1971, computer programmer and educator Seymour Papert made the widely heralded claim that computer science should be taught as a grade school subject so that children would learn to think about what they do with machines rather than being "processed" by them. He saw computers "as something the child himself will learn to manipulate, to extend, to apply to projects, thereby gaining a greater and more articulate mastery of the world, a sense of the power of applied knowledge and a self-confidently realistic image of himself as an intellectual agent" (Papert 1972). A decade later, in 1982, a trend report called *The Shape of the American Family in the Year 2000* was conducted by the American Council of Life Insurance. The authors projected that home computing technology would both empower and cement generational shifts. They wrote, "Like the children of immigrants learning the language of the new land, the first generation of children to have home computers may develop a literacy and an ability to communicate that their parents cannot match or even understand" (Cherlin and Furstenberg 1983). The notion of an empowered electronic generation is not such a new concept. It could perhaps even be traced to Radio Age popular mechanics/popular science, and promotion of what we now call STEM education through the twentieth century. The science fiction and pop science literature of the age inspired a massive investment in STEM education, rooted in very similar concerns to what Papert presents, and of course launched the cultural context of Atomic Age and Space Age fiction and pop science, with a goal of preparing people for and enticing them into the new electronic eras and the new media of radio, TV, computers, social media, etc.

5 David Phillips provides a very useful description of the desire to manage one's queer identity online (2002).

6 In the 1960s and 1970s the DIY video movement seemed to offer youth the opportunity to learn "not only how films are made or why they are art" (as was the emphasis of media literacy education in the early to mid-century), but, as Sol Worth argues, "how to manipulate images in his head, how to think with them, and how to communicate through them" (Worth and Gross 1981). Despite resistance from those who saw media production as a threat to the cognitive and creative skills gained through reading and writing literacies and as more aligned with technical skill and vocation than expression and education, media literacy education was increasingly recognized as a critical practice taken up in formal and informal educational environments not only as a technique of inquiry, but as a "critical practice of citizenship, part of the exercise of democratic rights and civic responsibilities." Influenced by the work of education scholars like Lev Vygotsky and Paolo Freire, media literacy education of the 1970s emphasized the power of literacy as a socio-cultural practice in which power relations could be examined and manipulated. As Postman and Weingartner argue, at stake is

The Problem with Youth Voices   49

the authority of the educator, as peer–peer education is encouraged, and a space is created for a multiplicity of truths and opinions about social and political issues that doesn't follow a logical progression outlined by the educator or institution's curriculum (Postman and Weingartner 1971).

7 Anthropologist Faye Ginsburg and other scholars of ethnographic and indigenous media have criticized the Navajo project researchers for prioritizing their inquiry into Navajo makers' relationship to the filmic text above the social process of producing films and the possible benefits to the Navajo community.

8 In *After the Death of Childhood*, David Buckingham makes excellent arguments for the persistence of this perception of youth as politically apathetic. He notes that contemporary political and media systems are structured to exclude youth participation, while young people tend to be discursively constructed as dependent, vulnerable subjects in need of protection by and from adults. Furthermore, age restrictions (such as voting, using certain participatory media, etc.) position youth as outside the realm of real political activity and, as such, the public sphere, suggesting that they are treated as second-class citizens (Buckingham 2000). For Buckingham, it is clear why youth are not more interested in engaging with politics: much of political life operates "over their heads." Sarah Banet-Weiser builds on this in her essay "We Pledge Allegiance to Kids: Nickelodeon and Citizenship," in which she illustrates how Nickelodeon television programming has worked to encourage youth voices through youth-targeted news programming (Banet-Weiser 2004).

9 See David Phillips for an excellent case study on the way individual internet users negotiate different layers of their identities online (2002).

References

Allen, Danielle, and Jennifer S. Light. 2015. *From Voice to Influence: Understanding Citizenship in a Digital Age*. Chicago: The University of Chicago Press.

Alper, Meryl. 2017. *Giving Voice: Mobile Communication, Disability, and Inequality*. Cambridge: MIT Press.

Bakhtin, Mikhail. 2004. "Discourse in the Novel." In *Literary Theory: An Anthology Second Edition*, edited by Julie Rivkin and Michael Ryan, 674–85. Malden: Blackwell Publishing.

Banet-Weiser, Sarah. 2004. "'We Pledge Allegiance to Kids': Nickelodeon and Citizenship." In *Nickelodeon Nation: The History, Politics, and Economics of America's only TV Channel for Kids*, edited by Heather Hendershot, 209–37. New York: New York University Press.

———. 2012. *Authentic TM: The Politics of Ambivalence in a Brand Culture*. New York: New York University Press.

———. 2015. "'Confidence You Can Carry!': Girls in Crisis and the Market for Girls' Empowerment Organizations." *Continuum* 29 (2):182–93. Doi: 10.1080/10304312.2015.1022938.

Barnhurst, Kevin G. 2007. *Media / Queered*. New York: Peter Lang.

Benkler, Yochai. 2006. *The Wealth of Networks: How Social Production Transforms Markets and Freedom*. New Haven: Yale University Press.

Berliner, Lauren. 2014. "Shooting for Profit: The Monetary Logic of the YouTube Home Movie." In *Amateur Filmmaking: the Home Movie, the Archive, the Web*,

50   The Problem with Youth Voices

edited by Laura Rascaroli, Gwenda Young, and Barry Monahan. New York: Bloomsbury.

Berliner, Lauren S., and Nora J. Kenworthy. 2017. "Producing a Worthy Illness: Personal Crowdfunding Amidst Financial Crisis." *Social Science & Medicine* 187:233–42. Doi: 10.1016/j.socscimed.2017.02.008.

Born, Georgina. 2006. "Digitising Democracy." In *What Can Be Done?: Making the Media and Politics Better*, edited by John Lloyd and Jean Seaton. Malden: Blackwell Publishing.

boyd, danah. 2007. "Why Youth Heart Social Network Sites: The role of Networked Publics in Teenage Social Life." Open Science Framework. Last accessed January 16, 2013. Doi: 10.17605/OSF.IO/22HQ2.

———. 2014. *It's Complicated: The Social Lives of Networked Teens.* New Haven: Yale University Press.

Buckingham, David. 2000. *After the Death of Childhood.* Cambridge: Polity Press.

———. 2008. *Youth, Identity, and Digital Media.* Cambridge: MIT Press.

Chalfen, Richard, Laura Sherman, and Michael Rich. 2010. "VIA's Visual Voices: The Awareness of a Dedicated Audience for Voices in Patient Video Narratives." *Visual Studies* 25 (3):201–9. Doi: 10.1080/1472586X.2010. 523271.

Cherlin, Andrew, and Frank F. Jr. Furstenberg. 1983. "The American Family in the Year 2000." *Futurist* 17 (3):7–14.

Couldry, Nick. 2010. *Why Voice Matters: Culture and Politics After Neoliberalism.* Los Angeles: SAGE.

Duggan, Lisa. 2003. *The Twilight of Equality?: Neoliberalism, Cultural Politics, and the Attack on Democracy.* Boston: Beacon Press.

Dussel, Inés, and Negin Dahya. 2017. "Introduction: Problematizing Voice and Representation in Youth Media Production." *Learning, Media and Technology* 42 (1):1–7. Doi: 10.1080/17439884.2016.1205602.

Ellsworth, Elizabeth. 1989. "Why Doesn't This Feel Empowering? Working Through the Repressive Myths of Critical Pedagogy." *Harvard Educational Review* 59 (3):297–325. Doi: 10.17763/haer.59.3.058342114k266250.

Foucault, Michel. 1977. *Discipline and Punish: The Birth of the Prison.* New York: Pantheon Books.

Giroux, Henry A. 1981. *Ideology, Culture & the Process of Schooling.* Philadelphia: Temple University Press.

Goldfarb, Brian. 2002. *Visual Pedagogy: Media Cultures in and Beyond the Classroom.* Durham: Duke University Press.

Gore, Jennifer. 1992. "What We Can Do For You! What *Can* 'We' Do For 'You'?" In *Feminisms and Critical Pedagogy*, edited by Carmen Luke and Jennifer Gore, 54–73. New York: Routledge.

Gray, Herman. 2013. "Subject(ed) to Recognition." *American Quarterly* 65 (4):771–98. Doi: 10.1353/aq.2013.0058.

Gross, Larry P. 2001. *Up from Invisibility: Lesbians, Gay Men, and the Media in America.* New York: Columbia University Press.

Grossberg, Lawrence. 1994. "The Political Status of Youth and Youth Culture." In *Adolescents and Their Music: If It's Too Loud, You're Too Old*, edited by Jonathon S. Epstein, 25–46. New York: Garland Publishing.

The Problem with Youth Voices 51

Halberstam, J. Jack. 2011. *The Queer Art of Failure.* Durham: Duke University Press.

Hauge, Chelsey, and Mary K. Bryson. 2015. "Gender Development in Youth Media." *Feminist Media Studies* 15 (2):287–305. Doi: 10.1080/14680777.2014.919333.

Hearn, Alison. 2008. "'Meat, Mask, Burden': Probing the Contours of the Branded 'Self.'" *Journal of Consumer Culture* 8 (2):197–217. Doi: 10.1177/1469540508090086.

Herring, Susan C. 2008. "Questioning the Generational Divide: Technological Exoticism and Adult Construction of Online Youth Identity." In *Youth, Identity, and Digital Media*, edited by David Buckingham. Cambridge: MIT Press.

Hobbs, Renee, and Amy Jensen. 2009. "The Past, Present, and Future of Media Literacy Education." *Journal of Media Literacy Education* 1 (1):1–11. Digitalcommons.uri.edu/jmle/vol1/iss1/1/.

Igo, Sarah Elizabeth. 2007. *The Averaged American: Surveys, Citizens, and the Making of a Mass Public.* Cambridge: Harvard University Press.

Jenkins, Henry. 2007. "Reconsidering Digital Immigrants..." *Confessions of an Aca-Fan* (blog). Last accessed December 4, 2011. http://henryjenkins.org/2007/12/reconsidering_digital_immigran.html.

Jenkins, Henry, Ravi Purushotma, Margaret Weigel, Katie Clinton, and Alice J. Robison. 2009. *Confronting the Challenges of Participatory Culture: Media Education for the 21st Century.* Cambridge: MIT Press.

Jenkins, Henry, Sangita Shresthova, Liana Gamber-Thompson, Neta Kligler-Vilenchik, and Arely Zimmerman. 2016. *By Any Media Necessary: The New Youth Activism.* New York: New York University Press.

Juhasz, Alexandra. 2008. "Learning the Five Lessons of YouTube: After Trying to Teach There, I Don't Believe the Hype." *Cinema Journal* (48) 2:145–50. Doi: http://dx.doi.org/10.1353/cj.0.0098.

Karppinen, Kari. 2008. "Media and the Paradoxes of Pluralism." In *The Media and Social Theory*, edited by David Hesmondhalgh and Jason Toynbee, 27–42. New York: Routledge.

Lange, Patricia G. 2007. "Publicly Private and Privately Public: Social Networking on YouTube." 13 (1):361–80. Doi: 10.1111/j.1083-6101.2007.00400.x

Lenhart, Amanda, and Mary Madden. 2005. "Teen Content Creators and Consumers." Pew Research Center. Last accessed November 2, 2011. www.pewinternet.org/2005/11/02/teen-content-creators-and-consumers/.

Livingstone, Sonia. 2008. "Taking Risky Opportunities in Youthful Content Creation: Teenagers' Use of Social Networking Sites for Intimacy, Privacy and Self-Expression." *New Media & Society* 10 (3):393–411. Doi: 10.1177/1461444808089415.

Livingstone, Sonia, and Julian Sefton-Green. 2016. *The Class: Living and Learning in the Digital Age.* New York: New York University Press.

Losh, Elizabeth, and Jonathan Alexander. 2010. "'A YouTube of One's Own?': 'Coming Out' Videos as Rhetorical Action." In *LGBT Identity and Online New Media*, edited by Christopher Pullen and Margaret Cooper, 37–50. New York: Routledge.

Luke, Carmen, and Jennifer Gore. 1992. *Feminisms and Critical Pedagogy.* New York: Routledge.

52 *The Problem with* Youth Voices

Malcolm, Beth. 2013. "Hey Girls, Let Your Voice Be Heard!" Canadian Women's Foundation Blog. Last accessed February 18, 2017. http://canadianwomen.org/blog/hey-girls-let-your-voice-be-heard.

Marchessault, Janine. 1995. *Mirror Machine: Video and Identity*. Toronto: YYZ Books.

Marshall, P. David. 2010. "The Promotion and Presentation of the Self: Celebrity as Marker of Presentational Media." *Celebrity Studies* 1 (1):35–48. Doi: 10.1080/19392390903519057.

Marwick, Alice, and danah boyd. 2011. "I Tweet Honestly, I Tweet Passionately: Twitter Users, Context Collapse, and the Imagined Audience." *New Media & Society* 13 (1):114–33. Doi: 10.1177/1461444810365313.

———. 2014. "Networked Privacy: How Teenagers Negotiate Context in Social Media." *New Media & Society* 16 (7):1051–67. Doi: 10.1177/1461444814543995.

Masterman, Len. 1985. *Teaching the Media*. London: Comedia Publishing Group.

Orner, Mimi. 1992. "Interrupting the Calls for Student Voice in 'Liberatory' Education: A Feminist Poststructuralist Perspective." In *Feminisms and Critical Pedagogy*, edited by Carmen Luke and Jennifer Gore, 74–89. New York: Routledge.

Papert, Seymour. 1972. "Teaching Children Thinking." *Innovations in Education & Training International* 9 (5):245–55. Doi: 10.1080/1355800720090503.

Phillips, David J. 2002. "Negotiating the Digital Closet: Online Pseudonymity and the Politics of Sexual Identity." *Information, Communication & Society* 5 (3):406–24. Doi: 10.1080/13691180210159337.

Postman, Neil, and Charles Weingartner. 1971. *The Soft Revolution: A Student Handbook for Turning Schools Around*. Delacorte Press.

Prensky, Marc. 2001. "Digital Natives, Digital Immigrants Part 1." *MCB UP Ltd* 9 (5):1–6. Doi: 10.1108/10748120110424816.

Rangan, Pooja. 2017. *Immediations: The Humanitarian Impulse in Documentary*. Durham: Duke University Press.

Rheingold, Howard. 2000a. *Tools for Thought: The History and Future of Mind-Expanding Technology*. Cambridge: MIT Press.

———. 2000b. *The Virtual Community: Homesteading on the Electronic Frontier*. Cambridge: MIT Press.

———. 2002. *Smart Mobs: The Next Social Revolution*. Cambridge: Basic Books.

———. 2008. "Using Participatory Media and Public Voice to Encourage Civic Engagement." In *Civic Life Online: Learning How Digital Media Can Engage Youth*, edited by W. Lance Bennett, 97–118. Cambridge: MIT Press.

———. 2014. *Net Smart: How to Thrive Online*. Cambridge: MIT Press.

Soep, Elisabeth. 2006. "Beyond Literacy and Voice in Youth Media Production." *McGill Journal of Education* 41 (3):197–213.

Spade, Dean. 2015. *Normal Life: Administrative Violence, Critical Trans Politics, and the Limits of Law*. Durham: Duke University Press.

Squires, Catherine R. 2002. "Rethinking the Black Public Sphere: An Alternative Vocabulary for Multiple Public Spheres." *Communication Theory* 12 (4):446–68. Doi: 10.1111/j.1468–2885.2002.tb00278.x.

Tapscott, Don. 1998. *Growing Up Digital: The Rise of the Net Generation*. New York: McGraw-Hill.

The Problem with Youth Voices 53

Tufekci, Zeynep. 2008. "Can You See Me Now? Audience and Disclosure Regulation in Online Social Network Sites." *Bulletin of Science, Technology & Society* 28 (1):20–36. Doi: 10.1177/0270467607311484.

Vaidhyanathan, Siva. 2008. "Generational Myth." *Chronicle of Higher Education* 55 (4):B7.

Worth, Sol, and John Adair. 1997. *Through Navajo Eyes: An Exploration in Film Communication and Anthropology*. Albuquerque: University of New Mexico Press.

Worth, Sol, and Larry Gross. 1981. *Studying Visual Communication*. Philadelphia: University of Pennsylvania Press.

2 "Look at Me, I'm Doing Fine!"

The Conundrum of Legibility, Visibility, and Identity Management in Queer Viral Videos*

Fourteen-year old Jamey Rodemeyer's voice trembles as he speaks to the camera from his bedroom in Buffalo, New York. He sits straight in front of the lens, nervously pushing the hair from his forehead, often looking down and to the side shyly as he tells viewers of his experience overcoming being bullied by his peers after he came out as bisexual at school.

> Hi, this is Jamey from New York. And I'm just here to tell you that it *does* get better. Here's a little bit of my story ... When I came out I got so much support from my friends ... I have so much support from people I don't even know online. I know that sounds creepy, but they're so nice ... and they don't ever want me to die. And just ... there is so much support for me. So just listen here—it gets better! Look at me, I'm doing fine.
> (Jamey Rodemeyer, "It Gets Better, I Promise!"
> [YouTube, May 4, 2011])

Jamey smiles, focuses on the positive, and refers to his feelings of oppression in the past tense. He concludes by shaping his hands into a heart, which he offers to the viewers, presumably other queer young people. The content and phrasing of Jamey's speech is consistent with the style and testimonial motif of the thousands of videos on the *It Gets Better Project* YouTube channel, where he first posted his video. His two minutes follow a familiar formula: a direct address to the viewer, a personal story about having been harassed and feeling alienated, a proclamation of hardship overcome by self-acceptance, and a plea for viewers to believe in themselves (Rodemeyer 2011).

The *It Gets Better Project* aims to reach struggling queer youth through videos made by people who have had the life experience to illustrate to viewers "what the future may have in store" when they have trouble

---

* A version of this chapter first appeared in Cuklanz, Lisa M., and Heather McIntosh, eds., *Documenting Gendered Violence: Representations, Collaborations, and Movements.* Bloomsbury Publishing USA, 2015.

Identity Management in Queer Viral Videos 55

Figure 2.1 Jamey Rodemeyer's *It Gets Better Project* video, May 4, 2011

imagining their own possibilities; Jamey's is one of dozens of videos made by teens. Intended as a recipient of the *It Gets Better* message, Jamey and so many of his peers have instead become messengers. His young age alone complicates the campaign's simple message that the passage of time is the ultimate antidote to queer suffering.

Understanding the function of Jamey's video in the context of his own life experience becomes more difficult when viewed alongside the other online postings he made during the same time period. Just five months after he contributed his video to the *It Gets Better Project*, Jamey left a very different kind of message about his experience of bullying on the Twitter feed of his muse, the pop star Lady Gaga. "I always say how bullied I am but no one listens, what do I have to do so people will listen to me?" The following morning, on September 12, 2011, Jamey's parents discovered his body in front of their family home (Hughes, 2011). Jamey's death leads us to question the narrative of overcoming that he presents in his *It Gets Better Project* video and his choice to participate in the campaign in the first place. What role might its production and circulation have played in his experience of homophobia and bullying? How might this production have figured into his self-acceptance, formation, and understanding of his sexual identity or imagined participation in a larger queer community?

Jamey Rodemeyer's account is a powerful illustration of the shortcomings of the social media approach to queer youth empowerment. Rather than being a representation of his lived reality, his video seems to communicate a desire to be included in an increasingly popular teleological narrative about queer lives and an aggregate of supportive voices. My aim in this chapter is to illuminate how the prerogatives of

56 *Identity Management in Queer Viral Videos*

the *It Gets Better Project* and its derivatives interfere with the emancipatory intent of the videos, ultimately advancing a type of queer visibility that threatens to sanitize or distract from the more urgent concerns of queer youth. This includes issues such as homelessness, domestic violence, depression, and forms of intimidation and humiliation that are not as visible within anti-gay-bullying discourse, which focuses primarily on in-school acts of bullying.[1] I argue that video "success" requires that makers achieve narrative coherence, legibility within the discourse of anti-gay-bullying, and what Jenkins, Ford, and Green call "spreadability," meaning that viewers will want to pass the videos on to others within their personal networks (2013).[2] With the expansion of bullying discourse, the focus has shifted away from the core concerns about the needs of queer youth that initiated the movement in the first place, and towards the publicity of a *movement*, thus further abstracting and reifying their specificity. Here the cultural logics of bullying discourse intersect with the logics of viral video production and circulation, which relies on marketing and publicity tactics. Through a discussion of the ways in which youth media production has been mobilized in response to the phenomenon of anti-gay-bullying, I will illustrate how youth-produced anti-gay-bullying videos may ultimately function more as pedagogy, propelling a discourse of anti-gay-bullying more than effectively resolving issues of queer strategies for survival or connection. I then turn to counter-examples in which the modes of production and circulation offer more possibilities for the performance and depiction of queer imaginings, connectivity, expression, and creativity.

Launched in late September 2010 by syndicated columnist Dan Savage and his partner Terry Miller, the *It Gets Better Project* (www.itgetsbetter.org) self-produced viral PSA video campaign was the couple's response to the string of highly-publicized queer suicides that had been reported in the few months prior (including Billy Lucas, Raymond Chase, Tyler Clementi, Ryan Halligan, Asher Brown, and Seth Walsh). The suicides, represented in the national news as evidence of an epidemic of queer teen suicide, were thrust even further into the media spotlight after the release of public health and education findings from the Gay, Lesbian, and Straight Education Network (GLSEN) (www.glsen.org) and the Pew Research Foundation (www.pewresearch.org) suggested that queer youth are more at risk for suicidal ideation compared to their heterosexual peers, in part due to their increased exposure to bullying. The campaign popularized the idea that online video (specifically imagined as "viral") can be an effective way to empower struggling queer youth and generate awareness as well as alliance. Arguably, it also advanced a particular form of participatory culture in which participants are encouraged to utilize messaging strategies that have long been used in traditional broadcast public service advertising in order to perform their investment in the well-being of queer youth and demonstrate their concerns about the impact of bullying.

While bullying is not the first social issue to be associated with a generation of American youth (drunk driving and drug use, for example, dominated educational and public health discourse in the 1980s and '90s respectively), it is perhaps the first to be articulated and, in some respects, experienced through digital social media. In particular, viral video—media produced expressly for intensive online circulation through networked publics—has become a central method through which people perform their concern about and investment in the issue of bullying. Understanding the *It Gets Better Project* as a *campaign* that has certain promotional objectives and relies on forms of publicity and reproducibility can help us to understand the underlying publicity priority of the many online anti-gay-bullying video projects intended for viral distribution that followed suit.

The *It Gets Better Project* began with a simple testimonial-style YouTube video featuring Savage and Miller (2010). Speaking into the camera in a two-shot, they talk about their painful experiences growing up gay and how much better things got for each of them after high school. "Honestly, things got better *the day* I left high school," Miller explains.

> I didn't see the bullies everyday, I didn't see the people who harassed me everyday, I didn't have to see the school administrators who would do nothing about it everyday. Life instantly got better.
> (Dan Savage and Terry Miller, "It Gets Better: Dan and Terry" [YouTube, September 21, 2010])

Figure 2.2 Dan Savage and Terry Miller's inaugural *It Gets Better Project* video, 2010

58 *Identity Management in Queer Viral Videos*

Using their own life trajectories as evidence, Miller and Savage try to reassure queer teen viewers that no matter how much pain and humiliation they may face in their teen years, their circumstances will inevitably improve. Then, over a montage of family photos, the couple describe how they first met, the acceptance they eventually received from their families, the joy they experience in raising their adopted son, and the happy memories they share from snowboarding trips and late-night strolls in Paris that Miller claims have made it "so worth sticking out the bullying and the pain and the despair of high school."

Following the structure of a traditional public service announcement, they close with an appeal to the target audience (queer youth). Savage declares:

> If there are 14- and 15- and 16-year-olds ... 13-year-olds, 12-year-olds out there watching this video, what I'd love you to take away from it really is that IT GETS BETTER [*emphasis taken from the video's subtitles*]. However bad it is now, it gets better. And it can get great. It can get awesome. Your life can be amazing, but you have to tough this period of your life out and you have to live your life so you're around for it to get amazing. And it can and it will.
>
> (Dan Savage and Terry Miller, "It Gets Better," 2010)

The video concludes with a call to action, directing viewers to the *It Gets Better Project* website where they will find links to more information on suicide prevention as well as anti-gay-bullying resources. At the time, the website invited other adults to share their stories of overcoming bullying by contributing a video aimed at queer youth. It was later revised to solicit videos from producers of any age who wish to contribute a message.

The campaign quickly comprised some of the most-circulated online content. In just one month, the *It Gets Better Project* became the second most popular channel on YouTube, with over 11,465 subscribers. Two years into the campaign, it claimed over 50,000 online videos posted and more than 50 million views.[3] The "it gets better" tagline became something of a rallying cry for the anti-gay-bullying movement.

In interviews, Savage has celebrated the campaign's ability to circumnavigate barriers that had formerly prevented the direct outreach of concerned adults to queer youth.

> We can't help them ... we can't barge into these schools ... Because of technology we don't need to wait for an invitation anymore to speak to these kids. We can speak to them directly.
>
> (Dan Savage and Terry Miller, *It Gets Better: Coming Out, Overcoming Bullying, and Creating a Life Worth Living* [New York: Penguin Books, 2011])

Identity Management in Queer Viral Videos   59

This intervention, he suggests, is made possible by using the "tools we have at our disposal right now" such as digital video technologies, Facebook, YouTube, and other social media. He imagines these technologies to be in the domain of youth and operating outside of the realm of formal education, the family, and the law. From Savage's perspective, the campaign has had the effect of bringing "the old order" (of how adults used to be able to support youth) "crashing down" (Savage and Miller 2011).

Savage claims that he was motivated to create the *It Gets Better Project* as a way to help make up for the scarcity of anti-gay-bullying programs and Gay–Straight Alliance clubs in most K-12 schools and the absence of legislation to protect young people from anti-LGBTQ discrimination (Savage and Miller 2011, 7). He attributes the high incidence of queer youth suicide to the lack of such programming and legal protections,[4] and positions viral video as offering something of a subterranean lifeline that can facilitate cathartic exchange between struggling youth and adults who can "give 'em hope" (Savage and Miller 2011, 4).[5] In this way, Savage imagines that online social media might mediate connections that were not otherwise possible. Absent from this discourse of hope—which is rooted in a belief in the possibility of meaningful exchange through viral video—is an articulation of the need for the work of these media practices to be sustained by relationships or face-to-face interactions between young people, their peers, and supportive adults. What's more, as with much uncritical appraisal of social media forms, high saturation or number of hits is facilely equated with social impact or efficacy.

The *It Gets Better Project*'s unprecedented level of participation initiated a sudden ubiquity of self-produced videos as a mode of expression and style of public discourse for addressing the concerns of queer youth. In particular, the format of the PSA campaign predominated over other ways of reaching youth while encouragement to produce "anti-gay-bullying PSAs" became the dominant means of addressing the issue in community groups, formal and informal educational environments, and action groups. Contests encouraging young people to make anti-gay-bullying PSAs soon peppered the philanthropic landscape as classrooms and community groups adapted their agendas and curricula to enable their students to produce relevant PSA videos. Educators, community organizations, and foundations writ large turned to viral video PSA production as a method of engaging the youth population in the issue of anti-gay-bullying, particularly because of the enhanced reach that the sharing function of viral video enables. The presumed efficacy, ease, and reach of the viral video approach has been considered so successful that, in a response to a perceived need to bring youth voices to the fore, many other sites have begun to encourage young people to make their own. This enthusiasm precipitated a proliferation of calls from organizations, film festivals, and educational institutions for queer youth for videos that address the perceived epidemic of "gay bullying." For instance, the *Make*

60   *Identity Management in Queer Viral Videos*

It Better campaign, initiated only nine days after the *It Gets Better Project* and endorsed by over 90 organizations nationwide, encouraged teens to produce videos in which they express their needs and describe what their schools and communities can do to support them (GSA Network 2010).[6] The campaign pivoted on the *It Gets Better Project*, specifically soliciting youth-produced videos in which young producers inform students, parents, teachers, school administrators, and adult allies about concrete actions they might take to make schools safer for all students.

Encouraging young people to produce videos themselves is an approach that assumes that agency and voice are engendered through the production process. The student/youth-centered "hands-on" production approach is presumably a self-perpetuating pedagogical model that expands learning outside of the school context by leveraging the widespread use of digital media technologies. With roots in the progressive Children's Rights Movement and the tradition of critical pedagogy, this model appears to be in the best interests of the youth producers. But does placing the means of (professional media) production into the hands of young people necessarily make viral video an ideal method for identifying and addressing their needs? Perhaps this equation persists due to the convenient coincidence between the popularity of engaged pedagogy and the inexpensive, fundable, reproducible nature of digital video projects. The completed video product, along with online streaming and sharing capabilities, serves as an effective tool for evidencing student engagement and enables educators and funders to claim impacts and outcomes beyond the scope of the smaller groups they support. In this way, youth-produced anti-gay-bullying videos could be said to fall into what some scholars of social justice movements have termed the "nonprofit industrial complex" (Gilmore 2007; Hawk 2007; Krabill 2012), a system of relationships in which the State, foundations, and other nonprofits, among other agencies, redirect energy and funding into career-based modes of organizing rather than societal transformation (www.incite-national.org).

Without a doubt, anti-gay-bullying campaigns have championed viral video as a powerful means of expression and connection that is paralleled by the unquestioning embrace of notions of the empowering dimensions of social media, but up to this point we have not examined exactly how viral video functions. The relevance and affective impact of a viral video is typically assessed in terms of the rate that it circulates. At present, the "success" of youth-produced anti-gay-bullying videos is measured more by the extent of their circulation than their ability to address the needs of the youth who produce and view them. When videos circulate widely through peer networks and achieve notoriety on a global scale, as many of the most famous anti-gay-bullying videos have, one might assume there to be a straightforward connection between the video content and its social, cultural, and personal significance. We might, as Dan Savage and many educators and community leaders have, go a step further and imagine an equivalency between the level of circulation and the impact on the person or people directly involved or depicted in the video. If broad reach is at once the strategy and goal of viral video campaigns like the *It Gets Better Project*, we must ask: what is it that makes such videos "viral," or, to borrow Jenkins, Ford, and Green's (2013) term here, "spreadable"?

Spreading the Message

I would like to turn our attention towards how video production that is intended from the outset for viral distribution (as in the case of the anti-gay-bullying videos mentioned above) obliges video producers to participate in a system of professionalizing practices that requires them to produce particular kinds of media in order to ensure circulation and legibility. Of central concern is how the prerogatives of viral or spreadable media may shape, and potentially impede, an individual's narrative and expressive possibilities. Specifically, what must participants understand about how to participate online in order to encourage visibility? What symbolic resources and shared meanings must be mobilized in the pursuit of legibility and publicity? What is happening on the level of production to ensure spreadability? Finally, how might these intuited expectations about what makes a video spreadable have an impact on self-representation?

While Dan Savage insists that streaming video technology enabled a paradigm shift in the way outreach and connection with queer youth is accomplished, Jenkins, Ford, and Green suggest that the rise of participatory circulation of online material cannot be explained solely (or even primarily) by a rise of technological infrastructure, "even as these new technologies play a key role in enabling shifts" (2013, 3). They claim, "media industries and marketing worlds are moving toward a model of circulation based on the logic of spreadability" (2013, 44). It might seem natural to think of the anti-gay-bullying viral video as an example of a *meme*, a term introduced by evolutionary biologist Richard Dawkins to describe cultural reproduction. Internet memes (like genes) rely on repetition and variation for their propagation and survival (Blackmore, 1999; Dawkins, 1989). But whereas memes often take unexpected and creative turns in their organic, rather rhizomatic developments, winding up altogether different from how they began, youth-produced anti-gay-bullying videos remain strikingly similar in their content, style, form, and, most importantly, message. Jenkins et al. find the concepts of viruses and memes particularly limiting, as they "often distort the human agency involved in spreading media content" (2013, 44). The spreadibility of online media, they suggest, is instead determined "by processes of social appraisal rather than technical or creative wizardry and on the active participation of engaged audiences" (Jenkins, Ford, and Green 2013,

62 *Identity Management in Queer Viral Videos*

196). Indeed, people circulate texts based on the perceived social value for their social circle, and how the circulated text may reflect upon them. In their words:

> Spreadability assumes a world where mass content is continually repositioned as it enters different niche communities. When material is produced according to a one-size-fits-all model, it imperfectly fits the needs of any given audience. Instead, audience members have to retrofit it to better serve their interests.
>
> (Jenkins, Ford, and Green, *Spreadable Media: Creating Value and Meaning in a Networked Culture* [New York: New York University Press, 2013], 27)

Yet whereas Jenkins et al. describe the spread of online material as motivated by audiences who retrofit to serve their interests, I would like to suggest that many videos have repurposed the anti-gay-bullying, pro-queer youth messages that originated with the *It Gets Better Project* in ways that do indeed suggest a "one size fits all" model. Across the numerous anti-gay-bullying videos that exist online, there are striking consistencies in the message ("Stop bullying!" or "Hold on if you're being bullied; life will get better!"), the positive tone, the call to action, and the digestible, sanitized approach to the topic of violence and oppression. We can see normalization explicitly encouraged by the *It Gets Better Project* in the guidelines it provides for contributors. These guidelines outline the visual and narrative parameters of successful (posts that won't be blocked) video contributions. These sanitizing guides and requisite "positive tone" are probably motivated by practical concerns, such as the perceived danger of posting videos that suggest justifications and techniques for suicide. But beyond this, there is a clear desire on the part of the foundation to maintain consistency across the campaign's style, tone, and message. So, despite the fact that the *It Gets Better Project* is comprised of videos from thousands of non-professional producers, their consistency aligns the campaign with traditional public service campaigns produced by advertising agencies and advocacy organizations.

For instance, contributors are offered advice on how to achieve the highest quality sound and lighting for their video. These aesthetic suggestions are based on a normative framing and style—the testimonial, seated, medium-shot documentary style that Savage and Miller first initiated. It is assumed that contributors will be shooting in a similar fashion and tacitly encourages such emulation. In addition, the *It Gets Better Project* website suggests "talking points" that contributors should cover. The broad categories include "Positive Messages of Hope for Queer Youth," "Using Safe Messaging Practices," and "Suggest Resources, Help, and Support." The campaign requests that contributors seek to "inspire" young people while staying "positive" and "uplifting" and avoiding

Identity Management in Queer Viral Videos   63

any "language that could be interpreted as negative or that specifically mentions self-harm."

In sum, message coherence and legibility seem to take precedence in ways that suggest that these videos and the campaigns of which they are a part have more in common with top-down traditional broadcast advertising than the positivist, techno-utopian discourse surrounding them suggests. This is perhaps the case because, similar to commercial advertisements, the PSA takes a uni-directional approach to a target audience about an issue and offers one discrete, often hard-hitting, uncomplicated message. Perhaps more than any other genre, the PSA seeks to homogenize a diversity of voices and experiences. To produce within this structure (even loosely) means to foreclose the possibility of ambivalence or contradictions in perspectives, which further shuts down possibilities for grappling with the trauma associated with bullying. Disqualified subjectivities or pathologized subject positions cannot be contained by this dominant narrative form. One's participation in an anti-bullying or anti-gay-bullying video, therefore, inevitably becomes a performance of a particular position with regard to (queer) youth pain and suicidal ideation. When one films, views, or circulates anti-gay-bullying PSA videos, one identifies as the "not-bully," the "ally," or the "survivor."

Legibility and Identity Management

Examining the outgrowth of the *It Gets Better Project* to offline channels illustrates the campaign's trajectory and clarifies the connection between online anti-gay-bullying videos and the role of anti-gay-bullying discourse in public identity management. We can see how the videos function as cultural objects that perform public legibility and can be commodified into a form of public relations capital as well as (acceptable) spectacle.

Soon after it had established an online presence, the *It Gets Better Project* extended its efforts into offline media. With several prominent funding backers, the campaign garnered the resources to advertise on prime-time network television, most notably during the Fox network's hit show *Glee*, which had featured storylines about anti-gay-bullying. The tie-in was reinforced by *It Gets Better* videos featuring actors from the show, including Max Adler (2010), who portrays the closeted football player who bullies Kurt, a beloved gay student.

The campaign continued to expand in the form of clothing merchandise and a book, *It Gets Better: Coming Out, Overcoming Bullying and Creating a Life Worth Living* (Savage and Miller, 2011), a compendium of the online campaign designed to reach young people lacking reliable internet access. The book includes expanded testimonials and essays from dozens of prominent queer adults and allies, such as Ellen DeGeneres and Senator Al Franken. In 2012, the campaign also delved into broadcast distribution with two *It Gets Better* documentary specials

64 *Identity Management in Queer Viral Videos*

that aired on MTV and LOGO. These programs featured stories of three queer young adults in the process of coming out to their families and friends. The MTV-hosted website that streamed the documentaries described the specials as the network's way of contributing to the "worldwide movement" initiated by Savage and Miller.

> Now, it's MTV's turn to add to the movement with the It Gets Better special, a reminder to teens across the country that it will get better, and we're standing right by them until it does.
> (Veronica Brezina, "New Shows For Lesbians to Look Forward to!," Lez Talk [hypeorlando, 2014])

In its notoriety, the *It Gets Better Project* quickly became something of an obligatory rite of passage for expressing support for queer youth, to the extent that appearing in a video for the campaign seems to have become compulsory for politicians, actors, professional athletes, and employees of corporations like Facebook (2010) and Pixar (2010) who wish to be included on this public roster of individuals and institutions who care. The campaign encourages people to perform their support for queer teens while also providing an opportunity to identify themselves as "not the bullies" (ItGetsBetter.org). In his column for Seattle's *The Stranger*, Savage insists that the campaign forced straight people—politicians, teachers, preachers, and parents—to decide whose side they were on. It arguably became what I call a campaign of "conspicuous concern," in which participants and funders alike could register their support for queer youth. Participation became, as one Salon.com columnist put it, "hip," "de rigueur," and, for some public figures, a facet of their image management (D'Addario, 2013).

The *It Gets Better Project*'s objective of rallying support from as many people as possible perhaps worked *too* well, as by 2013 it became clear that there were people contributing videos to the campaign whose interest in publicity eclipsed their intent. The most notable example is the video that was made by players from the San Francisco 49ers football team (2013).[7] When players were interviewed in the locker room following homophobic remarks that had been made by a teammate after a former 49er was revealed to be gay, the team had to be reminded that they had publicly offered support to queer youth through the video they had made. Players Ahmad Brooks and Isaac Sopoaga, who appear in the video, disavowed their participation in anything of the sort. Brooks insisted to reporters that what he had participated in was "an anti-gay-bullying video, not a gay video." Dan Savage promptly removed the team's video from the site. When, shortly afterwards, the team lost in the SuperBowl, headlines read "It Gets Worse," connecting their defeat on the field to their fumbles in public relations (Barmann, 2013). This underscores that the *It Gets Better Project* campaign has resulted in a cultural performance that assumes that

Identity Management in Queer Viral Videos   65

there are only two sides—the bullied and the bullies—rather than allowing for a more complex understanding of how the 49ers were trying position themselves. It became necessary to see their distancing themselves from the *It Gets Better Project* as effectively siding with the bullies.

Queer Youth and Visibility

For queer youth, who have historically used media to forge social connections, peer recognition, and identity formation, YouTube has had a particular gravitational pull.[8] Mary L. Gray's ethnographic work with rural queer youth suggests that media are often the primary site of production for social knowledge about queer identities—it is the first point of contact for some youth who will come to identify as queer. For Gray, it is through media that young people "circulate the social grammar, appearance, and sites of LGBT-ness" (2009a; 2009b). As queer youth produce themselves in the social media world, it becomes apparent that an assortment of narratives is needed to construct different kinds of queer identities and experiences. Surveying the diversity of queer-produced YouTube videos provides a lens for recognizing the ways in which queer youth are not limited to being one kind of (documentary/social media) subject.

Queer visibility (in social life and the media), widely understood to be the pathway to queer liberation and social justice, gets deployed in several ways through youth-produced viral video anti-gay-bullying campaigns. These campaigns offer the opportunity for queer youth to connect with others around their gender and sexual identities, while potentially adding to the visibility of queer people in society. As the Jamey Rodemeyer case indicates, the popularity of a video does not necessarily correspond to the effectiveness of improving the life of its producer. We must look at the ways in which viral videos depend on already extant hegemonic and market techniques that work to reinforce power structures even when their stated purpose is to challenge them. Altogether, what is reinforced by queer youth-produced anti-gay-bullying videos is a normalizing narrative about queer youth experience that often belies the reality of the individual lives they represent. The specific sets of issues and intersectional identities that have an impact on their lives get eclipsed. Class, race, gender, ethnicity, religion, and disability get shut out of the framework that the *It Gets Better Project* presents, and concerns such as dating anxieties, abuse, homelessness, and financial struggles do not have a place in the narrative. Viewing queer youth participation in campaigns like *It Gets Better* through the lens of identity management and performance can shed light on discrepancies in young people's motivation to participate and the benefits to them.

It is critical to consider the *pedagogical* work these viral video projects perform. Here I am using a capacious definition of pedagogy

66   *Identity Management in Queer Viral Videos*

that emphasizes the structures and methods by which knowledge about subjects is produced (as opposed to how subjects are taught or instructed).[9] The theme and content of pedagogical videos are generally ascribed from outside, rather than emerging from existing local publics, and explicitly aim to change thinking or behavior related to queer identity.

The discourse surrounding the *It Gets Better Project* suggests that YouTube is a mechanism for cohering queer youth and forging intergenerational connections that can buttress those who are struggling. Participation in the anti-bullying discourse through video production appears to enable queer youth to leverage themselves as visible—both in their identities *and* as successful media-makers. The testimonial-style video campaign was formed as a tool for aiding queer youth in their identity formation, their connection to each other and to a broader queer community, and their visibility through an aggregate of their individual voices.

Yet, as several critics have asserted, in the attempt to normalize queer narratives, the *It Gets Better Project* simultaneously homogenizes and sensationalizes them (Gal, Shifman, and Kampf 2016). The *It Gets Better Project*, and the many spinoff online video projects it has inspired, fix a narrative that suggests that, at its core, queer life is inherently rooted in the experience of suffering and emergence. So, despite the *It Gets Better Project*'s intent to discourage queer youth from suicidal ideation, the structure of the campaign nonetheless reinforces the logics of queer youth suicide. The *It Gets Better Project* does not challenge heteronormative social structures in which queer youth may feel excluded; rather, it takes suicidal ideation as the problem rather than the symptom. Dustin Bradley Goltz has identified the differential logics of queer and straight teen suicide, in which queer suicide is naturalized in mediated representations and presented as "sensible" within the context of normative forms of belonging. Goltz compares this to representations of straight teen suicide, paradoxically represented as "selfish" within normative familial bonds (Goltz 2013a; 2013b). The discursive logic of queer youth suicide, he argues, mitigates against the possibility of queer relational systems that elide this logic. This discourse, predicated on queer identity being rooted in struggle due to non-normativity, belies other ways of understanding queerness as a project of worldmaking and a *destabilizing* of collective identity (Cohen 1997). As Chistopher Pullen claims, queer youth are "less interested in finding an assured future, or some sense of resistance to the 'straight world', and are more interested in the 'unfixed' potential of life chances, as mobile and enabling" (Pullen 2014, 80). Therefore, while the campaign may encourage connection between queer-identified people, it ultimately does not challenge heteronormativity or structural injustice. Furthermore, the campaign has been proven to disproportionately feature white, normatively gendered males, who in general are most likely to be represented in the mainstream media as the face of sexuality-based bullying (Phillips 2013).

The resulting representation is of "queer" as an identity that is quintessentially about *survival*, which not only comes to stand in for what it means to be a queer-identified youth, but which is also often assumed to be definitive of how this segment of the population uses media technologies in their own negotiations of identity. Indeed, the sizeable viewership of *It Gets Better Project* videos suggests tremendous relevance to queer youth experience. Moreover, due to the consistency of talking points across the videos ("life is hard for queer youth, but hold on and it will get better"), their wide circulation on the internet, and celebrity, corporate, nonprofit, and broadcast media tie-ins and promotions, the "it gets better" message is affectively and algorithmically set up to circulate successfully. This is in part because videos like these traffic in broadcast strategies of publicity, circulating to an imagined universal queer public that is assumed to share common experiences of bullying, self-loathing, and forms of structural violence.

Pedagogical videos present common logics of a broadcast genre in a social media environment that imagines and addresses a universal queer public with a consistent narrative about queer experience (Gal et al. 2016). The emphasis on message cohesion and legibility in pedagogical videos seems to take precedence in ways that suggest that these videos and the campaigns they are a part of have, in fact, more in common with top-down traditional broadcast advertising that is interested in singular, comprehensive narratives. This is perhaps because the commonly utilized public service announcement (PSA) form, similar to commercial advertisements, takes a uni-directional approach to a target audience about an issue and offers one discrete, often hard-hitting, uncomplicated message.

We may also consider queer youth participation as the production of a form of visibility that facilitates online social connections for the participant. The *It Gets Better Project* leverages the ubiquity of online social media in the search for connections. In recent years, online video has been widely embraced as a method of connecting and giving voice to marginalized subjects. YouTube, in particular, has been celebrated as a platform that seemingly affords everyday users the opportunity to circumnavigate the formal barriers of institutional spaces and the constraints of mass communications with self-generated and self-directed videos, or what Manuel Castells has referred to as "mass self-communication" (Burgess et al. 2009; Castells 2009). With relatively low barriers to participation, opportunities for informal mentorship, and strong support for collaboration with others, YouTube is seen by many educators and activists as a model platform for facilitating interaction among those with shared affinities (Jenkins 2009). Through the act of producing and circulating videos, YouTube invites everyday users

68   Identity Management in Queer Viral Videos

to engage in what Peters and Seier have described as a "self-staging" of identities, in which producers can reflect on how they perform in the world (Peters and Seier 2009). Jenkins et al.'s concept of the participatory "media franchise" (2013, 209) helps us to explain the work the campaign does in acting as "a cultural attractor, drawing like-minded people together to form an audience, but also a cultural activator, giving that community something to do." Media studies scholar Larry Gross argues that electronic media have always played a central role in helping to forge connections between queer people. He refers to these networks as the "submerged archipelago of queer life across the United States" (Gross 2007, vii). Other media studies scholars who have also studied the relationship between queer identity formation and online media use have described the existence of queer communication networks that are made possible through social media as simply more visible extensions of already-mediated queer networks (Gray 2009a; Phillips 2002; Pullen 2009; Pullen and Cooper 2010; Driver 2007).

Driver's (2007) ethnographic research on queer youth and popular culture emphasizes the value and importance of informality and spontaneity in young people's connections and feelings of belonging. She writes:

> For queer youth, informal public modes of community are especially valuable in the face of a lack of social recognition and support within both formal public institutions and private family realms. Queer youth are often in a predicament of having literally nowhere to go in order to physically experience the pleasure of feeling at home with others. And it is precisely those improvised, casual, and open forms of sociality to which young people turn for a sense of laid back, spontaneous belonging.
>
> (Susan Driver, *Queer Girls and Popular Culture: Reading, Resisting, and Creating Media* [New York: Peter Lang, 2007], 174)

Might we understand anti-gay-bullying videos online as a form of sociality that facilitates the sense of belonging that Driver describes, so that even if the anti-gay-bullying videos do nothing to perform the social change they purport to make through awareness-building and connection, they may provide new opportunities for young people to seek out and be in touch with others and possibly build alliances? At the same time, if we interpret celebrities' and public figures' participation in anti-gay-bullying campaigns to be (at least partially) a form of identity management, can we assume that the same motivations apply to the youth who participate in the campaigns?

Spreadable media may appear to offer queer youth similar cultural capital and a form of authority. At the very least it provides a way for them to imagine and perform their own successful survival of the challenges that

Identity Management in Queer Viral Videos 69

can come with being young and queer. By posting a video that resembles those of celebrities, youth producers can seemingly align themselves with the stars. It endows participants with what Howard Rheingold (2008) calls a "public voice"—one that can be leveraged in the projection of a coherent, self-confident, reflective self. Media scholars Peter Levine (2008) and Tara McPherson (2008) have both noted the ways in which *participation* (through media that is participatory in nature) is often cast as evidence of a healthy citizenry. Taking this position into account, might we also understand participation in anti-gay-bullying video production as the performance of a compliant, legible citizen? In other words, someone who *belongs*.

From Pedagogical to Performative Queer Videos

When we disentangle the spread and mainstream visibility that the *It Gets Better Project* video campaign enjoys from the sheer number of videos that exist for and about queer youth, we begin to see a profuse and diverse representation of queer youth life that effectually counters the homogenizing, oppression-based narrative that the campaign and its derivatives further. A second category of videos can, therefore, be characterized as more informal, improvisational, and typically posted for an already-invested local public of viewers (rather than an imagined homogenous queer youth public). These videos, which I call *performative*, are characteristically disjointed, non-linear, and work against any particular script. In so doing, they work to direct the viewer away from notions of any essentialized interiority associated with being queer.[10] So rather than describing a universal narrative of what it means to be queer, as pedagogical videos are apt to do, performative videos actively *enact* queer publics (Butler 1999). Through a multiplicity of narratives, styles, tone, and genres, the net of queer legitimacy and identity is cast much wider (Cohen 1997).

Indeed, the filming styles, content, metadata, and circulation of performative videos consummate queer youth publics online, and in turn complicate the proscribed, teleogical narrative that the *It Gets Better Project* and similar pedagogical videos further. It thus moves us away from monolithic narratives rooted in violence and oppression and towards multiple narratives of possibility. Taken together, *performative* queer youth videos confound the narrative of a singular queer public that the *It Gets Better Project* seeks to cohere. In so doing, they point to different forms of queer sociality and futurity, evidencing multiple queer publics that are responsive to change and invested in transformation. To wit, these videos encourage alternative ways of thinking about the potential role of participatory video in the lives of queer youth. As the variety of *performative* queer youth videos illustrate, YouTube is a site where marginal positions, narratives, and experiences are performed and circulated. These appear

70 *Identity Management in Queer Viral Videos*

to emerge from local publics that have pre-existing audiences and knowledge that is embedded in the production process. For these reasons, such videos rarely circulate beyond an already-invested viewership. But as local queer youth publics continue to use YouTube, the multiplicity of narratives, coalitions, symbolic representations, and mimetic re-imaginings they create can help form the basis for transformative social change. These videos realize a world in which many other possibilities and ways of being queer emerge, de-emphasizing bullying, violence, and suicidal ideation as the most legible shared narrative.

Performative queer youth videos take many forms, reflecting the overall diversity of existing genres. They include home video-like documentation of local queer community events, group webcasts, participations in mainstream internet video memes, personal video blogs, intergenerational community-produced videos, and more. Like so much user-generated content on YouTube, the circulation of each particular video is often quite weak. This is in part due to the sheer ubiquity of videos online, but it is also because most of these videos do not follow the templates that ensure spreadability. Pedagogical videos require spreadability because their social value is imagined to be located in the content (a message). Performative videos, on the other hand, are typically directed towards representing community and queer diversity while activating local publics.

What are the possibilities for social connection, identity formation, and social recognition when the goals of production shift away from consolidating a shared public narrative of emergence from suffering towards a deeper engagement among more localized, pre-existing communities of affinity? What are the possibilities when queer youth video production is thought of as constituting local, already-invested mediated queer publics rather than a mass audience that self-broadcasts efforts such as those that the *It Gets Better Project* encourages? What follows are examples of performative video projects that serve as counterpoints to pedagogical videos like those of the *It Gets Better Project*.

Vlogs

If pedagogical videos work to reinforce cohesive narratives about queer lives, queer youth video blogs (vlogs) and webcasts confound them. Typically featuring individuals or pairs of youth who answer questions their viewers have posted or emailed to them across a series of episodes, these videos present a spectrum of ways to be queer. A digital age rendering of the call-in peer helpline or advice column, crossed with the television talk show genre, peer education videos offer an opportunity for informal peer-to-peer advising, knowledge sharing, and the chance for young producers to perform queer identity for others who are learning what it means to be queer. These videos speak to a self-identified audience of viewers and fans, rather than a generalized imagined community.

Identity Management in Queer Viral Videos   71

Altogether, these works present an expansive and varied picture of queer youth (Berliner 2011).

One popular silo for peer education vlogs was LGBTeens, a YouTube channel which consisted of more than 600 videos and had 36,000 subscribers and 10,493,655 views (www.youtube.com/user/LGBTeens). The webcast's tagline, "We offer a younger perspective of the LGBT community," gestured to the often-criticized approach of video campaigns like the *It Gets Better Project* that are initiated and shaped by adults. In LGBTeens, viewers typically emailed questions to the vloggers, which were subsequently answered on camera. No information about who was asking the questions was provided in the vlog, but the sense of individual viewers standing by to hear their questions answered was evoked. Topics varied from specific practical and logistical concerns, such as "where to hang out" and "where to buy a chest binder," to broader issues of identity, such as "how to identify within the queer community." Videos were generally unscripted and did not appear to include editing, and often incorporated unplanned appearances from pets and friends who entered the frame and interrupted the conversation. Videos ranged in length, and typically devoted only a portion of onscreen time to the designated topic. Most of the videos involved the vloggers simply interacting with each other onscreen—they were so informal that in some cases it felt as if they may have forgotten to turn off the camera. Their onscreen performance of ease suggested the absence of immediate danger and threat in their environment while representing the world of the LGBTeen as safe and comforting. The improvisational nature of the videos signaled the makers' inclination to depart from a script, signifying their willingness to represent their lives as more disjointed and complex than might be offered by a scripted (pedagogical) video that tries to encapsulate an overarching narrative of the lives of queer youth.

Violence and loss are issues that also emerged, although from within nonlinear, intimate conversations. In the wake of the 2010 suicides, many YouTube channels took up issues of bullying and suicidal ideation, but on LGBTeens, mention of these topics was typically buried within other discussions. In the channel's popular video, "Dumbledore is a Raging Homosexual with a Unicycle," vloggers Anna and Amanda briefly addressed the recent youth suicides after a playful opening in which they told a joke while the video cut back and forth between settings (2010). A minute in, Amanda addressed the topic:

> Before we start with the questions, we have to touch on kind of a serious note. Lately there have been five suicides in the past I think, week ... somebody said six, but I am going to go with five because it is less sad ... by gay youth and gay teens and, uh, I just want ... if that's a problem that any of you are having, just know that there is

72   *Identity Management in Queer Viral Videos*

always something better for you to do and that suicide is never, ever, the answer.

> (Anna and Amanda, "Dumbledore is a Raging
> Homosexual with a Unicycle" [YouTube, 2010])

Up to this point in the video, the message and approach were similar to those of pedagogical videos. But as she continued, it became clear that her intent was to inspire action more than to circulate a message. First, she presented herself as a resource: "If any of you are having issues, you can come to me and talk to me, all you millions of people." Second, she mentioned ways to participate in a suicide awareness campaign that was happening offline, in different cities. There did not appear to be any organizations or foundations behind Amanda's message; rather, it seemed she had independently gathered the resources at her disposal to share with other young people. The video actively built on already established connections, making links between the talking heads on YouTube and actions and connections that can happen offline.

Another way in which the video departed from the pedagogical template was that discussion of queer youth bullying and suicide was mentioned alongside several other discussion threads. Anna and Amanda addressed the topic briefly (but solemnly) at the head of the video, but then continued for six more minutes, laughing and chatting about a range of things, like whose pack of cigarettes they were smoking. They frequently interrupted each other—sometimes with a kiss—and took a break to show Anna riding—and subsequently falling off—a unicycle. They shouted back and forth to Anna's younger brother who was outside of the frame, and whispered about whose car they would use to make out in after they turned off the camera.

Amidst the playfulness they also addressed three of the questions sent in by viewers: "Do you think society's view of the gay community is slowly changing?" "After coming out did you become *really* gay? For example, buying lots of rainbow stuff?" and "What did you think about Dumbledore being gay in *Harry Potter*?" These questions indicated a range of ways in which viewers were connecting with Amanda and Anna, and served to spark discussion between the vloggers rather than to elicit certain answers. In addressing the questions onscreen, the pair demonstrate the ways in which both they and their viewers are making sense of what it means to identify as queer. If the viewers learn anything from the vlog, it is that there are no simple answers to the question of what it means to be queer.

Community Collaborations

While the *It Gets Better Project* and similar spin-off pedagogical videos reify generational divides in the queer community, others have used online video production as a tool for enhancing intergenerational alliances and social justice activities in their communities.

Identity Management in Queer Viral Videos 73

On November 23, 2010, only a month into the *It Gets Better Project*, Seattle-based community educators/media-makers Sid Jordan and Megan Kennedy launched a YouTube PSA, "ReTeaching Gender and Sexuality," that they had written in conjunction with youth in their community. In the three-minute video, diverse young people each utter a sentence of a statement that implicitly stages a critique of the *It Gets Better Project* while offering an alternative framing of queer youth in relation to bullying and suicidal ideation. They begin:

- This is about way more than bullies in our schools.
- This is about our school boards, our homes, and our country.
- This is about every small town, every suburb, and every city.
- This is about how people talk about us and treat us.
- This is about how we talk about ourselves and treat ourselves.
- This is not just about how "it gets better" when you get older.
- Do you want me to wait 'til later?
- Hell, no!
- This is not just about being picked on for being different.
- It's about being ... queer.

At first glance the video might appear to be aligned with the more didactic pedagogical videos like those of the *It Gets Better Project*, but upon watching the video all the way through it soon becomes apparent that the filmmakers have strategically utilized the conventions of the PSA to draw attention to their project's radical departure from the dominant style of narrative proffered by the *It Gets Better Project*. And while this PSA quite literally presents a number of disparate voices coming together to produce a unified message, it ultimately differs from the more explicitly pedagogical videos in that its message is precisely that making life better for queer youth requires a complex set of approaches and actions that extend beyond the realm of YouTube. To boot, "ReTeaching Gender and Sexuality" does not purport to represent queer youth; instead, it encourages young people to participate in a *movement* aimed at changing the ways in which queer young people speak for themselves and are spoken about. It seeks to "contribute additional queer/trans youth voices to the national conversations about queer/trans youth lives" and "intends to steer the conversation beyond the symptom of bullying, to consider systemic issues and deeper beliefs about gender and sexuality that impact queer youth" (www.reteachinggenderandsexuality.org). Promotional stickers supporting the *Reteaching Gender and Sexuality* campaign speak directly to the promise that "it gets better" by advocating that "this is not about waiting." It is clear from the video's message that the *ReTeaching Gender and Sexuality* team's aim is to identify strategies within communities that can address the "root causes of violence and isolation in our communities" rather than passively accepting them as realities of queer life (Jordan and Kennedy 2010).

Figure 2.3, 2.4, and 2.5 Posters associated with "ReTeaching Gender and Sexuality" promotional materials

Credit: Sid Jordan and Megan Kennedy, "ReTeaching Gender and Sexuality," YouTube, 2010

The *ReTeaching Gender and Sexuality* YouTube page includes a link to the group's website, which provides facilitator discussion guides, definitions of preferred language, and information about the composition of the volunteer advisory team, which they describe as "intentionally multi-generational, multi-racial, and multi-faith," who are "a majority people of color, under 23 years old, and trans/gender-variant" (www.putthisonthemap.org). They claim, "we collectively speak 7+ languages; are from diasporic histories; are people with disabilities; and are people who have experienced homelessness." This description illustrates the group's breadth of experience and their value they place on different variations and circumstances of queer life experience, and by contrast calls out the *It Gets Better Project*'s overwhelmingly white, normatively-gendered, middle-class, older representation.

Another media action organization, *Global Action Project*, has been facilitating social justice work with New York City youth since 1991. Their mission is "to work with young people most affected by injustice to build the knowledge, tools, and relationships needed to create media for community power, cultural expression, and political change" (www.global-action.org). The organization hosts a variety of media education programs, including one for queer youth called *SupaFriends*, through which participants have produced dozens of videos that now circulate on YouTube Utilizing a range of genres, from drama to science fiction to animation, *SupaFriends* producers explore justice issues by imagining queer worlds that draw heavily on documentary footage from their communities.

One film, "SupaFriends: The Fight for Acceptance," is a nine-minute live-action comic book story that centers the drama on the trials facing queer teens (St. Clair et al. 2013). Juxtaposing mainstream news footage and clips of youth speaking at the "LGBTQ communities against 'stop and frisk' press conference" with dramatic sequences, the teens re-imagine their universe as subject to evil forces that are enacted through gentrification, violence, and the criminalization of queer youth of color. The video relies on science fiction tropes to distance the audience from the otherwise archetypal narrative about queer youth experience upon which pedagogical videos often insist, while it incorporates documentary footage from the filmmakers' communities as a way of explicitly making links back to their lived realities. Quick cuts, special effects, and bombastic costumes and set decoration also establish a tone that is more playful than pedantic. The synopsis for the movie reads:

> When one member of the Superheros loses hope for justice on earth and decides to escape to the moon, other members of the team have their beliefs tested. In the process an unlikely hero discovers their own powers to heal, connect, and stop cycles of violence.
> (St. Clair et al., "SupaFriends: The Fight for Acceptance"
> [YouTube, 2013])

Figure 2.6 Still from "SupaFriends: The Fight for Acceptance" (Global Action Project), St. Clair et al., 2013, YouTube video still

The prevalent themes of self-doubt, isolation, and violence resemble those of queer youth pedagogical videos, but by blending the supernatural and the spectacular, these producers distance the content from an otherwise didactic message about overcoming self-hate with self-love: "Sometimes the best way to live," the main character explains in voiceover narration, "is to leave the world entirely—to find a way to escape, rather than to sustain yourself." Here we see that the youth filmmakers have chosen to represent suicidal ideation and feelings of oppression through an abstraction of social forces, imagining "leaving the world" as flying to the moon. Choosing to live, represented here as "sustaining," is characterized as an active process that requires community collaboration and the utilization of existing powers. Through the narrative, we might imagine that the video is hailing the communities around queer youth, encouraging them to fight for justice.

Like most youth-produced videos on YouTube, *SupaFriends* videos have each garnered relatively few views, averaging just a few hundred hits per video. This suggests that, unlike campaign-based videos like those of the *It Gets Better Project*, which in many cases has facilitated a generous number of hits, the *SupaFriends* audience is probably local and already invested in the topic (including the people who produce and appear in the videos). This extended viewing community is explicitly rewarded for their insider knowledge through content that references inside jokes, nicknames, and slang that would not necessarily register as meaningful to outside viewers. Videos often close with long credit sequences that celebrate the filmmakers. While these sequences appear to exist more for the benefit of the makers and their friends and families than for an imagined public, they have the potential added effect of demonstrating

Identity Management in Queer Viral Videos   77

queer relationality to other queer youth who are looking for examples of real teens who appear to live fun and fulfilling lives.

Global Action Project emphasizes the production process as knowledge creation and the exercising of community power. The expressed priority of the process of adding pedagogical and social value (over the aesthetic quality and distributive potential of the movie that is produced) aligns their work with a history of youth cultural expression and media activism that extends back before the existence of YouTube (and digital media, for that matter).

Other Video Memes

Branching out from the popularity of viral internet memes, the *WeHappyTrans* project has circulated a video chain called 7 *Questions* which the site contributors describe as "a set of questions for trans people framed to prompt positive responses." According to the site, over 50 participants have submitted responses, "spreading the word that trans people are just people, with many talents, who all deserve to be happy" (http://wehappytrans.com [last accessed November 11, 2014]). Open-ended questions prompt participants to provide extensive responses. Questions encourage participants to situate their experience in ways that emphasize identity-based self-awareness and joy over stories of violence and dejection. The prompts include: "Who has been most supportive of your transition or gender expression?" and "What do you most enjoy about your life since beginning transition? If you're not there yet, what about the possibility of transition excites you the most? What do you look forward to? Alternatively, what about your current gender expression is most satisfying?" Participants are asked to name their trans role models and identify the change they would most like to see in the world. They are asked to speak about how they are "the change they [you] want to see."

The 7 *Questions* videos encourage participants to imagine and perform the world they wish to live in and resist simple narratives. They are asked to speak the change they wish to see. This is made apparent in the way that the organizers imagine the site, both as a way of convening the trans community and as a way to contradict normative narratives about trans people. They explain that *WeHappyTrans* is an organized community effort of trans people "talking to one another, reaching out to one another to create something together … it's a communal consciousness raising project, an effort to destroy the idea that trans lives are exclusively comprised of suffering."

One highly circulated 7 *Questions* video features (then) Vassar College student Stephen Ira, who opens his video by introducing himself as "a transman, a faggy queen, a homosexual, a queer, nerdfighter, a writer,

78   Identity Management in Queer Viral Videos

an artist, and a guy who needs a haircut." This video garnered widespread attention and circulation through mainstream media outlets due to public interest in Ira's celebrity parentage (he is a child of actors Annette Benning and Warren Beatty). In this coverage, the media framed the *WeHappyTrans* project as simply a site for trans people to talk about their feelings. In his blog, *Supermattachine Review*, titled in homage to the radical pre-Stonewall queer activist group *Mattachine Society*, Ira reflects upon his reasons for participating, insisting that he was motivated by a desire for discursive and structural change (2012). He writes:

> Of course trans people need space to talk about our feelings, both our suffering and our joy. That's part of why *WeHappyTrans* exists, but don't make the mistake of thinking that this makes *WeHappyTrans* an apolitical project.
> The media talks about trans people only in very specific contexts. They talk about trans people when we are murdered, when we're connected to famous cis people, or when cis writers feel the need to discuss our aberrant bodies for purposes of sensationalism and exploitation.
> When trans people talk about our feelings to one another—really talk about them, not through a cis lens—we're doing profoundly political work. That's why *WeHappyTrans* is political, subversive, and valuable. What could be more subversive than a happy transsexual?
> (Stephen Ira, "Unpacking the Media Coverage of My
> WeHappyTrans Video," [Supermattachine Review, 2012])

Here Ira directly expresses the need for trans people to imagine themselves outside of media narratives that perform a sort of discursive violence against them by depicting them as victims. *7 Questions* calls on trans-identified people to use online video to articulate a transgender public that is committed to exploring the possibilities and joys of transgender experience while creating a form of self-representation that provides a dimension and texture not available in dominant depictions of trans people.

A very different but also popular queer youth meme, referred to as "The Girlfriend Tag" and "The Boyfriend Tag," appears prominently on the LGBTeens YouTube channel and elsewhere on YouTube.[11] In this series, young queer couples casually answer self-directed questions about their relationships, covering everything from what they watch on TV to what kinds of drinks they order when they go out to eat to what characteristics attracted them to each other. In these videos, the couples discuss the intimacies and ordinary details of their relationships for their imagined peer viewers while answering questions that are addressed across all the videos in this meme. As each couple answers the questions, they provide a range of representations of what it is like to

Identity Management in Queer Viral Videos   79

be in a relationship with another queer-identified person. The intimacy they create punctuates the content they discuss, demonstrating what it means to find love and support in the queer community and modeling relationships for queer young people who may be finding their independence. These images stand distinct from the persistent archetype of the bullied and suicidal queer youth and diminish the power of the master narrative of the anti-gay-bullying pedagogical video.

Conclusion

Anti-gay-bullying viral video media production has become central to the emergence of the discourse of queer youth empowerment and is bound at the nexus of identity politics and the bloated promises of participatory media. Shares, video clicks, and favorable comments from viewers seemingly affirm one's worth. Yet it is crucial that we do not assume an equivalency between the perceived value of the spreadable media that queer youth produce about bullying and the ways in which they internalize their own social value through the distribution of their videos. Self-produced video is certainly a useful tool for mediating identity, but its empowering properties must always be understood within the context of its production and distribution.

Whereas pedagogical videos work to fix particular kinds of understandings of what it means to be young and queer, performative videos reflect varied and sometimes even contradictory ways of identifying as queer. The range of video representations produce a diverse set of meanings about what it means to be queer and, in effect, *realizes* the potential for joy, connection, and social action, often precluded by pedagogical videos that center around violence and oppression. While violence and suicidal ideation are indeed very real concerns for the queer youth population, they are not necessarily central to, or definitive of, the experience of being a young queer person. Performative videos challenge the pedagogical video genre's ability to speak to and about queer youth. Performative videos position themselves less as a panacea for queer youth pain, but rather as just one of many possible outlets for expression, social cohesion, and perhaps even reflexivity. These videos perform the narrative multiplicity that exists among and between queer youth and, in so doing, encourage us to divest ourselves of the master narrative of oppression-based experience that is proffered by pedagogical videos such as those of the *It Gets Better Project*.

Notes

1 While *bullying* is often cited as a driving force in queer teen suicidal ideation, scholars such as sociologist Jessie Klein, author of *The Bully Society*, have noted that the contemporary bullying epidemic is really an epidemic in

80 *Identity Management in Queer Viral Videos*

the culture as a whole, not just among adolescents. Cultural Studies scholar Roddey Reid has described this as an overall American culture of public bullying which traffics in "intimidation and disrespect." To wit, bullying is not necessarily the core issue for queer youth, who make up 20–40 percent of the homeless population in the United States (Powell 2011).

2 The authors make a point to distinguish between "viral" and what they call "spreadable" media. "Spreadability" takes agency into account. They write, "we use terms such as 'spread,' 'spreadable' or 'spreadability' to describe these increasingly pervasive forms of media circulation. 'Spreadibility' refers to the potential—both technical and cultural—for audiences to share content for their own purposes, sometimes with the permission of rights holders, sometimes against their wishes."

3 This data appeared on the *It Gets Better Project* website in late 2012–early 2013, and is mentioned in Savage's voiceover narration in the trailer for the documentary *It Gets Better 2*.

4 Another main goal of the campaign is to raise money for the Trevor Project (aimed at preventing queer youth suicide), GLSEN (the Gay, Lesbian and Straight Education Network), and the American Civil Liberties Union LGBTQ Project's Youth and Schools Program—organizations that have established histories of working to support LGBTQ youth.

5 When using this phrase, Savage gestures to a famous quote from the pre-eminent gay rights activist Harvey Milk.

6 On the *Make It Better* website they address what differentiates their campaign from the *It Gets Better Project*: "Columnist Dan Savage started the 'It Gets Better' video campaign to send a message of hope to queer youth who are experiencing bullying and contemplating suicide. His project, along with a swell in media coverage of youth deaths by suicide in the fall of 2010, ignited dialogue across the country about the epidemic of bullying in our schools. But it left an important question unaddressed: what can we do to make it better? GSA Network launched the *Make It Better Project* to let students, parents, teachers, school administrators, and adult allies know that there are concrete actions they can take right now to make schools safer for all students." Unfortunately, the Make It Better website is no longer available.

7 Due to the disavowment of the video production by multiple players, the *It Gets Better Project* removed the original video from their website. However, it can be located by re-publishings on YouTube, one of which is referenced here.

8 Media studies scholar Larry Gross argues that electronic media have always played a central role in helping to forge connections between queer people.

9 I am drawing on Michel Foucault's concept of power/knowledge and Paolo Freire's and Henry Giroux's concepts of critical pedagogy (Freire 2000).

10 While it is possible to consider all videos on YouTube to be in some sense performative, I aim to highlight the ways in which particular narrative templates bring into being the queer experiences they seek to represent.

11 Examples of the dozens of videos in this genre include: "Boyfriend Tag!" www.youtube.com/watch?v=oe_eZkmELjo and "Girlfriend Tag LGBT edition" www.youtube.com/watch?v=iQb13LbDajo.

Bibliography

Adler, Max. 2010. "Glee's Max Adler: It Gets Better." YouTube, 1:50. Posted by It Gets Better Project, November 16. www.youtube.com/watch?v=aHfM_iV-554.

Anna and Amanda. 2010. "Dumbledore is a Raging Homosexual with a Unicycle." YouTube, 7:48. Posted by That's Gay, October 5. www.youtube.com/watch?v=yTm76oOj84I.

Barmann, Jay. 2013. "It Gets Worse: 49ers Who Appeared in 'It Gets Better' Video Deny Making Video [Update]." *Sfist*. January 31. http://sfist.com/2013/01/31/49ers_deny_it_gets_better.php.

Berliner, Lauren. 2011. "When Your Curriculum Shuts a Door, Open a (YouTube) Window: What Queer Youth Video Bloggers Can Teach Us About Necessary Shifts in Media Pedagogy." *The New Everyday*, March 30. http://mediacommons.futureofthebook.org/tne/pieces/where-your-curriculum-shuts-door-open-youtube-window.

Blackmore, Susan. 1999. *The Meme Machine*. Oxford: Oxford University Press.

Burgess, Jean, John Hartley, Henry Jenkins, and Joshua Green. 2009. *YouTube: Online Video and Participatory Culture*. Cambridge: Polity Press.

Butler, Judith. 1999. "Bodies that Matter." In *Feminist Theory and the Body: A Reader*, edited by Janet Price and Margrit Shildrick, 235–45. New York: Routledge.

Castells, Manuel. 2009. *Communication Power*. Oxford: Oxford University Press.

Chalfen, R. 1987. *Snapshot Versions of Life*. Bowling Green: Bowling Green State University Popular Press.

Cohen, Cathy J. 1997. "Punks, Bulldaggers, and Welfare Queens: The Radical Potential of Queer Politics." *GLQ: A Journal of Lesbian and Gay Studies* 3 (4):437–65. Doi: http://dx.doi.org/10.1215/10642684-3-4-437.

Couldry, Nick, Mary L. Gray, and Tarleton Gillespie. 2013. "Culture Digitally: Digital In/Justice." *Journal of Broadcasting & Electronic Media* 57 (4):608–17. Doi: 10.1080/08838151.2013.846343.

D'Addario, Daneil. 2013. "'It Gets Better' Pulls 49ers' PSA After Players Deny Their Involvement." Salon.com. February 1. www.salon.com/2013/02/01/it_gets_better_pulls_49ers_psa_after_players_deny_their_involvement/.

Dawkins, Richard, ed. 1989. *The Selfish Gene*. Oxford: Oxford University Press.

Driver, Susan. 2007. *Queer Girls and Popular Culture: Reading, Resisting, and Creating Media*. New York: Peter Lang.

Facebook. 2010. "It Gets Better: Facebook Employees." YouTube, 6:07. Posted by Facebook, October 26. www.youtube.com/watch?v=aHfM_iV-554.

Foucault, Michel. 1977. *Discipline and Punish: The Birth of the Prison*. New York: Pantheon Books.

Freire, Paulo, ed. 2000. *Pedagogy of the Oppressed*. New York: Continuum.

Gal, Noam, Limor Shifman, and Zohar Kampf. 2016. "'It Gets Better': Internet Memes and the Construction of Collective Identity." *New Media & Society* 18 (8):1698–714. Doi:10.1177/1461444814568784.

Gilmore, Ruth Wilson. 2007. "In the Shadow of the Shadow State." In *The Revolution Will Not Be Funded*, edited by INCITE!, 41–52. Durham: Duke University Press.

82 *Identity Management in Queer Viral Videos*

Giroux, Henry A. 2003. "Public Pedagogy and the Politics of Resistance: Notes on a Critical Theory of Educational Struggle." *Educational Philosophy and Theory* 35 (1):5–16. Doi: 10.1111/1469–5812.00002.

Goltz, Dustin Bradley. 2013a. "'Sensible' Suicide, Brutal Selfishness, and John Hughes's Queer Bonds." *Cultural Studies ↔ Critical Methodologies* 13 (2):99–109. Doi: 10.1177/1532708612471317.

———. 2013b. "It Gets Better: Queer Futures, Critical Frustrations, and Radical Potentials." *Critical Studies in Media Communication* 30 (2):135–51. Doi: 10.1080/15295036.2012.701012.

Gray, Mary L. 2009a. *Out in the Country: Youth, Media, and Queer Visibility in Rural America*. New York: New York University Press.

———. 2009b. "Negotiating Identities/Queering Desires: Coming Out Online and the Remediation of the Coming-Out Story." *Journal of Computer-Mediated Communication* 14 (4):1162–89. Doi: 10.1111/j.1083-6101.2009.01485.x.

Gross, Larry. 2007. "Forward." In *Queer Online: Media Technology and Sexuality*, edited by Kate O'Riordan and David J. Phillips. New York: Peter Lang.

GSA Network. 2010. "Youth Suicides Prompt Make It Better Project." GSA Network. Last modified October 3. https://gsanetwork.org/news/youth-suicides-prompt-make-it-better-project/100310.

Halleck, DeeDee. 2002. *Hand-Held Visions: The Impossible Possibilities of Community Media*. New York: Fordham University Press.

Hawk, Madonna Thunder. 2007. "Native Organizing Before the Nonprofit Industrial Complex." In *The Revolution Will Not Be Funded*, edited by INCITE!, 101–6. Durham: Duke University Press.

Hughes, Sarah Anne. 2011. "Jamey Rodemeyer, Bullied Teen Who Made 'It Gets Better' Video, Commits Suicide." *The Washington Post*, September 21. www.washingtonpost.com/blogs/blogpost/post/jamey-rodemeyer-bullied-teen-who-made-it-gets-better-video-commits-suicide/2011/09/21/gIQAVVzxkK_blog.html?utm_term=.cf24f07a3fae.

Ira, Stephen. 2012. "Unpacking the Media Coverage of My WeHappyTrans Video." *Supermattachine Review* (blog), July 30. https://supermattachine.wordpress.com/2012/07/30/278/.

Jenkins, Henry. 2009. *Confronting the challenges of Participatory Culture: Media Education for the 21st Century*. Cambridge, MA: MIT Press.

Jenkins, Henry, Sam Ford, and Joshua Green. 2013. *Spreadable Media: Creating Value and Meaning in a Networked Culture*. New York: New York University Press.

Jordan, Sid and Megan Kennedy. 2010. "ReTeaching Gender and Sexuality." YouTube video.

Ketchum, Karyl. 2014. "'We've Got Big News': Creating Media to Empower Queer Youth in Schools." In *Queer Youth and Media Cultures*, edited by Christopher Pullen, 98–112. London: Palgrave Macmillan UK.

Krabill, Ron. 2012. "American Sentimentalism and the Production of Global Citizens." *Contexts* 11 (4):52–54. Doi: 10.1177/1536504212466332.

Levine, Peter. 2008. "A Public Voice for Youth: The Audience Problem in Digital Media and Civic Education." In *Civic Life Online: Learning How Digital Media Can Engage Youth*, edited by W. Lance Bennett, 119–38. Cambridge, MA: MIT Press.

Identity Management in Queer Viral Videos 83

McPherson, Tara. 2008. "A Rule Set for the Future." In *Digital Youth, Innovation, and the Unexpected*, edited by Tara McPherson, 1–26. Cambridge, MA: MIT Press.

Muller, Amber. 2011. "Virtual Communities and Translation into Physical Reality in the 'It Gets Better' Project." *Journal of Media Practice* 12 (3):269–77. Doi: 10.1386/jmpr.12.3.269_1.

Peters, Kathrin, and Andrea Seier. 2009. "Home Dance: Mediacy and Aesthetics of the Self on YouTube." In *The YouTube Reader*, edited by Pelle Snickars and Patrick Vonderau, 187–203. Stockholm: National Library of Sweden.

Phillips, David J. 2002. "Negotiating the Digital Closet: Online Pseudonymity and the Politics of Sexual Identity." *Information, Communication & Society* 5 (3):406–24. Doi: 10.1080/13691180210159337.

Phillips, Laurie M. 2013. "Offering Hope and Making Attributions through YouTube: An Exploratory Ethnographic Content Analysis of the Social Change-Oriented 'It Gets Better Project.'" *The Journal of Social Media in Society* 2 (1):30–65. Thejsms.org/index.php/TSMRI/article/view/11.

Pixar Animation Studios. 2010. "'It Gets Better' – Love, Pixar." YouTube, 8:01. Posted by PixGetsBetter, November 22. www.youtube.com/watch?v=aHfM_iV-554.

Powell, Nicholas. 2011. "LGBT Youth Empowered by Victories." *Liberation News*, June 21. www.liberationnews.org/lgbt-youth-empowered-html/.

Puar, Jasbir K. 2012. "Coda: The Cost of Getting Better: Suicide, Sensation, Switchpoints." *GLQ: A Journal of Lesbian and Gay Studies* 18 (1):149–58. https://muse.jhu.edu/article/460796.

Pullen, Christopher. 2009. *Gay Identity, New Storytelling and the Media*. London: Palgrave Macmillan.

———. 2014. "Media Responses to Queer Youth Suicide: Trauma, Therapeutic Discourse and Co-Presence." In *Queer Youth and Media Cultures*, edited by Christopher Pullen, 63–85. London: Palgrave Macmillan UK.

Pullen, Christopher and Margaret Cooper. 2010. *LGBT Identity and Online New Media*. New York: Routledge.

Reid, Roddey. 2009. "The American Culture of Public Bullying." *Black Renaissance Noire* 9 (2):174–87. http://go.galegroup.com.offcampus.lib.washington.edu/ps/i.do?&id=GALE%7CA271406204&v=2.1&u=wash_main&it=r&p=LitRC&sw=w&authCount=1.

Rheingold, Howard. 2008. "Using Participatory Media and Public Voice to Encourage Civic Engagement." In *Civic Life Online: Learning How Digital Media Can Engage Youth*, edited by W. Lance Bennett, 97–118. Cambridge, MA: MIT Press.

Rodemeyer, Jamey. 2011. "It Gets Better, I Promise!" YouTube, 2:04. Posted by xgothemo99xx, May 4. www.youtube.com/watch?v=-Pb1CaGMdWk.

San Francisco 49ers. 2013. "San Francisco 49ers' Ahmad Brooks Deny Participating in 'It Gets Better' Gay Youth Video." YouTube, 0:59. Posted by keepinguuptodate, February 1. www.youtube.com/watch?v=h86A3N78uHs.

Savage, Dan. 2011. "How it Happened: The Genesis of a YouTube Movement." *The Stranger*, April 13. www.thestranger.com/seattle/how-it-happened/Content?oid=7654378.

Savage, Dan, and Terry Miller. 2010. "It Gets Better: Dan and Terry." YouTube, 8:31. Posted by It Gets Better Project, September 21. www.youtube.com/watch?v=7IcVyvg2Qlo.

84   *Identity Management in Queer Viral Videos*

———. 2011. *It Gets Better: Coming Out, Overcoming Bullying, and Creating a Life Worth Living.* New York: Penguin Books.

Shifman, Limor. 2012. "An Anatomy of a YouTube Meme." *New Media & Society* 14 (2):187–203. Doi: 10.1177/1461444811412160.

St. Clair, Abena, Esai Lopez, Gabby Valdez, Jace Romello, Juan Guadalupe, Maria Santana, Rene A. Jaquez, and Scotty Zinifire. 2013. "SupaFriends: The Fight for Acceptance." YouTube, 9:11. Posted by GlobalActionProject, July 16. www.youtube.com/watch?v=W8meG60pqis.

3 Vernacular Voices

Business Gets Personal in Public Service Announcements

In a January 1985 commercial slot, during the height of the deregulation period of the US media industry, American television stations broadcast an interview with actor Yul Brynner, a figure beloved by audiences for his performance in the leading role of Rogers and Hammerstein's *The King and I*. The appearance of Brynner chilled viewers: at the time of its first airing, Brynner had been dead for months. The spot opens with the epitaph "Yul Brynner: 1920–1985" as a male voice announces, "Ladies and gentlemen, the late Yul Brynner." White type dissolves to black as Brynner's face fades into a close-up. Famously aloof, Brynner now emotes up close and personal into the camera, stern and pleading:

> I really wanted to make a commercial when I discovered that I was that sick and my time was so limited. I want to make that commercial that says simply "now that I'm gone, I tell you, don't smoke. Whatever you do, just don't smoke."
>
> (Yul Brynner, American Cancer Society
> public service announcement, 1985)

An American Cancer Society logo fades in to replace the image of Brynner as he continues emphatically in voiceover: "If I could take back that smoking, we wouldn't be talking about any cancer. I'm convinced of that" (2006).[1] It was no doubt startling for audiences to encounter this image of the typically private and dispassionate Brynner returned from the dead to confess personal regret about smoking and to urge viewers to give up the habit (Brynner 200610).

The Brynner public service announcement (PSA) was remarkable for its time because it relied on the authority of a different kind of first-person perspective from that which viewers were accustomed to hearing in commercial and cause-related advertising of the era.[2] Most PSAs—noncommercial messages aimed at changing audience behavior—up until that point had used authoritative expert voices. In contrast, Brynner's voice and affect was vernacular and personal. The PSA puts forth Brynner not just as a lofty spokesperson performing a script for a venerated national

Figure 3.1 Yul Brynner addresses smokers in a 1985 American Cancer Society public service announcement (PSA)

society. Rather, he speaks subjectively about his experiences and feelings and delivers a personal message to other smokers like himself, bypassing institutional signifiers of authority and scientific knowledge.

The more direct relationship Yul Brynner had with the audience can be understood through the advertising strategy of *resemblances*, or *perceived similarity*, which refers to "the extent to which individuals perceive a portrayal as realistically reflecting their own experiences or as similar to themselves based on different attributes" (Austin and Meili 1994; Andsager et al. 2006). These attributes may include demographics, shared values and ideas, and common experiences (Toncar, Reid, and Anderson 2007; Salmon and Atkin 2003). Industry research into advertising and affect shows that the more personal approach of the Brynner spot had a greater impact on viewers than earlier PSAs with similar messages but a less directly personal appeal (Goodwill 2017).[3] Researchers noted a correlation between a drop in smoking rates and the airing of the specific PSA featuring Brynner's personal appeal.

The Brynner PSA introduced a new element to the industry repertoire of *resemblance*. Not only did audience members find Brynner's emotive image uniquely relatable, they sensed that the spoken message was from him personally—and in fact he had played a significant role in the conceptualization of the PSA. Brynner's PSA testimony is an example of the advertising industry's attempts during this period to close the emotional gap between the subject on the screen and the audience. The success of this spot helped to popularize the advertising industry's strategy of using documentary elements and testimonies of people who have real-life investment in the issues at hand to enhance resemblances in PSAs and other forms of advertisement.

Since the 1980s, an investment in the PSA genre as both a pedagogical and an expressive form has emerged. Many educators, community leaders, and social issue activists have celebrated self-produced, self-distributed PSA videos as a venue for youth producers to share personal experiences. The expectation is that the messages will circulate and find resonance with others who are looking for information or advice.[4] In both popular and education discourse, the participatory nature of YouTube is often equated with democratic practice; producing social-issue-based content for the site has been conflated with forms of civic action and personal expression and heralded as a political shift to a more democratic model of media. Others have suggested that the proliferation of PSAs in particular is evidence of an epistemological turn, where user-generated content performs a reproach to the pre-digital, more centralized production of knowledge about social issues, and replaces that authoritative mode with a diversity of first-person accounts (Serlin 2010). Just as Yul Brynner's message to smokers was set up to be interpreted as coming from the heart and not from an objective authority, it also served the American Cancer Society's campaign goal of discouraging smoking. Similarly, many self-produced online PSAs derive authority through the voice of the speaker but acquire their ultimate visibility and circulation through alignments with existing institutions. It is precisely the contemporary banality of the use of the personal in the PSA that I would like to bring our attention to in order to interrogate its function in public service announcements.

Historical context allows us to see the ways the PSA form has transformed in accordance with changing media policies and regulations, as well as fluctuations in funding for particular public health and other social issues. The vernacular mode of expression in many contemporary user-produced online PSAs contains remnants of the style and formal approach to content historically used by PSAs. I use the term *vernacular voices* to refer to the personal message and subjective style of address used in PSAs which cast figures who explicitly identify themselves as being a member of the PSA's target demographic, speak candidly from their experiences and feelings as individuals (not as authorities from a place of objective knowledge and authority), and who interpellate members of the audience as individuals rather than as a generalized collective group. While it may seem as if there has been a shift in authority from authoritative to vernacular voices in contemporary public service campaigns, when we examine recent online PSAs in the context of the institutional history of PSA media we can see how their content has been informed by a longstanding public service media business model that has evolved along with changing technologies and affective regimes.

88 *Vernacular Voices*

The Business of Public Service Advertising

Broadcast public service announcements first emerged in the United States during World War II in the form of home-front propaganda produced by the War Advertising Council, an organization of advertising agencies and broadcasters commissioned by the government to generate support for various war efforts (Jackall and Hirota 2000). Towards the end of the war, the council evaluated its role and opportunities, sensing a need to change its role to postwar campaigns that would have a "feel of the future." A memorandum from T. S. Repplier, the executive director of the council, to Chairman Harold B. Thomas suggests that the council hoped that its members could leverage for the postwar commercial industry tactics advertisers had used successfully in wartime persuasion (Jackall and Hirota 2000, 44). In the wake of war, the council had identified the opportunity for the business world to align its interests with those of the commonwealth, and to leverage media persuasion towards other ends. The document also suggests that members of the council took the position that if advertisers and broadcasters did not address the "human problems" wrought by the machine age, they would have to rely on centralized governmental solutions to those problems, at a perceived cost to the freedoms and liberties of both individuals and businesses. The council document also introduces the important notion of public service as a job explicitly in the purview of the advertising industry. The document proposes that advertising could continue to "help solve national problems" by providing information on issues such as public health and conservation of the environment, thereby elevating the status of the entire advertising enterprise in the minds of various publics and the ever-dubious business community. It further suggests that advertising plays a role in maintaining a free market ideology, a principle that would bloom in the later move towards a neoliberal free-market: by providing information about the "free exchange of goods," it is suggested, advertisers and broadcasters could provide reassurance about the "stability of the private enterprise system" (Jackall and Hirota 2000, 45). Indeed, this and other documents produced by the council suggest that rationalizing public service work to the business community was the council's postwar public relations strategy for bolstering the entire advertising enterprise, which at that time was still a growing industry with little esteem among other more established and financially commanding industries.

The postwar mission of the council coalesced around a surprisingly prescient idea captured in the statement that "the best public relations advertising is public service advertising" (Jackall and Hirota 2000, 45). In a 1945 speech to the American Association of Advertising Agencies (AAAA), James W. Young, the newly elected chairman of the council and consultant to the ad agency J. Walter Thompson, emphasized that the council's mission was not to push advertisers and their agencies into

Vernacular Voices 89

"a Boy Scout program of doing a good deed daily," but rather, to help the image of the advertiser who wished to enhance his corporate reputation (McCarthy 2010).[5] For contemporary historians Robert Jackall and Janice Hirota, the act of consuming the PSA was, and continues to be, inextricably intertwined with the goodwill payoff for the sponsoring company or organization:

> Public service advertising, whether it advocates support for Liberty Bonds, victory, the Red Cross, or the United Negro College Fund, implicitly divides the world into sheeps and goats, into clusters of patriotic or compassionate souls, on one hand, and, on the other, clusters of unconcerned or selfish egoists unmindful of the sacrifice and plight of others. It triggers among those who choose to "do the right thing" self-images of moral superiority complete with self-congratulation, a desirable goal for all advertising and public relations.
> (Robert Jackall and Janice M. Hirota, *Image Makers: Advertising, Public Relations, and the Ethos of Advocacy* [University of Chicago Press, 2000])

Through PSAs, businesses and advertisers could represent their industry as being on the side of good. Through strategic association with public causes such as health and the environment, advertisers and broadcasters were able to counter the profession's stigma of mercenariness and rebrand itself as collaboratively philanthropic.

Major American opinion leaders informed the direction of the council. In 1946, the council's leaders put together a Public Advisory Committee (later called the Public Policy Committee) which at various times included distinguished intellectuals and affairs leaders such as Eugene Meyer, chairman of the Washington Post; James B. Conant, president of Harvard University; and the gurus of public-opinion polling, George Gallup and Elmo Roper (McCarthy 2010, 47). The policy group helped link the council to a range of publics as they worked together to address non-controversial issues. In their account of the council's history, Jackall and Hirota argue that the organization helped play "a decisive part in shaping the contemporary apparatus and ethos of advocacy" while it welded "business and government interests into a single institutional complex through expertise with mass symbols ... filling our public arena with highly emotional and moralistic ideals" (McCarthy 2010, 62). Indeed, some of the same successful strategies and tactics used by advertisers to sell products were taken up by government agencies and charities (with the help of advertising agencies) to make emotional appeals about social issues of the day (Berger 2002). Topics included, for example, recruiting student nurses and ending drunk driving. Smokey the Bear, the cartoon character who even to this day educates the public about forest fires, emerged during

90 *Vernacular Voices*

this period. The early success of this campaign convinced advertisers that commercial tactics could be applied to the realm of advocacy (Berger 1991).

It was not just the messaging tactics of successful commercial advertising campaigns that the Ad Council sought to reproduce in public service campaigns; they also mimicked its distribution strategies. By the 1950s, this meant broadcasting PSAs on television. Taking advantage of the particularities of the American broadcasting system's unique hybrid commercial and public service model, the Ad Council made use of the industry's federal directive to provide evidence of its service to the community through "public interest" programming. This mandate, first established through the Federal Radio Act of 1927 (which was reinstated with the near-verbatim 1934 Communications Act that established the Federal Communications Commission), required that, in exchange for the use of the electromagnetic spectrum, broadcasters were obligated to serve "public interest, convenience, and necessity" over profit maximization[6]. Broadcast historian Michelle Hilmes claims that the definition of "public interest" was intended to be vague, making it difficult to fully enforce— for to enforce content would both violate First Amendment protections and interfere with corporate interests and competition (Hilmes 2007). It is what Robert Horwitz has referred to as an "irony of regulatory reform" (Horwitz 1989). As Anna McCarthy convincingly argues in her history of the postwar broadcasting era, the public service model offered a way for the government to legitimize the corporate structure of broadcast media (McCarthy 2010).

The explosion of the public service advertising genre as we know it today had everything to do with the strategic partnership that the Ad Council formed with advocacy groups and broadcasters during the postwar era. Through PSAs, the Ad Council offered something of a marriage of convenience for advertising agencies, social issue advocates, and the broadcast industry. Nonprofits or government agencies could seek out help from the Ad Council to develop a public education effort to promote their message (often covering production costs), advertising agencies produced ads pro bono (thereby enhancing their corporate image), and media organizations donated space to run the ads, helping broadcasters to fill empty airtime and meet their public service obligations. The Federal Communications Commission (FCC) defines public service announcements as:

> any announcement (including network) for which no charge is made and which promotes programs, activities, or services of federal, state, or local governments (e.g., recruiting, sale of bonds, etc.) or the programs, activities or services of non-profit organizations (e.g., United Way, Red Cross blood donations, etc.) and other announcements regarded as serving community interests, excluding

time signals, routine weather announcements and promotional announcements.

(Craig LaMay, "Public Service Advertising, Broadcasters, and the Public Interest: Regulatory Background and the Digital Future," in *Shouting to be Heard: Public Service Advertising in a New Media Age* [The Henry J. Kaiser Foundation, 2002])[6]

PSAs were not the only way that broadcasters met the public interest, but they were a widely used strategy. Easy to program, they were perceived by broadcasters to be well worth the donated time. At different times in broadcast history, this form dominated public interest airtime over, for example, discussion-based community programs. The success of the early broadcast PSA model gave rise to the PSA format as a mainstay of broadcasting. Thus was born the PSA formula of a single-message, commercial-length ad explicitly devoted to public advocacy rather than commercial gain. While the business model of broadcasting would change over the course of the following decades, the existence of PSAs has remained constant through the 2010s. I propose that this is in part due to the format's perceived effectiveness, but also simply because more attention has been paid to introducing techniques for effectively executing PSAs messages than to studying the social value of the PSA itself.[7]

A blossoming of advertising creativity and social activism in the immediate postwar years and through the 1950s met with changing broadcast legislation in the 1960s. This legislative challenge was organized around the promotion of media—and, specifically, television—for the public good, and it manifested in part in a surge of broadcast public service announcements. Much of the increase in PSAs in the US in the late 1960s and early 1970s can be attributed to a 1967 Federal Communications Commission ruling that upheld the "fairness doctrine," which required broadcasters to ensure a balance of perspectives in their programming (Ford 1963, 3–16). To balance the glut of tobacco advertising, for example, broadcasters were required to donate time to anti-smoking messages. As a result, during the years 1967 through 1970, broadcasters aired one anti-smoking PSA for every three tobacco ads, with anti-smoking ads comprising the majority of PSAs on television. With so much airtime mandated for public service messages, broadcasters showed spots produced by organizations such as the American Cancer Society, which worked with major advertising firms that volunteered their services, experimenting with a range of approaches beyond those used to promote commercial products. PSA messages during this time included warnings to parents who smoked about the role model they presented for their children; an emphasis on the unglamorous aspects of smoking, such as the smell and stains; characterizing cigarette smoke as an indoor pollutant; and satirizing some of the aspirational images that the tobacco industry

92 *Vernacular Voices*

used to sell cigarettes. During this period, the testimonial approach was put to use through hard-hitting and poignant messages that featured everyone from families of people who had died as a result of smoking-related diseases, to smokers who attested to the harms of smoking and their struggles to quit, to the terminally ill. These early testimonial ads were a precursor to the Brynner ad with which I began this chapter, and the first steps of a now-common strategy of explicitly linking the subject of the PSA with the viewer through perceived similarity.

The golden age of free airtime for anti-smoking ads ceased in 1970 when the tobacco industry reactively withdrew all broadcast advertising, drastically reducing the corresponding requirement for donated air-time for anti-smoking PSAs. The form was relegated to off-peak hours of commercial broadcasting (Aufderheide 1999; Croteau and Hoynes 2006; Leys 2003). Despite this change, the testimonial mode prevailed, and would continue to be used as a dominant messaging strategy in future PSA campaigns. During this decrease in media saturation of anti-smoking PSAs, researchers discovered a correlation between the drop in anti-smoking PSAs and an increase in smoking rates. This data boosted advertisers' and advocates' confidence in the effectiveness of PSA adver-tising so much that some charities and public health organizations determined that it was worth the cost to pay for PSA airtime, and at prime time to boot (Reid 2005). Advertising worked for promoting spending on charity and increasing identification with public-good messages as well as for promoting consumption and brand identification. Over the course of the next few decades, media buys for PSA airtime would become more prevalent, to the extent that by the 2010s the majority of PSAs on the air would be paid, not donated, slots.[8]

Throughout the 1970s and 1980s, the PSA form continued to have a strong presence during commercial airtime, as independent charities and organizations started creating their own PSAs without the aid of the Ad Council, sometimes through in-house production staff and sometimes through contracts with advertising agencies, which now saw charity nonprofits as a client sector. Many of these charity organizations paid for commercial ad time to obtain spots that would ensure a high view-ership and frequent repetition, using funds obtained by the increasingly successful model of private charitable giving to nonprofit foundations and public charities that escalated during the same period and during which media industry deregulation and privatization escalated. By the mid-1970s, Ad Council PSA production had declined to the point where their ads accounted for only a fraction of the total PSAs on air, yet throughout the 1970s and into the 1980s it was still almost impossible to watch an hour of television without encountering a PSA. The Partnership for a Drug Free America, which emerged in 1987, is a particularly note-worthy example of an organization that created highly successful and widely viewed PSAs independent of the Ad Council. Throughout the late 1980s and 1990s, the Partnership produced so many PSAs that they were second only to McDonald's in the number of ads simultaneously in circulation. Not only did the Partnership's PSAs saturate the media market, they were quite popular and memorable. One of their most famous ads, "Fried Egg," is reported to have been viewed by 92 percent of American teens during one period of the campaign (Levine 1991) "This is your brain," informs a male voice over an image of an un-cracked egg. A hand then breaks the egg into a frying pan where it sizzles. "This is your brain on drugs," he declares. "Any questions?" The impact of this ad helped to popularize the PSA strategy of visually depicting negative outcomes through shocking graphic association. Yet, whereas the Partnership used the egg as a metaphoric illustration of the human brain, anti-smoking advertising of the period went a step further, putting out ads that included people demonstrating against Big Tobacco and talking about the effects tobacco had had on their bodies and psychological states. By the early 1990s, the prevailing anti-tobacco PSA strategy was, in the words of Assistant Secretary of Health and Human Services Howard Koh, to "tap into the authenticity of true stories that were graphic, negative and emotional to capture the public's attention" (Koh et al. 2005). The strategy used in anti-tobacco campaigns was consequential because by the late 1990s, anti-smoking ads would once again dominate the PSA landscape and, as a result of the new paid PSA placement approach, had a very visible presence in broadcast advertising.[9]

In the late 1990s through the early 2000s, a sudden influx of funding for anti-smoking advertising, paired with advocates' interest in paying to secure airtime, led to impressive PSA circulation on both the local and national level (Koh et al. 2005).[10] Several PSA campaigns that had proven to be effective on the state level became very recognizable during this time as other states integrated them into their tobacco control programs and aired the PSAs (Reid 2005). Ongoing public health research revealed that young people and adults considered campaigns that portrayed the serious effects of smoking by "real people telling real stories" to be the most effective, and so campaigns that delivered this strategy were put in high rotation. Two such campaigns emerged out of Massachusetts, where at the time funding for anti-tobacco media was abnormally robust compared to other states (Koh et al. 2005).[11] One series featured a man named Rick Stoddard whose wife had died from lung cancer at the age of 46. The other followed Pam Laffin, a young woman with emphysema awaiting her second lung transplant. The campaign followed her at different points over the course of several years, illustrating the physical and psychological toll that the smoking-related disease was taking on her life and her two children (Biener and Taylor 2002). Each spot had a different message conveyed within thirty seconds. Gregory Connolly of the Massachusetts Department of Public Health describes how Laffin's story developed into a winning campaign strategy:

> We tried humor ... we had Roger Clemmons in a Red Sox uniform, and Pedro Martinez! And kids turned to us and said, "If you think this is a serious problem, you've got to treat it seriously." And so we came back and said, you know, maybe we've got to tell real stories talking about empathy and communicating real risk. Humor, no. Role models, no. What you have to do in the messaging is link the real people, real stories, negative emotion. We needed a face to make this work. So Pam became not only our face, she became our poster child.[12]
>
> (Greg Connolly, "Life Cycle of an Anti-Smoking Campaign" [YouTube, 2007])

Based on the documented success the Laffin campaign had had with young people, the Massachusetts Department of Public Health created a school curriculum kit that included a documentary about Laffin's experience. When Laffin died at 31, the campaign continued, playing back clips of Laffin from earlier spots and revealing her fate as the ultimate tagline. The CDC then circulated a curriculum to schools across the nation and the documentary was aired on MTV (Koh et al. 2005).

Through the PSAs, Laffin's story went national. Laffin had exposed personal details about her life, confessed her fears, and described her pain, fulfilling the Massachusetts Department of Public Health's strategy of presenting her as a negative role model for smokers and potential smokers. Her face became synonymous with a message of the hazards of

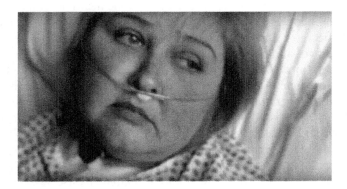

Figure 3.2 Pam Laffin in "I Can't Breathe," Massachusetts Department of Public Health, 1999

smoking as it performed the vernacular voice for the campaign. Yet, despite her divulgence and candor, her story has been structured by messaging strategies and agendas since the campaign's beginning. Viewers can see the scar on her back where her lung had been removed, her photos from her youth, her children crying as they talk about her failing health. The campaign's high rotation of ads led these aspects of Laffin's life to be revealed, framed by taglines and calls-to-action. Through Laffin, the campaign successfully executed a strategy of resemblance with their target cohorts, but did very little to affect her circumstances. Nevertheless, the Laffin campaign was determined by anti-tobacco advocates and advertisers to be a successful public health case study. But the success of the campaign also pointed to some of the limitations on supporting people like Laffin whose personal confessions and exposure perform the campaign message. The authority of the campaign message emerges from the apparent truth in Laffin's story, yet its ultimate articulation was in the hands of the institutions and organizations that produced and circulated the ads.

Even the Doctor is an Amateur: PSAs on YouTube

Seeking to respond to the challenges to traditional broadcast dissemination presented by the introduction of digital cable and the growing popularity of online social media and video sharing, in the 2000s public health and other social issue advocacy campaigns increasingly turned to websites that featured user-generated content as an alternative distribution model for PSAs. In 2008 the Ad Council released a research report based on a study of the effectiveness of PSA advertising with youth viewers that underscored the need to narrowcast this group through online media. The study notes a trend in broadcast PSAs to "not necessarily gear the advertisement to any one demographic," but to aim for "an umbrella effect to all demographics." They conclude that "narrowcasting [to] Millennials and constructing PSA messages that specifically speak to [these young Americans] is crucial" for effectiveness"[13] (Ellazar et al. 2011). The Ad Council report follows online PSA dissemination since 2007, which began when the Clinton Global Initiative first used YouTube as an official video delivery channel. Other organizations followed suit. For example, the US government's National Youth Anti-Drug Media Campaign's 100 million dollar budget contained significant funding for internet advertising in order to pay "particular attention to youth social settings where pro-drug messages are increasingly prevalent" (Walther et al. 2010).

The Ad Council report indicates that social media websites are the answer for PSA distribution, not just because they are where this demographic engages most often with media, but because the websites themselves traffic in the circulation of distinctive messages.

96 *Vernacular Voices*

Most respondents mentioned their indifference towards a public service announcement on the whole. However, behavioral changes may occur when Millenials receive information about social issues by word of mouth, making individual adaptation of particular social issues much more motivating in terms of action ...

(Aaron Ellazar et al., "Youth Public Service Advertising Effectiveness Research" [Ad Council, 2011])

The Ad Council report suggests that in order to reach youth, public service campaigns need to not only gravitate to online spaces, but also seek to circulate through existing peer-to-peer online networks. Like the perceived similarity model that drove campaigns like the one that featured Pam Laffin, the Ad Council's online recommendations emphasize the importance of the message source while taking the *personal* message a step further by having it passed on through one's networks. In online PSA advertising, it is not just the question of *who speaks* within the spot that is perceived to be important to its success, but *who produces* or *who circulates* the campaign message.

Advertising researchers have offered theoretical models to explain how perceived similarity leads to persuasion. According to the *source attractiveness model*, introduced by Kelman in 1961, viewers evaluate messages based on how much they identify with the sources that are delivering the messages (Kelman 1961). The social influence process suggests that all people, and youth in particular, base their thinking and behaviors on what others think and how they behave. And, according to reference group theory, perceived similarity leads people to assume that others belong to their reference group and thereby respond to their opinions and messages (Sherif and Sherif 1964; Hyman and Singer 1968). Young people in particular are thought to rely on others in their age cohort as having more significant influence. Since 2008, many public service advertisers have sought to engage everyday people from their target groups in the construction of online campaign messages (Paek et al. 2011).

Advertisers have come to believe in the power of perceived similarity engendered through user-generated content to the extent that some have even attempted to simulate it (Paek et al. 2011, 181). For example, the Canadian company NB Liquor created a series of video diaries by a teen named Paul Underhill who had killed his friends while driving under the influence. The campaign also featured video responses from Paul's friends. Only later was it made public that "Paul" was an actor, and that the scenarios were fictions intended to be perceived by viewers to be real-life confessionals (Paek et al. 2011, 181).

In 2011, advertising and public relations researchers Hye-Jin Paek, Thomas Hove, Hyun Ju Jeong, and Mikyoung Kim of Michigan State University designed a study to test the extent to which who produces a

PSA influences persuasiveness. Their article shifts the trajectory of PSA effectiveness studies by drawing attention to the proliferation of youth-produced PSAs. In their study with college students they screened a series of youth-produced PSAs on the topic of child abuse alongside professionally made PSAs on the same topic. They sought to measure not only the audience's perceived similarity with the person who delivered the message within the ad, but their level of identification with the PSA's producers. The researchers concluded that, compared to child abuse prevention PSAs produced by experts, those produced by perceivably similar peers were more effective in the enhancement of attitudes towards the PSA and issue importance (Paek et al. 2011, 179).

Ultimately, the researchers found that audiences felt that the PSAs that appeared to have been made by nonprofessionals of their cohorts were more effective. The viewers who had the lowest level of involvement with the issue of child abuse were significantly more likely to look to the peer-produced PSAs for answers. While the researchers entered the study unsure of whether or not the question of who produced the ad would be of concern to the audience, their mere interest in the impact of the PSA producer suggests that message effectiveness evaluation has shifted to include the PSA producer as a critical component of the credibility, authenticity, and persuasiveness of PSA messages. This marks a shift, where the vernacular voice is no longer accessible to the audience simply based on who *appears* in the PSA spot; in the age of digital video it must now also represent the person or people behind the camera. Here we can begin to see the authenticity, believability, and persuasiveness of the vernacular voice entwining with modes of PSA *production*.

Overlooked in the study by Paek et al., and in literature on PSAs as a whole, is the relationship of the young PSA producers to their subject matter. What are the producers' relationships to the topic at hand and how are they affected by the production experience? The sheer quantity of nonprofessional PSAs on YouTube and other file sharing channels indicates a significant number of people who, through their production of videos, have demonstrated involvement with certain issues, at the very least by going to the trouble of making a PSA and posting it online. Nonprofessional PSA producers are considered by advertisers to be on the producer side of the effects model, rather than on the side of those they hope will be affected by the ads. Yet it appears that young PSA producers often fill the role of both producer and target demographic. For many of them, identifying as part of the target demographic was precisely their impetus for production.

Researchers interested in ad effectiveness might find it useful to reframe their models for evaluating youth-produced PSAs in order to understand the effects that the act of making a PSA may have on its producers. When advertising researchers measure professionally produced PSAs against youth-produced PSAs, they tend to cast young producers

98 *Vernacular Voices*

as an equivalent set of producers rather than addressing the complex motivations for their production. The PSA production process can be used by youth to confront and work through the issues that the PSAs are designed to address. This is precisely why so many pedagogues and community leaders continue to encourage young people to produce videos in this form. Yet we should ask: to what extent do young people and other nonprofessional PSA producers consciously present themselves as similar to their imagined audiences? Might young producers strategize just like advertisers have been doing for decades while taking their own subjectivity into account as a factor in their PSA's persuasiveness? Answering these questions can help add complexity to our understanding of the relationship between youth PSA production, personal expression, and power.

A 2009 PSA contest initiated by the United States Health and Human Services (HHS) agency to promote flu prevention measures exemplifies the strategy of migrating to YouTube to promote a perceived similarity between PSA producers and their audiences. On July 9, 2009, HHS secretary Kathleen Sebelius appeared on YouTube to appeal to Americans to help her department create a PSA contest on flu prevention for a $2,500 prize and the chance to have the video broadcast on national television (Sebelius 2009).

> We want you to help us to create a 15 or 30 second PSA. And I'm not talking another boring, educational video—this is your chance to be funny, dramatic, or whatever you think would make the most positive impact. I'm organizing an expert panel to evaluate submissions, and we'll present the best ones back to the public, so everyone can vote for their favorite.
>
> (Kathleen Sebelius, "Create a Flu Video and
> Be Eligible to Win $2,500" [YouTube, 2012])

Here, Sebelius appeals to everyday Americans to encourage flu prevention by exalting their ability to "help" the government create a public health message, suggesting that the average citizen is uniquely qualified to develop a messaging strategy, appear on camera, and manage all aspects of video production towards affective and effective ends. Later in the video she refers to the contest as a way to "tap into the nation's creativity."

On the face of it, the flu PSA contest appears to be a departure from the dominant model of public health campaign advertising, historically the product of collaboration between state officials, medical experts, advertising firms, and the broadcast industry. But while the appeal for lay participation offers the impression that the government agency aims to channel the authority of laypeople, on closer inspection we can see how the HHS harnessed nonprofessional video within a campaign that continued to involve all of those institutions. This example shows the strong imbrication of institutional and vernacular voices in the production of online PSAs.

Indeed, the flu prevention campaign's effectiveness was hitched to the success of the delivery of its message from a vernacular rather than an authoritative voice. The HHS leveraged perceived similarity in order to achieve the "look" and character of non-governmental intervention. In this way, the vernacular voice was appropriated as an extension of state-authorized medical authority, the infrastructure of the national television broadcast industry, and the input of media professionals. By having the winning PSAs presented and circulated on social media platforms as the work of individual producers, the campaign appeared to have been wholly directed by nonprofessionals. In this way, the HHS communicated accessibility, distancing itself from an authoritative role.

The selection process and plans for distributing the winning PSA were key factors in pairing vernacular voices and the agency's objectives. Participating producers were guided to articulate the agency's key points about the issue in much the same way that an advertising agency would be called upon to do in the creation of a message for broadcast. Participants were required to use the government's flu.gov website as the primary source of their information.[14] The winning PSA would be aired on national television and the winner would appear in television interviews. All video submissions, which were required to be uploaded to YouTube, were tagged as associated with the HHS, and, therefore, were poised to do exponential advertising for flu.gov. The Health and Human Services department appointed a committee of communication and health experts to select the finalists from the 240 entries. These "experts" represented areas of knowledge and skills that have historically been called upon to create strategy and implement execution in traditional public health media campaigns. The same state and media institutions that have historically produced broadcast PSAs are still involved, albeit in the background, of user-produced online PSA campaign execution. Though traditional PSA institutions did not ventriloquize the flu message through their video contributors, the vernacular and the institutional intertwined.

In their research on trends in the related area of healthcare journalism, Briggs and Hallin noted a shift away from traditional forms of medical authority that prevailed until recent decades, in which the public was encouraged to accept medical information only from physicians. The authors suggest that this model, which they refer to as "patient-consumer centered," has been to a large extent displaced by one that de-centers medical authority, placing the onus on patients to seek out the appropriate medical information, evaluate the sources they find, and control their own health choices according to what they have discovered (Briggs and Hallin 2010).

What is particularly noteworthy about the HHS contest approach is that it used viral video strategies to effectively spread its flu message. The

100 *Vernacular Voices*

contest motivated the creation and distribution of 240 YouTube PSAs on the subject of the flu, in many different styles and tones, and featuring comic and artistic devices. It is easy to imagine that these videos might have caught viewers' attention for reasons other than the health-related information they convey. One of the entries features a girl in elementary school and her puppy, which she treats as her flu patient. Another includes homemade hand puppets. A third features macabre animated imagery of animals and a foreboding warning about exposure to swine flu. With 240 videos, the chances that the information might have spread as a side effect of the videos that were circulated through peer networks was promising. The information that the HHS hoped to convey could potentially circulate to a wider net of health consumers than would have been possible through earlier forms of media distribution.

Turning to the winning entry, we can see how forms of authority entwine in this new mode of PSA production. As advertising researchers Cialdini and Perloff have argued, people sometimes favor experts in situations where they expect sources that are "higher in quality" or more "authoritative," for example, a doctor delivering medical information as opposed to a patient (Perloff 2003; Cialdini 2001). The winning entry, "H1N1 Rap by Dr. Clarke," written, composed, produced, and performed by John D. Clarke, MD, FAAFP, hybridizes forms of authority in both form and content (Clarke 2009). The video opens with a medium shot of the name Dr. John D. Clarke, MD embroidered on a white medical coat. The camera zooms out to reveal that the coat is worn by a young African–American physician who, like many doctors, wears a tie and a collared shirt underneath. But unlike most doctors—certainly the majority of medical professionals who have appeared in traditional health-related public service announcements—this doctor is sporting sunglasses and rapping about the flu.

A low-fi handheld video camera moves with him as he performs, New York City buildings framing him as he forms hand gestures that illustrate his lyrics about how to prevent the spread of the H1N1 virus.

> H1N1, Swine Flu infection, for intervention, I bring prevention,
> Dr. Clarke here I come, to make your head numb!
> Health Hop, lesson one, to stop the bedlam.
> If you think you're infected, seek attention,
> If you have it stay at home, so you don't spread none,
> Use tissues when you sneeze, 'cause you could spread some,
> 'Cause coughed-up germs is where it spreads from!
> I'm recommending, washing hands for protection,
> Front and back, real thorough, while you count 20 seconds.
> Hand sanitizer, I advise you, get it, why?
> It makes germs die, when you rub and let it dry.
> Don't touch your eyes, your mouth, your nose, your face,

Figure 3.3 Dr. John Clarke raps about how to prevent H1N1 in "H1N1 Rap by Dr. Clarke," 2009, YouTube video still

> That's how you get infected so you'd better play it safe!
> Long-term outcome, we'll see the end come,
> Never sick again from the H1N1!
> (Dr. John Clarke, "H1N1 Rap by Dr. Clarke", YouTube, 2009)

The PSA closes with Dr. Clarke seated in a medical office with its staid maroon leather chair, fireplace, and mahogany desk. He has lost the sunglasses and no longer raps, but instead speaks in a friendly, familiar tone, instructing viewers to do as he did and go to the flu.gov website for "some great information" about H1N1. "Log onto flu.gov, and together we can stop the H1N1," he says.

While Clarke's lab coat and formal office space point to his association with medical institutions, his performative style evokes forms of credibility typically associated with mainstream hip-hop culture. He emphasizes his relatability to the layperson by disabusing his medical expertise, claiming that he wrote his lyrics based on knowledge gained from reading the flu.gov website as opposed to years of medical training and practice. Instead, he derives legitimacy to give advice about flu prevention through bravado. Playing on a popular motif from hip-hop and rap in which artists brag about their skills and status, Clarke describes himself as someone who will "bring[s] prevention" to "bedlam." Whereas most broadcast PSAs that feature actual doctors strike a sober tone as they deliver advice, Clarke describes himself as a powerful force whose knowledge will overwhelm the viewer: "Dr. Clarke here I come, to make your head numb!" Clarke's bombastic and playful performance, paired with a video style that signals "amateur" artist and producer, conveys that he is more like the layperson than the professionals (the doctors, the government, etc.).

102   *Vernacular Voices*

Dr. Clarke's active dissociation from the didactic, professional form of address helps the HHS to actively work against the "boring educational" video message against which Sebelius sought to define the 2009 flu.gov campaign. The medical authority driving the overall campaign (HHS) is intentionally eclipsed by a style and aesthetic through which medical authority masquerades as the authority of the everyday person. Dr. Clarke's winning PSA is successful at presenting medical authority as emerging from the realm of the amateur/consumer/patient. It is not made explicit in the video, but Dr. Clarke is a practicing medical doctor. To boot, he has a side career professionally distributing his original health-related songs. The considerable press he received due to the HHS contest win must certainly have increased the number of visits to his website, and may have boosted his recording sales. His win draws our attention to the user-generated PSA's unique interplay between the nonprofessional and the professional, and formerly contradictory forms of authorial voice.

While the flu.gov campaign provides a very clear example of how institutional messages are circulated through vernacular forms of authority, in other online user-produced PSAs the line between institutional and everyday producer content is more opaque. The 2011 National Eating Disorders Association (NEDA) PSA Video Competition, established as part of the organization's largest national outreach campaign called "It's Time to Talk About It," provides another example of an organization that has used nonprofessional PSA production as a way of increasing perceived similarity with their target population. The contest, established by NEDA as a way to "raise consciousness about the realities and seriousness" of eating disorders, prompted dozens of nonprofessional filmmakers to create YouTube PSAs about eating disorders. "The idea behind the PSA competition is to give entrants a voice and ask them, 'How would you talk about it?'" explains Lynn Grefe, president and CEO of NEDA, in a press release about the contest (Greenleaf & Associates 2010). The NEDA competition specifically called for the filmmakers to use "all original material" in order to respond to provide a "helpful, hopeful or informative message about eating disorders."

The NEDA competition rules, paired with what I have been suggesting are limitations of the PSA form, structure how the participants "talk about it [eating disorders]." Examining the structure of the contest as well as the video submissions gives us another way to see how the organization's initiatives, paired with YouTube's business model, combined with traditional public relations efforts work to popularize the PSA formula and further the organization's messaging strategy. But this is not just a case of an institution bearing down on a young video-maker's expression. By comparing one entrant's NEDA submission to another video she made on the same topic, we begin to see some of the ways that participating in the campaign and framing her message and style according to their

Vernacular Voices 103

framework might appear to her as a way to leverage her visibility as a video artist, aspiring actor, and someone with thoughts about eating disorders. NEDA offers the chance of publicity perhaps more than personal expression.

NEDA used traditional media distribution strategies to help popularize the personal PSA style. The contest required all participants to submit their PSAs on DVDs or tapes, but also asked for signed release forms, which gave NEDA permission to freely distribute the videos through YouTube and other outlets. While the number of hits for the three winning videos hosted on YouTube is not especially impressive (a year after the videos were first posted they had received approximately 2,000 views each), NEDA has extended viewing possibilities by circulating the PSAs offline as part of their "It's Time to Talk About It" national outreach campaign, presumably extending viewing exponentially. By circulating the PSAs beyond YouTube and on DVD, NEDA has been able to extend the reach of their message beyond what was possible with broadcast television PSAs or on YouTube alone. More than a year after the close of the competition, the NEDA website still advertised that the winning PSA videos were available to any interested media outlets or organizations for further broadcast and distribution. Additionally, NEDA used the 2011 PSA contest to enhance publicity for the overall campaign. Press releases and online advertisements announced lavish prizes (an expenses-paid round trip to New York City, recognition at NEDA's annual benefit dinner, and cash prizes), a promise of extended media exposure (videos screened at the annual NEDA conference, featured online, etc.) and the existence of a "celebrity media" judging panel, which included George Larrimore, managing editor of Access Hollywood (Greenleaf & Associates 2010).

All three winning PSAs rely on *vernacular voices* to convey the "It's Time To Talk About It" message (NEDA 2011).[15] Two videos feature children in a school context while a third features a family who tell the story of learning of their daughter's eating disorder. The generic conventions of the PSA formula that is promoted through the YouTube PSA business model become most apparent when compared to non-PSA videos on the same topics. By *generic conventions* of the PSA, I am referring to the genre's orientation towards singular, brief, simple, and positive messages with memorable taglines. Through this comparison I aim to elucidate the ways in which the traditional PSA's tendency towards soundbites limits the possibilities of what can be said.

By comparing a 2011 NEDA YouTube video PSA called "I am..." that was produced by and features 23-year-old Sascha Sternecker, to another of her short YouTube videos called "goodbye, scale!" in which she departs from the PSA structure but delivers the same message about recovering from an eating disorder, we can see the ways in which the PSAs generic conventions bear on her expression (Fiercee 2011a). I am not suggesting that Sternecker was necessarily constrained by these conventions; rather,

104 *Vernacular Voices*

I would like to consider her participation in the PSA formula as part of the campaign as a strategy of visibility that is part of her overall self-expression. With this in mind, we might move away from thinking of the institutionally prompted PSA as a vehicle for youth expression in and of itself.

Institutional factors that affect video circulation are key to determining the visibility and relative popularity of these two videos, more so than the differences in the content or form of the individual videos. With only 75 views at the time of writing, "goodbye, scale!" has had little more circulation than the average home movie on YouTube (Fiercee 2011b). Conversely, "I am…" has received over 800 hits, which, while still relatively low compared to famous YouTube videos, represents a number that probably exceeds Sascha's personal network. While it is impossible to know exactly what motivated those 800-plus people to click on "I am…," it seems plausible that its inclusion in the NEDA competition increased its circulation. We might consider how metadata on YouTube (how users title and tag their videos with keywords that affect its place in the archive) effects where those videos will appear in searches. The fact that "I am…" is tagged with the NEDA name already increases its standing in the hierarchy of search terms related to eating disorders.

Media historian Pelle Snickars notes that despite the common use of metaphors of "sharing" to refer to user-generated video distribution on YouTube, it is perhaps more useful and appropriate to consider the mechanisms of how "sharing" occurs and how technological, business, and social factors determine which files are circulated and to what extent (Snickars and Vonderau 2009). Critical legal studies scholar Lawrence Lessig suggests that what most people call "sharing" is indeed a "new mode of production" that has emerged through a "non-market economy" as opposed to a purely social endeavor, as the term implies. Rather than dichotomously separating the "commercial" from "sharing," he suggests we may benefit from thinking more deeply about what factors govern video exchange on YouTube (Lessig 2008). Bearing this in mind, we may consider the role that YouTube's search engine infrastructure plays in promoting the circulation of some videos more than others. In other words, instead of thinking of YouTube as a digital archive in which videos are seen simply because they have been shared (which implies generosity or a democratic forum), we should keep in mind how video sharing is motivated by already-established personal and business networks, as well as algorithms that affect which particular videos get circulated most often (Berliner 2014; Gillespie 2010; Juhasz 2011).

It is not just social networks that shape which videos prevail and predominate on YouTube. As Siva Vaidhyanathan reminds us in his polemic tome *The Googlization of Everything (And Why We Should Worry)*, the business model of YouTube's parent company Google is designed

Vernacular Voices 105

to algorithmically categorize user-generated content (Vaidhyanathan 2011). Like Google, the YouTube search engine sorts videos based on how recent the video is and the total number of hits it has received; it also censors videos that have been deemed "offensive" by Google employees whose job it is to weed out such content. According to Vaidhyanathan, a video's views are also increased when links elsewhere on the internet connect back to it on YouTube. Videos also receive greater circulation when they are tagged and titled with keywords that link them to other, more popular videos. In effect, one video's popularity begets a related video's popularity. And, like any popularity contest, popularity is not necessarily commensurate with the quality of the object in question as much as it is with how often and where it circulates. The popularity of a YouTube PSA video can be achieved when a producer links it to social issue organizations and causes that have a presence both on and off YouTube. The circulation of Sascha Sternecker's "I am..." video has probably benefited from its association with NEDA and the NEDA PSA competition. The official NEDA website links to the winning entries, while in turn, those videos are algorithmically linked to other NEDA entries that have been uploaded and tagged by their producers as related to the contest. Cumulatively, the NEDA PSAs popularize each other, and in doing so, they advance the common PSA form that was tacitly promoted by the competition that inspired their creation. The generic conventions are ultimately reinforced through popularity. As Alexandra Juhasz, Siva Vaidhyanathan, and José Van Dijck have argued, this is also true in general of content on YouTube, Facebook and other social media (Juhasz 2011; Van Dijck 2009; Vaidhyanathan 2011).

Comparing the two videos makes it apparent that the PSA testimonial presents a homogenized style of address that ultimately provides the viewer with less information about Sascha's experience and arguably has less direct impact on her own relationship to the issue. If the goal of the PSA contest was to encourage producers and viewers to "talk about" eating disorders, we should evaluate how discourse is produced through the institutionally prompted youth-produced PSA.

"I'm just a girl next door," are the first words that appear in the video titled "I am..." They appear in lower-case lilac-colored script font over a black screen as an upbeat jazz piano refrain plays. We then see a black-and-white shot of a woman in her early twenties. She sits confidentially with her legs dangling over an arm of the office chair she is sitting on. "I want to be on Broadway," she says with gusto. We then cut to a head-on close up of another young woman who also speaks directly into the camera. "I am a future social worker," she says. Her statement is followed by that of another young woman, who smiles widely as she tells us, "I love to play guitar." Text appears again. "But I have a secret," it reads.

We return to the three women, who again appear one at a time to speak. The camera angles have remained the same as the earlier shots,

Figure 3.4 Sascha Sternecker in "I am..." 2011, YouTube video still

but now each woman has shifted her body so that she is leaning towards the lens. "I am in recovery from an eating disorder," confesses the first. "I am currently struggling with an eating disorder," says the second. "I'm recovering from an eating disorder," says the third. "It's time to talk about it" all three say in synchronization and with conviction over a screen that provides information about how to contact NEDA for help.

In contrast to the rather formulaic "I am...," Sascha's video "goodbye, scale!" which she posted on YouTube months after her NEDA PSA offers a more creative and personal approach to her continued effort to reach out to her peers about eating disorders. While "goodbye, scale!" also shows its maker clearly devoted to inspiring open discussion about eating disorders, it would probably not have qualified for the NEDA competition for which she entered "I am..." earlier that year. Unlike other winners selected by NEDA, it breaks from the traditional PSA formula in many ways. Even though it resembles "I am..." in terms of its message, it has more in common with a tradition of feminist performance art than with the PSA genre.

In "goodbye, scale!" Sascha appears seated in front of a white curtain photography studio backdrop. "I'm Sascha, I'm twenty-three years old and I'm from Lafayette, New Jersey," she tells us. A title card appears with her signature lilac font: "because of thirteen years spent battling anorexia nervosa, I will be smashing my scale." We cut to a deck at nighttime, a white-and-grey digital scale centered in the frame. All we can see of Sascha are her pink sheepskin boots as her hammer swings down on

Vernacular Voices   107

the scale. "That was a fail!" she says in an amused but self-effacing tone when her first swing only produces a chip the size of a dime. She curses as little pieces of plastic fly off. "Oh shit!" she shouts when the force of her second swing sends her sunglasses flying to the ground.

At this point in the video, the link between Sacha's anorexia and her act of scale-smashing is only implied. Unlike with the rote and predictable "I am…" PSA, the viewer must work to understand the connection between Sacha's experience with anorexia and her message. We are caught up in the physicality of the act, her raw energy, and the intimacy of the moment that we have been given access to.

Off-screen we hear the voice of an avuncular male camera operator (perhaps her father) who makes wisecracks while he gives her advice and encouragement. "Did you break your glasses?" the man asks in a protective tone. As her hammer swings upwards for a second try he interrupts: "Whoa, whoa, whoa! Close your eyes while you do it!" She swings again, and remarks that she's not making much headway. "Close your eyes," he demands. "I *am* closing my eyes!" she says defiantly. She continues to aggressively swing the hammer, and then gently puts a foot on the scale to see if it is actually broken. "Damn it! It still works!" she declares in frustration. "Go for the LED meter! Close your eyes," advises the man.

Sascha continues to hit the scale with great vigor. Upbeat instrumental music fades in. It is the riff that comes with Apple Computer's iMovie editing package and gets used often in nonprofessional videos. Pieces fly everywhere. She steps on the scale again, asking, "Does it still work?" The numbers don't move. "Yes! I broke it!" she exclaims. "Now leave it there as a warning for all other scales," he says. "Ha! Victorious!" Sascha sings with great pride. The camera tilts up as she rises while holding the hammer over her head under the porch's floodlight. She takes a bow. "Point down to your kill," says the man. "Take that, fuckerhead! Take that!" she says with a mock-angry face. The segment ends with her holding the hammer like it is a smoking gun.

The video doesn't end there. We cut away to Sascha facing the camera in a brightly-lit bedroom. Her tone is both casual and sincere as she continues to encourage others like her to "rise against eating disorders":

> To anyone who has ever experienced an eating disorder, I urge you from the bottom of my heart to do what I've done tonight. Take a step that propels you in the direction of your values and makes life worth living. So take my advice, and take up your hammers [she raises her right fist in the air] and rise against eating disorders.

"Why? Because eating disorders? We can do better than that," reads a title card. And, then, as her other videos have prepared us to expect, the Broadway-bound Sascha returns on camera for a brief moment to sing those same words in a voice fit for the stage.

Figure 3.5 Sascha Sternecker threatens her scale with a hammer in "goodbye, scale!" 2011, YouTube video still

With a message and a call to action, "goodbye, scale!" shares some characteristics of the traditional testimonial-style PSA, but it also departs from the PSA formula in significant ways. Drawing out these distinctions helps us to recognize how the traditional PSA format limits and directs the way in which personal perspective and voice is expressed. A significant marker of the voice of "goodbye, scale!" is its pacing and duration. The total running time is almost twice that of the longest PSA. At 1:41 minutes in length (as opposed to the standard 30- or 60-second length) there is time for a developed interaction between Sascha and the man offscreen. We get a sense of their rapport and mutual investment in breaking the scale. It is unclear when and how the scale will break and what their reactions will be. The scale-breaking scene seems unscripted and in the moment, which promotes a less presumptuous overall viewing experience. Through their intimate exchange we learn that the symbolism of the scale seems to mean as much to him as it does to her. Their relationship allows us to imagine the ways that Sascha's eating disorder must have affected people beside herself. The relationship between Sascha and this male figure brings to life the NEDA "It's Time to Talk About It" message. Their moment over the scale suggests that they have talked about it at great length and, as a result, Sascha has had support throughout her recovery. The emotional impact of their shared experience with her eating disorder is only implied; unlike "I am..." and other formulaic message-based PSA videos where the testimonial style tends toward the predictable and rote, in "goodbye, scale!" the viewer must work harder to make meaning out of the relationships between signs onscreen.

Compared to the didactic "It's Time to Talk About It" message and tag that Sascha was required to use in her NEDA PSA video submission, "goodbye, scale!" offers a more complex message about eating disorders.

Sascha doesn't explain the symbolism of breaking the scale. There is no need, as it references symbolic acts of defiance, from rock stars smashing guitars to '70s feminist demonstrators burning their bras. The breaking of the scale is an action that has clear significance and magnitude for Sascha. Her visible thrill at having been "victorious" over the scale suggests how much power the scale once had over her. The significance of her scale-smashing may perhaps be best understood by viewers who have experienced their own weight-related struggle. Whereas "I am…" speaks to a nonspecific audience (people in general need to "talk about it"), "goodbye, scale!" speaks more directly to people who have been or are troubled by their weight.

Like the more formulaic PSAs, "goodbye, scale!" includes a personal appeal. But it appears after the scale scene, through which Sascha established herself as having a more casual, genuine affect than is typically conveyed in formulaic, message-based testimonial PSAs that tend towards the earnest. The juxtaposition of the scale and the message scenes undercuts the potential for the appeal to read as overly earnest or dramatic. Her exhibition of spontaneous emotion in the scale scene establishes a foundation that helps the viewer to read her appeal as genuinely passionate and, as she suggests, "from the heart." Further, calling on viewers to "raise up your hammers!" could be read as a play on the PSA call-to-action formula, or possibly an attempt to start a movement of scale-breaking as a way to throw a wrench (or a hammer, as the case may be) into popular discourses around bodyweight. Unlike the *It Gets Better Project* videos discussed in earlier chapters, or the NEDA campaign that she participated in with "I am…," Sascha's message in "goodbye, scale!" is unconnected to a broader campaign or narrative framework. Her message and her call to action is original and exists outside of any institutional campaign agenda. Likewise, her message and tone are not tethered to any institutional expectations. It is impossible to know which video, if any, was more empowering for Sascha or her viewers. But through "goodbye, scale!" we can see a different form of expression penetrate the landscape of videos about eating disorders, potentially opening up discourses about the female body that transcend the traditional PSA message.

This comparative analysis allows us to identify two distinct kinds of online testimonial-style PSAs. On the one hand are PSAs like "H1N1 Rap" and "I am…" that are connected to and promoted by institutions (such as those prompted by nonprofit organizations like Health and Human Services or NEDA, funded by a grant, or the product of a school assignment). In these, institutions promote a set of desired messages through these nonprofessional videos and the amateur aesthetics that authenticate the message as coming from everyday people. On the other hand there are message-based testimonial videos like "goodbye, scale!" that do not seem to have been created in response to an institutional call for

110   *Vernacular Voices*

a PSA but which nonetheless use elements of the PSA form. In "goodbye, scale!" Sascha appears to use the testimony and call-to-action features of the PSA formula that NEDA and other nonprofits have promoted as a narrative device that intentionally mimics the authorial frame that the formula has come to represent. In other words, while in "I am…" NEDA draws its authority from the PSA form and the perceived authenticity of Sascha's expression about her eating disorder, in her independent project "goodbye, scale!" Sascha seems to derive her own authority from the PSA form. These separate forms of authority have different potentials. In "I am…" Sascha becomes an object of the NEDA campaign. Like Pam Laffin and the many testimonial voices of PSAs past, she is the mouthpiece and face of the message, working for the organization to reach the audience. In "goodbye, scale!" Sascha becomes a subject, drawing on traditions outside of the PSA form, remixing styles and experimenting with many inflections of her own voice. Whereas her choice to make a video for the campaign shows her desire to contribute to the NEDA effort to combat eating disorders, her actions within "goodbye, scale!" appear to be a part of her actual recovery process.

"Goodbye, scale!" breaks from the PSA form in important ways that point to the range of expressive possibilities for youth who produce videos on issues that concern them. When young producers like Sascha depart from the often-recycled PSA-style testimonial, they challenge the longstanding PSA media model, producing videos that are more likely to circulate and have meaning within their peer networks rather than to operate in the service of larger organizations or hosting media sites. And perhaps the power in the video transcends widespread circulation, existing in the moments of creation.

The content and circulation of nonprofessional online PSAs is determined by more than just producers' imaginations and viewer interest. I have been suggesting that a combination of intrapersonal, organizational, and business agendas have driven the popularity of the nonprofessional, confessional, and ultimately formulaic PSA style. The self-produced YouTube PSA is not a new form of media, but rather, an evolutionary development in the century-long history of the public service announcement. While the production of nonprofessional PSAs may often be used to fulfill some of the publicity priorities for cause-related organizations and aid pedagogical efforts in educational and community settings, it must also be acknowledged that it is ultimately the producers as agents who make choices about the style and content of their videos. I have attempted to identify some of the factors that influence what kinds of PSAs are produced, but this has not answered the question of why non-professional producers continue to use so many of the tropes that have existed for decades, particularly in an era where the PSA genre has been lampooned to the point of threatening to cast all recent PSAs in an ironic light.[16]

Vernacular Voices   111

The generic conventions of the PSA may grant the producer a sense of authority that is not as available through other forms. Performing the authoritative role under the auspices of using a vernacular voice is the particular style of the PSA and perhaps part of what has made it such an accessible and attractive model to new producers and pedagogues alike. A key factor in why so many nonprofessionals continue to employ the common PSA formula may in fact be evident in the trope of mobilizing the "face" not just as a sign of the "real" but a sign of the production of the real. The public service announcement has always been a technique of authority (whether it be the state, nonprofit organizations, advocacy groups, etc.) that seeks to persuade viewers; then we must consider the work that youth producers do when they contribute to campaigns and deploy the PSA structure as a way to authorize their experiences and their right to communicate a message or idea. But if we look to videos like "goodbye, scale!" for direction, we will see that when youth producers step aside from the PSA structure and add more complexity to their exploration of the topic at hand, they engage in ways that imbue them with an authority that is derived from the creative content of their videos rather than the generic conventions of the PSA.

Notes

1 Brynner had first made these statements during an appearance on *Good Morning America* nine months prior to his death and agreed to let the American Cancer Society release his statements posthumously in the form of a public service announcement. The PSA is available for viewing on YouTube.
2 The majority of public service announcements and commercials of the time used an authoritative (typically male) voiceover or an actor speaking scripted lines directly to the audience.
3 On their website www.PSAresearch.com, Goodwill Communications brings together current history and research on public service announcements. I am grateful to their organization for the service they provide through this site. It has inspired my research while pointing to avenues for deeper engagement with the topic.
4 Youth media pedagogy in particular has long been a site where nonprofessional PSA production has been encouraged. In fact, PSA video production as a classroom or community group activity has been popular as far back as the late 1970s, when video cameras and VCRs first became commercially available and affordable. The simple, easily recognizable, and reproducible message-oriented narrative style of the PSA has made it a particularly efficient tool for merging media into the curriculum. It is precisely the simplicity of the form and the blatancy of the desired response that has made it both a useful introductory media production exercise and a method for engaging target youth populations around social issues. A simple search online reveals dozens of educators sharing curricula that integrates PSA production with goals that include teaching young people the language of media production, engaging them in critiques of media messages, and providing a platform for

112   *Vernacular Voices*

them to become more deeply involved in "issues they care about." PSA production has also become a popular assignment within humanities education more generally as education researchers have promoted PSA production as a way to engage students in a form of multimodal composition (podcasts, digital video, audio essays, etc.) and an efficient way to teach students how to organize research and information in persuasive ways. Among media educators and, increasingly, in the area of composition studies, student PSA production is commonly thought to be a way to enable them to acquire multiple forms of literacy and engage in different composing modalities that are critical to contemporary communication. For writing and humanities scholars Richard J. Selfe and Cynthia L. Selfe, who have published on the value of teaching public service announcement production in English and language arts classrooms, argue that the exercise is ideal for teaching persuasive communication and responsive action, which they see as necessary for learning how to participate as "effective and literate citizens of the 21st century." They believe that by producing PSAs, students gain a sophisticated understanding of audience expectations and needs so that they can "commit to ethical standards of persuasion" (Selfe and Selfe 2008).

5 Anna McCarthy provides thorough and engaging case studies that illuminate the payoff for companies that sponsored public service programming in the postwar era, including the DuPont Corporation and the Ford Foundation.

6 Indeed, the FCC has always defined in terms of broadcasters' responsibility to air them, but the US has only twice evaluated that responsibility; the FCC inquiry in the late 1970s in which they examined the role that PSAs had played or should play in fulfilling broadcasting's public service requirement, and the Gore Commission, a presidential committee charged with examining the public interest obligations of broadcasters in the digital age. The inquiry in 1978 was based on self-reporting by the broadcasting stations. It found that the average television and radio station aired one to two PSAs an hour, about 200 per week, the equivalent of one percent to two percent of advertising time (Craig 2002, 9). Through the study, the FCC determined that "PSAs concerning controversial matters are usually not aired." Ultimately, all that changed were reporting procedures, broadening what kind of content licensees could receive public service credit for. During the Gore Commission, FCC Chair Reed Hundt testified that "The FCC lacks the will to impose public service regulations and rules that are clear and specific and that apply equally to everyone. Instead, we've continued to rely on an unwritten agreement by broadcasters to run PSAs—and unwritten deals are bound to be broken, especially as the competition for eyeballs becomes more fierce" (Berger 2002, 3).

7 Of course, there have always been skeptics when it comes to believing in the effectiveness of the PSA genre overall (Hyman and Sheatsley 1947) and concerns about the tendency for advocates to treat PSAs as a magic bullet, or what public health professor Lawrence Wallack calls a "media fantasy" (1989, 353–68). Others have argued for less emphasis to be placed on PSA advertising in the course of a public health campaign (Wallack et al. 1993). For a concise history of effects research in public service advertising, see Charles Atkin, "The Impact of Public Service Advertising: Research Evidence and Effective Strategies," prepared for the Kaiser Family Foundation (2001).

Vernacular Voices   113

8   According to research conducted by the Kaiser Family Foundation in 2008, at the time broadcasters donated 17 seconds an hour to public service announcements. The report was released on Thursday, January 24, 2008, at a forum that featured Federal Communications Commission members Michael Copps, Jonathan Adelstein, and Deborah Taylor Tate along with representatives from News Corporation, CBS, Time Warner, Univision, the Ad Council, and the American Legacy Foundation.

9   The increase in anti-smoking advertising was in part due to the 1998 Tobacco Master Settlement Agreement, when 46 states sued the tobacco industry and won. The American Legacy Group was created with the funds, leading to the creation of anti-smoking advocacy such as the "legacy" campaign aimed at women smokers, and the "truth" campaign, aimed at teens and young adults.

10 Two important things changed during the late 1980s and 1990s that increased the circulation and visibility of anti-smoking PSA campaigns. First, Massachusetts DPH funding went up in 1992 when voters passed a tax on cigarettes to fund anti-smoking efforts, but the campaigns were later drastically reduced by state budget cuts in the 2003 fiscal year when the program was defunded by 95 percent. Second, there was the redistribution of successful state campaigns and the establishment of the American Legacy Foundation to combat smoking, formed with money won when 46 states sued the tobacco industry in 1998 for Medicaid costs due to smoking (called the Master Settlement Agreement). The American Legacy Foundation directed its efforts towards two target demographics—adult women and teens. The teen-specific effort was what became the "truth" campaign, which sought to discourage smoking by vilifying the tobacco industry, thereby appealing to teens' natural sense of rebelliousness.

11 Between 1993 and 2001 the Massachusetts Department of Public Health Tobacco Control program oversaw the production of approximately 150 thirty-second television spots.

12 During the years 2000–2002 I worked directly on the advertising strategy and market testing for the campaigns mentioned here on behalf of the Massachusetts Department of Public Health anti-smoking campaigns, in my role as an Account Planner at Arnold Worldwide. My knowledge of the strategy to involve "real people" in the ads is something I acquired firsthand.

13 In a 2011 analysis of prize-winning communication campaigns in Asia, Warc (www.warc.com), the largest database of online advertising case studies, declared the "death of global campaigns." The most successful, they declared, were ones that targeted their audience in specific ways, "speaking directly and distinctively to them." In a 2011 blog entry giving advice to the social marketing community, the Noral Social Marketing Group observed that "the campaigns that increasingly work hardest are the ones that drive the most buzz and sharing—and these are almost without exception very local." This information was gathered from the Noral Group International social marketing group blog (www.noralgroup.com/user_generated_psas, 2012). For a more extensive look at narrowcasted PSAs through YouTube, see http://thenextweb.com/shareables/2011/06/22/user-generated-content-by-the-numbers-infographic/, www.warc.com/Topics/Asian Strategy.topic, and the Ad Council: Annual Reports (2003–2008) (https://archives.library.illinois.edu/archon/?p=digitallibrary/digitalcontent&id=4263).

114 *Vernacular Voices*

14 These recommendations possess a set of inherent cultural biases towards illness-prevention methods, as they advance a particular model of hygiene that places the responsibility of prevention (and, by extension, spread) on individuals. To boot, they obscure the role of class and environmental conditions.

15 The NEDA website notes that "2011 NEDA PSA Contest Winning videos are available for use by media outlets." The Grand Prize Winner was "Perceptions," by Savannah Dickson, Lexington, KY. First Prize Winner: "The Letter," by Kent Jones, Edmond, OK. Second Prize Winner: "Self-Esteem: Breaking the Status Quo," by Paula Cruz, Bellevue, WA. The winning videos can be found on the NEDA website (NEDA 2011).

16 Examples of plays on the PSA can be found in decades worth of televised sketch comedy (*Saturday Night Live* and *MadTV* have each provided dozens of examples); in experimental video (in the 1990s Laurie Anderson produced a particularly affective series called the "Personal Service Announcement" in which she performed the testimonial PSA formula to make political commentary); and on YouTube itself, where there are hundreds of mock PSAs, such as those warning people against the dangers of "Vertical Video Syndrome" (the tendency for people with iPhone cameras to shoot vertically instead of adjusting in order to shoot the standard 16x9 aspect ratio). There is even a PSA of Looney Toons cartoon characters advocating for the protection of the hapless pig characters in the popular video game Angry Birds. At this point in time it would be surprising if any media consumer has managed to miss one of the many existing PSA spoofs.

References

Andsager, Julie L., Victoria Bemker, Hong-Lim Choi, and Vitalis Torwel. 2006. "Perceived Similarity of Exemplar Traits and Behavior: Effects on Message Evaluation." *Communication Research* 33 (1):3–18.

Atkin, Charles. 2001. "Impact of Public Service Advertising: Research Evidence and Effective Strategies." Project conducted for the Henry J. Kaiser Family Foundation. www.learningace.com/doc/1648360/0c951c8e031ecccdef0a8f83e26afd7b/impact-of-public-service-advertising_-research-evidence-and-effective-strategies.

Aufderheide, Patricia. 1999. *Communications Policy and the Public Interest: The Telecommunications Act of 1996*. New York: Guildford Press.

Austin, Erica Weintraub, and Heidi Kay Meili. 1994. "Effects of Interpretations of Televised Alcohol Portrayals on Children's Alcohol Beliefs." *Journal of Broadcasting & Electronic Media* 38 (4):417–35. Doi: 10.1080/08838159409364276.

Berger, Warren. 1991. "The Advertising Council: 50 Years of Public Service." *Advertising Age* 62 (48):A2.

———. 2002. "Public Service Advertising in America: An Overview." *Shouting to be Heard: Public Service Advertising in a New Media Age* by the Henry J. Kaiser Family Foundation. Last accessed February 20, 2011. https://web.archive.org/web/20030605154904/wwwkff.org/content/2002/20020221a/.

Berliner, Lauren. 2014. "Shooting for Profit: The Monetary Logic of the YouTube Home Movie." In *Amateur Filmmaking: the Home Movie, the Archive, the Web*, edited by Laura Rascaroli, Gwenda Young, and Barry Monahan. New York: Bloomsbury.

Vernacular Voices   115

Biener, L., and T. M. Taylor. 2002. "The Continuing Importance of Emotion in Tobacco Control Media Campaigns: A Response to Hastings and MacFadyen." *BMJ Publishing Group Ltd* 11 (1):75–77. Doi: 10.1136/tc.11.1.75.

Briggs, Charles L., and Daniel C. Hallin. 2010. "Health Reporting as Political Reporting: A Biocommunicability and the Public Sphere." *Journalism: Theory, Practice, and Criticism* 11 (2):149–65. Doi: 10.1177/1464884909355732.

Brynner, Yul. 1985. "Anti-Smoking Commercial." American Cancer Society. Posted by DutchTornado, October 21, 2006. YouTube, 0:29. www.youtube. com/watch?v=JNjunlWUJJI&list=LLceYX13VIyDaLQPLrXpZ0nQ&feature =mh_lolz.

Cialdini, Robert B. 2001. "Harnessing the Science of Persuasion." *Harvard Business Review* 79 (9):72–79. Shli.sccs-sa.org/documents/2/Harnessing%20 the%20Scienceof%20Persuasion.pdf.

Clarke, John. 2009. "H1N1 Rap by Dr. Clarke." YouTube, 1:00. Posted by Dr. John Clarke, August 16. www.youtube.com/watch?v=_gwUdmPl0bU.

Connolly, Greg. 2007. "Life Cycle of an Anti-Smoking Campaign." YouTube, 2:49. Posted by anddoit and alteredmediaimpact.com, March 1. www.youtube. com/watch?v=EypLrQf3rAA.

Croteau, David, and William Hoynes, eds. 2006. *The Business of Media: Corporate Media and the Public Interest*. Thousand Oaks: Pine Forge Press.

Ellazar, Aaron, Jason Hawkes, Josh Heim, Jen Kennedy, Jillian Vandehey, Christian Varg, and Arielle Watts. 2011. "Youth Public Service Advertising Effectiveness Research." Ad Council.

Fiercee, Sascha. 2011a. "NEDA PSA—'I am…' " YouTube, 0:31. Posted by sascha fiercee, February 14. www.youtube.com/watch?v=Ru5juBQy5yk&feature=en dscreen.

———. 2011b. "goodbye, scale!" YouTube, 1:41. Posted by sascha fiercee, October 5. www.youtube.com/watch?v=5KB-jsgDvkw.

Ford, Frederick W. 1963. "The Fairness Doctrine." *Journal of Broadcasting* 8 (1):3–16. Doi: 10.1080/08838156309386083.

Gillespie, Tarleton. 2010. "The Politics of 'Platforms.'" *New Media & Society* 12 (3):347–64. Doi: 10.1177/1461444809342738.

Goodwill, Bill. Last accessed 2017. "Public Service Advertising – Background & Future." PSA Bibliography. www.psaresearch.com/bib9830.html.

Greenleaf & Associates. 2010. "NEDA Announces PSA Competition to be Judged by Celebrity Media Panel." Online Form Press Release. December 21. www. onlineformpressrelease.com/201091876/NEDA-Announces-PSA-Competition-to-be-Judged-by-Celebrity-Media-Panel/news.html.

Hilmes, Michele. 2007. *Only Connect: A Cultural History of Broadcasting in the United States*. Belmont: Wadsworth/Thomson Learning.

Horwitz, Robert Britt. 1989. *The Irony of Regulatory Reform: The Deregulation of American Telecommunications*. Oxford: Oxford University Press.

Hyman, Herbert H., and Paul B. Sheatsley. 1947. "Some Reasons Why Information Campaigns Fail." *The Public Opinion Quarterly* 11 (3):412–23. www. jstor. org/stable/2745237.

Hyman, Herbert H., and Eleanor Singer. 1968. *Readings in Reference Group Theory and Research*. New York: Free Press.

Jackall, Robert, and Janice M. Hirota. 2000. *Image Makers: Advertising, Public Relations, and the Ethos of Advocacy*. Chicago: University of Chicago Press.

116 *Vernacular Voices*

Juhasz, Alexandra. 2011. *Learning from YouTube*. Cambridge, MA: MIT Press.

Kelman, Herbert C. 1961. "Processes of Opinion Change." *The Public Opinion Quarterly* 25 (1):57–78. www.jstor.org/stable/2746461.

Koh, Howard K., Christine M. Judge, Harriet Robbins, Carolyn Cobb Celebucki, Deborah K. Walker, and Gregory N. Connolly. 2005. "The First Decade of the Massachusetts Tobacco Control Program." *Public Health Reports* 120 (5):482–95. Doi: 10.1177/003335490512000503.

LaMay, Craig. 2002. "Public Service Advertising, Broadcasters, and the Public Interest: Regulatory Background and the Digital Future." *Shouting to be Heard: Public Service Advertising in a New Media Age* by The Henry J. Kaiser Family Foundation. https://web.archive.org/web/20020611075632/www.kff. org/content/2002/20020221a/.

Lessig, Lawrence. 2008. *Remix: Making Art and Commerce Thrive in the Hybrid Economy*. New York: Penguin Press.

Levine, Joshua. 1991. "Don't Fry Your Brain." *Forbes*, February 4.

Leys, Colin. 2003. *Market-Driven Politics: Neoliberal Democracy and the Public Interest*. London: Verso.

McCarthy, Anna. 2010. *The Citizen Machine: Governing by Television in 1950s America*. New York: NYU Press.

National Eating Disorders Association (NEDA). 2011. "National Eating Disorders Association Announces PSA Contest Winners." National Eating Disorders Association. Last accessed March 29, 2012. www.nationaleatingdisorders.org/press-room/press-releases/2011-press-releases/national-eating-disorders-association-announces-psa-contest-winners.

Paek, Hy-Jin, Hyun Ju Jeong, Thomas Hove, and Mikyoung Kim. 2011. "Peer or Expert?: The Persuasive Impact of YouTube Public Service Announcement Producers." *International Journal of Advertising* 30 (1):161–88. Doi: 10.2501/ IJA-30-1-161-188.

Perloff, Richard M. ed. 2003. *The Dynamics of Persuasion: Communication and Attitudes in the 21st Century*. Mahwah: Lawrence Erlbaum Associates.

Reid, Roddey. 2005. *Globalizing Tobacco Control: Anti-Smoking Campaigns in California, France, and Japan*. Bloomington: Indiana University Press.

Salmon, Charles T., and Charles Atkin. 2003. "Using Media Campaigns for Health Promotion." In *the Handbook of Health Communication*, edited by Teresa L. Thompson, Alicia M. Dorsey, Roxanne Parrott, and Katherine I. Miller, 449–72. Mahwah: Lawrence Erlbaum Associates.

Sebelius, Kathleen. 2009. "Create a Flu Video & Be Eligible to Win $2,500." YouTube, 1:16. Posted by US Department of Health and Services, July 8. www. youtube.com/watch?v=gteC4AALn08.

Selfe, Richard J., and Cynthia L. Selfe. 2008. "'Convince Me!' Valuing Multimodal Literacies and Composing Public Service Announcements." *Theory Into Practice* 47 (2):83–92. www.jstor.org/stable/40071528.

Serlin, David. 2010. *Imagining Illness: Public Health and Visual Culture*. Minneapolis: University of Minnesota Press.

Sherif, Muzafer, and Carolyn W. Sherif. 1964. *Reference Groups: Exploration into Conformity and Deviation of Adolescents*. New York: Harper and Row.

Snickars, Pelle, and Patrick Vonderau. 2009. "The Archial Cloud." In *The YouTube Reader*, edited by Pelle Snickars and Patrick Vonderau, 292–313. Stockholm: National Library of Sweden.

Toncar, Mark, Jane S. Reid, and Cynthia E. Anderson. 2007. "Effective Spokespersons in a Public Service Announcement: National Celebrities, Local Celebrities and Victims." *Journal of Communication Management* 11 (3):258–75.

Vaidhyanathan, Siva. 2011. *The Googlization of Everything: (And Why We Should Worry)*. Berkeley: University of California Press.

Van Dijck, José. 2009. "Users Like You? Theorizing Agency in User-Generated Content." *Media, Culture & Society* 31 (1):41–58. Doi: 10.1177/0163443708098245.

Wallack, Lawrence. 1989. "Mass Communication and Health Promotion: A Critical Perspective." In *Public Communication Campaigns*, edited by Ronal E. Rice and Charles K. Atkin, 353–68. Los Angeles: Sage Publications.

Wallack, Lawrence, Lori Dorfman, David Jernigan, and Makani Themba. 1993. *Media Advocacy and Public Health: Power for Prevention*. Newbury Park: Sage Publications.

Walther, Joseph B., David Deandrea, Jinsuk Kim, and James C. Anthony. 2010. "The Influence of Online Comments on Perceptions of Antimarijuana Public Service Announcements on YouTube." *Human Communication Research* 36 (4):469–92. Doi: 10.1111/j.1468-2958.2010.01384.x.

4 "I Can't Talk When I'm Supposed to Say Something"

Negotiating Expression in a Queer-Youth-Produced Anti-Bullying Video

Michael stares intently at the LCD screen of a handheld video camera.[1] His rigid posture and stern expression speak to the intensity of his engagement. He squints his eyes to see the video image as it plays, presses the pause button with his left hand, then furiously scribbles on the scratch pad next to him with his right: "Here's the thing about being gay ..." He labels this quote "A" to indicate it should go in the section of the video called "coming out stories." The face on the screen is his own.

Jo sits across the room on a plush blue footstool that looks like it belongs on the soundstage of a children's television show. Slumped over her laptop with one hand on the keyboard and the other on a super-sized Amp energy drink, Jo shifts in place, using her t-shirt to cover places where some of the holes in her ripped jeans have become too big to cinch together with their array of large safety pins. "If I want to make the clip bigger I think I press 'control z,' " she says tentatively. She tries those keys and it works. "*Yes!*" she cheers, and proceeds to edit down a soundbite from an interview she had conducted with another teen during the previous week. "I think this one goes in the section on bullying stories," she declares confidently. She uses the trackpad on the laptop to pull the clip down into the sequence. This is only the second time she has ever used video editing software and she makes this move slowly and deliberately. Michael brings Jo his sheets of coded interview quotes for her to locate and digitize to include in their edit. Pieces of kettle corn and fragments of chile limón-flavored potato chips are sprinkled on the carpet around their workstations. Towards the front of the youth center an episode of *The Simpsons* is playing on a giant television screen. No one is watching.

Michael and Jo wear headphones while they work to block out the noise of other people who may drop in at the three-room Hillcrest Youth Center (HYC), a recreational center for queer teens and their allies. No matter where they sit, the two are likely to get caught with other people talking or hovering over them. But it is Wednesday, which is typically a slow night at the HYC, and it's still early, so they happen to be the only ones there. When Michael and Jo are concentrating it is quiet enough to hear the fluorescent overhead lights humming. Along with the muted TV

Negotiating Expression 119

and the occasional anxious sigh, there is a quiet symphony of tension building in the room. The teens are on a deadline, with only two weeks until April 20, the date by which they have agreed to have complete a public service announcement video on the topic of anti-gay-bullying. Waiting for the video are administrators at the San Diego LGBT community center (The Center), who plan to upload the PSA online (with hopes it will go viral), screen it at a local film festival, and provide DVD copies to Gay/Straight Alliance clubs throughout San Diego's high schools.

Anyone who has ever shot and edited a video with a team knows that the process involves a tremendous amount of labor. Even a short video—in fact, especially a short video—necessitates elaborate coordination, concentration, and cooperation. This is the story of the making of one such video by frequent visitors to the HYC who were also part of a weekly media workshop I founded and facilitated there called *Changing Reels*. While on the one hand it depicts how queer youth collaborated towards creative expression and social justice activism, it also reveals a chain of negotiations between many institutional actors and imperatives that prompted the youth to produce this particular media artifact in the first place. Examining the chain of events that led to the making of the video, as well as the production choices along the way, illuminates multiple investments in youth media production as an emancipatory practice and shows how two seemingly entwined pedagogical priorities—youth expression and participation in production—are actually often at odds with each other.

Behind the Scenes

I started *Changing Reels* with donated equipment and outside start-up funds in January of 2010.[2] Already an active member of The Center, the queer adult community organization that sponsors the HYC, I designed the workshop, with feedback from HYC staff, as a way to provide an activity for what had been functioning as mainly a youth drop-in social center.

At the time, I was a graduate student with almost a decade's worth of experience as a filmmaker and director of youth film programs. I had designed the workshop as a space for encounters with experimental media forms as a technique of socialization and self-reflection. My goal was to enhance the activity already at the HYC rather than to impose a vocational or scholastic environment or staged opportunity to interact with new media for educational purposes. Legalities and logistics prevented us from filming or editing offsite, so I sought to make good use of the intimacy of working together in a relatively small space. Together we examined individual and collective queer identity, engaged in play, and studied the legacy of media activism. Most of our early activities consisted of film screenings and short production exercises; the PSA

120 *Negotiating Expression*

was our first foray into a larger-scale production. My involvement with *Changing Reels* took place over a three-year period; the PSA production was six months of that time. All of the youth involved in the program were aware of my interest in writing about our work together and we engaged in discussions of what I would be writing and why. Several of the students visited my campus, joined me in undergraduate media classes, and even attended an academic Cultural Studies conference that took place in the area.

The building was located in a small San Diego strip mall on the edge of the increasingly gentrified "gayborhood" of Hillcrest. They refrained from using any signage on the building in order to protect the privacy of visiting teens. Adults, including parents—aside from those of us volunteers who had been pre-screened and fingerprinted—were not permitted on the premises unless given special permission. At the time, the HYC hosted approximately 300 visits from youth each month. They were primarily (80 percent) youth of color from all over San Diego county, representing almost every zip code. Some were from affluent homes, others were homeless and living in transitional housing run by The Center. More than 70 percent came from low-income and underserved backgrounds. The media workshop included a cross-section of this population. Some of the youth at the HYC had media production courses in their schools, and almost all of them used social networking sites like Facebook and Tumblr, either on their phones or on one of the HYC's two desktop computers. Oftentimes teens would communicate with other people in the room through Facebook or texting. Engaging with digital media technologies in itself was not novel for the group— but the access to prosumer camera and editing equipment and instruction was. Participation in the workshop was free and open to any teen visitors to the youth center.

While over 50 teens were casually involved in the workshop's activities throughout the PSA production, a group of ten teens from diverse racial, ethnic, and class backgrounds established themselves as core participants through their activity over many months. These teens had joined the workshop with an already-established interest in audiovisual media production and a stated interest in skill development.

I am a white, able-bodied, cis-gendered, queer woman who the youth came to know as a graduate student and teacher, but I was at first taken to be younger than I was, and confused for an HYC youth. In reading what follows, it is worth considering how my performance of identity and presence as a white educator in the space may have had an impact on the youth's choices.

Amy joined the media workshop to learn more about editing in order to enhance the aesthetic and technical quality of the music videos she makes for her favorite band. She was planning to graduate high school

Negotiating Expression 121

in June and was building a portfolio to submit as part of her college applications. She would eventually try to transfer from community college to a four-year university that focused on the arts. She frequently asked to borrow the hard drive to edit the footage on her laptop during her spare time at home, using a copy of the editing software that had been obtained through our funding.

Keisha, 18 years old, was also a high school senior and was set on becoming an on-camera political host like Rachel Maddow of MSNBC or Jon Stewart of *The Daily Show*. She had even created an email signature that read "Aspiring Political Analyst and Filmmaker." She hoped the workshop would help her get a foot in the door of the news media field and took it upon herself to help direct the activities of the rest of the group, making sure that we stayed on schedule.

Jo, 18 years old, came to the program wanting to be a professional cinematographer. She had an exceptionally keen eye and was eager for formal training. Living in transitional housing for homeless queer youth, she planned to start at a local city college the following semester. She had limited access to a computer and no access to video technology other than at the youth center.

Michael, 16 years old, was trying to get his GED so he could leave high school as soon as possible to pursue acting. He was drawn to the workshop because he desired to appear on camera and wanted to build his reel. Yet during the workshop he discovered he had an interest in operating the camera and directing, and began talking about pursuing video production as a fallback career. Michael, Amy, Jo, and Keisha were the most committed to seeing the PSA through to completion and putting in the work to see it through.

Many others had become casually involved in the shoots and editing critiques, and some, like Layna and Marianne, demonstrated a strong work ethic which seemed to be a side effect of their being exceptionally responsible and eager to work hard at anything they participated in. Both were leaders at their school, recipients of several merit-based scholarships, and found it challenging to find time for the youth center between athletic practices, music lessons, and school activities. Participating in the workshop was their chosen way of socializing with other youth at the center, perhaps because it was the only structured activity. They each expressed that they didn't feel any particular ownership over the content and were just participating "to help."

Enrique, who had almost aged out of the HYC, was always present for the workshops and expressed interest in media, but, as this account will illustrate, was ultimately not interested in participating in the productions. His simultaneous enthusiasm and ambivalence reveals key tensions between production as a means of personal expression and as a form of labor.

122   *Negotiating Expression*

Administrative Prerogatives

The PSA first came to my attention when administrators at The Center pitched a youth-produced video to the telecommunications company AT&T in their bid for a $20,000 grant to establish anti-bullying programs for youth and requested the involvement of the *Changing Reels* group. While the original proposal specified an education program in which community leaders, lawyers, policymakers, youth advocates, and media production specialists would hold workshops with queer youth in the area to teach them how to prevent and respond to bullying, once the grant was won, The Center administrators decided that making a video would not merely be a component of the proposed anti-bullying program, but could replace it entirely. They had determined that there was the same amount of pedagogical and social value in the self-production and circulation of a PSA about anti-gay-bullying as there was in the previously proposed mentoring workshop. AT&T agreed. From an administrative point of view, it had the twofold benefit of allowing the program to be reframed to allow them to recoup overheads for facilities and staffing, and providing a new pedagogical goal for the group that could also provide exposure for the organization. The Center had endured funding losses due to significant state budget cuts and a drop in donor contributions. This was a cost-effective way to proceed and one commonly pursued by social and cultural nonprofit organizations that find educational programs to be attractive to funding agencies.

At the same time, since much of the funding available to nonprofit agencies was targeted at "new" projects and not at sustaining established programs, not to mention operating expenses, there was a strong incentive, if not a necessity, to repackage existing activities or programs into new deliverables. Not only would the AT&T grant-support the project and the HYC itself, it could also be tapped to funnel portions to other vital areas of the organization where funding holes urgently needed to be plugged. Having a small group of youth produce a PSA was going to be a lot easier and more cost-efficient for The Center to execute than a coordinated, multi-faceted, multiple-day workshop for youth across the county.

The specific date for the launch was significant, as it marked the *National Day of Silence*, an annual day of action founded and promoted by the Gay, Lesbian and Straight Education Network (GLSEN). On this day, as per GLSEN's directive, queer youth and allies are encouraged to perform some form of self-silencing as a way to "call attention to the silencing effect of anti-LGBT bullying and harassment in schools." This typically takes the form of silent marches, performances, and other activities that enhance the visibility of queer youth. In the 15 years since the day was first observed, April 20 has become something of a national holiday to honor the lives of queer youth. Initially established as a way to

Negotiating Expression 123

raise awareness of perceived common wounds in the queer youth community, it is also often used by educational institutions that support youth as something of a catch-all day for celebrating queer youth. For queer-specific educational and community groups that serve youth, there is an expectation that they will host activities to mark the day. Historically, the Hillcrest Youth Center has organized a silent march on April 20. For 2012, the administrators decided to also kick off a county-wide initiative meant to educate and empower queer youth and their allies about their legal and civil rights and the resources available to them. The public service announcement was at the center of this initiative.[3] It could be circulated like the literature typically distributed to advertise The Center's youth resources, and became a visible representation of The Center's investment in queer youth—a calling card of sorts.

Asking youth to use video to respond to the phenomenon of anti-gay-bullying was a strategy for addressing and working to solve the problem. To the administrators, the program seemed to have tremendous potential reach. Once their PSA was posted and circulated online, they hoped that its impact would extend beyond both the HYC's constituents and San Diego queer youth. Because of my already-established role at the HYC, I was asked to convey the assignment to the group.

As the facilitator, I could see some of the potential benefits that the administration was suggesting, and understood how popular discourses of digital media pedagogy made this seem unproblematic. At the same time, I was aware that this approach eclipsed some of the objectives that shaped my approach to teaching the workshop and certainly imagined the needs and desires of the youth participants in ways that were not derived from interaction with them. So when I agreed to guide the PSA production I understood that it would entail additional work and rethinking to merge the needs of the administration with my goals of developing a pedagogy that emerged from sensitivity to my interactions with the youth.

The simple, message-bound form of the PSA made it an especially good first project for new makers, so, from a pedagogical perspective, it seemed like an appropriate challenge for the group, who up until this point had been primarily learning how to use equipment while becoming familiar with the language of cinema through screenings, production exercises, and discussions. The workshop participants had not yet tried to make a complete video, so why not have the first one be one that was commissioned by our parent organization? For all of us in the *Changing Reels* media workshop, the PSA assignment felt like an honor and a responsibility to the community. The PSA gave us a focused objective and suggested an avenue for continued support from The Center. It was important that our workshop goals be as closely aligned with the direction of The Center as possible. We shared a dedication to supporting the youth and to helping them to forge

124 *Negotiating Expression*

connections within the greater queer community. Our location within the space of the youth center was one way in which we had already established this link; producing the PSA at our parent organization's request was another important way to enact our affiliation and unified commitments. The youth could presumably go on to make projects of their choosing once the PSA was complete.

Together the program administrators and I decided that the project prompt should be conveyed to the youth in an open-ended way so as to encourage creativity and original expression. The only requirements were that the final video should be under six minutes long (a standard maximum length for viral distribution and incorporation of video into in-school presentations) and focused on the topic of anti-gay-bullying. The particular message, style and execution would be at the discretion of the youth producers. I also hoped that the youth would take a creative stylistic approach to the public service announcement, and so instead of reviewing other PSAs as an introduction to the project, I engaged them in discussions about their feelings about gay bullying and, for inspiration, screened films and videos that conveyed different forms of anti-gay-bullying messages.

The idea that I could convey a PSA assignment without outlining or modeling conventions of the PSA form speaks to my (and perhaps our group's collective) assumption that PSA conventions are commonly understood. This approach is reflective of trends towards integrating PSAs into activities and agendas with youth where the pedagogical emphasis is on the content rather than the form. My choice to refrain from giving more explicit guidance regarding the video's content and structure was intentional, as it meant that the youth had to articulate their own interpretation of both the issue and the PSA form. As it turned out, their interpretation of what a PSA should contain and look like was very much in keeping with conventional broadcast public service announcements— brief, emotionally triggering, and aimed towards delivering one simple, explicit message. Their understanding of the constraints of the PSA genre actively worked against any desire they may have had to include a diversity of experiences and perspectives, particularly those that were unemotional, complex, or ambivalent about the topic. What liberatory or expressive possibilities are possible when producing within this genre and under these production constraints? If the video production is a form of queer youth empowerment, who exactly is being empowered and in what ways?

Ultimately, the completed PSA was barely circulated, even by its creators and participants, receiving under 500 views in a four-year period.[4] And when they had finished making it, the youth quickly moved on to other projects, including a cooking show, several narrative shorts, and a contribution to two popular comedic video memes. Their continued interest was in play and creative possibility through collaboration more than overt identity-related video activism. Bullying was a topic that never came up again once the PSA was sent off to the administrators.

"Let's Get Back to Work": Production Imperatives and Pressures

Organizing the production process required the producers to take the initiative to structure the use of time and space at the HYC as they considered multiple approaches to completing the video within a limited timeframe. They decided to begin the project by interviewing each other on camera about their personal experiences of anti-gay bullying. The interviews, they claimed, could help to reveal some common themes on the subject of bullying. From there they would determine their message for the video. The filming of these initial interviews would also double as a way for the group to become more proficient in using the camera, lighting and sound equipment. Once those who had agreed to go on camera had been interviewed (three people), they actively sought out other youth at the center to interview. Only one other person agreed, so they began recruiting new people who walked through the door. This resulted in a collection of interviews from an array of teens, many of whom were completely new to the space and didn't know anyone. The teens in general seemed very eager to expand their community and the majority of the group was very sensitive to newcomers' comfort. All production stopped as the new focus became welcoming the person and attempting to integrate them into our activities. The interview tapings became something of an "icebreaker" for the new person and the group, and the workshop participants now found that they had interviews from people from a wide variety of backgrounds, schools, and communities within San Diego.

The workshop group devised a list of questions to ask the interviewees about their experiences of being targeted for identifying as queer. While the interviewers would typically stick to the discussion guide during the interviews, the filmmakers and subjects would often continue the on-camera discussion once the camera had been shut off. They would ask the new person more questions about the stories they had told and would often pick up on details mentioned during the interview to get to know the new person better. Phone numbers were exchanged, and the newcomer often returned the following week as a participant in the media workshop, there to help make the PSA. As the size of the group ballooned, the two and a half hours of workshop time came to be dominated by interviews and discussion. Suddenly there were more people visiting the youth center on Wednesday nights than there had been in a year. Meaningful conversations were beginning to emerge out of the interviews and often blossomed into intense group discussions begun when the camera was turned off. The video project seemed to be helping to enliven the space and enhance communication among the youth. At this point in the production process there were clear benefits that matched the intentions of

126   *Negotiating Expression*

the grant. Yet social connection took time away from our deadline, and at a certain point, as the facilitator, I had to cut discussions short in order to keep the producers on track with our timelines. The expectation of producing a final product imposed time constraints that made it difficult to pay attention to unforeseen issues that might have been valuable to work through, such as what to do when an interview strayed from the original topic or how to compensate for poor lighting or sound in post-production. As one might imagine, this was particularly true in the case of this population of teens because many of them came to the youth center expressly to engage in conversations about their identity-based issues, which is not always best facilitated through production exercises. Yet the interview process itself revealed opportunities to enhance the lives of the specific teens at the youth center.

In his on-camera interview, Michael spoke about the traumatic experience of being rejected by his family. When the cameras were turned off, the group of us moved in closer to Michael to show our support. Other teens who weren't involved in the shoot but had been listening from across the room came to join us. People asked concerned follow-up questions and applauded Michael for his strength and courage. Keisha, a close friend of Michael's, told him that she had never heard that whole story. Michael mentioned that he was especially sad because his birthday was coming up and he didn't think his mother was going to call him. We asked him when his birthday was and a few weeks later, on his birthday, we surprised him with a cake. The interview had clearly affected those of us who were at the youth center that night and provided an impetus for a type of sharing that had apparently not happened there since a few years back when there were weekly "coming out" support groups. At the time of the interview the youth center was primarily a recreational space with very few organized activities other than holiday parties and the occasional Friday night open mic. The post-interview discussion brought the need for more youth support groups (or at least some more organized discussions) to the attention of Jen, the youth center coordinator, while it also helped us to identify some of the specific needs of the youth who frequented the center.

While the video interviews dynamized relationships and interactivity at the youth center, they were inevitably evaluated by the makers not just on the level of content, but on technical merit. Decisions on which interviews to include were sometimes based on sound and image quality and compositional elements. The youth had determined that the first few interviews that had been recorded had several technical problems and were therefore "unusable."[5] For instance, Michael decided to cut his own video from the PSA, deciding that the audio was not as sharp as some of the other interviews.

However, these "unusable" interviews were in fact extremely useful in providing the pretext for the teens' meaningful engagement around their experiences of bullying and harassment. They directly enhanced the level of expression in the youth center. New personal connections were formed and relationships were deepened. In this way, the PSA assignment encouraged youth expression and was, therefore, potentially empowering to the youth (and adults) involved. Yet by virtue of their exclusion from the final cut, these interviews only remained beneficial to the participating youth within the context of the center itself. In this way, the process of making the video and the excluded content probably had more impact than the finished product itself. The finished PSA was the justification for trying a range of communicative practices that enhanced the participants' experiences in the HYC. The video stands more as an artifact of their engagement than a piece of media whose power is readily available to others through its circulation.

Making Editing Choices

As Educational Video Center executive director and youth media educator Steven Goodman has noted, it is precisely during the process of reviewing and logging interview tapes that youth producers become more critical about the content they have produced. In his work with students who make videos in a community setting he found that through discussing what they have shot and where to place their footage in their editing timeline, his students are able to achieve some distance from their subjects, shifting their social position "from being a *participant in the community to a participant-observer* of the content" (Goodman 2003). In other words, the young people gained perspective by holding members of their community up to a "critical light" and comparing the stories on the screen to their own experiences and having to reconcile the narratives with their own. While the *Changing Reels* group, like Goodman's students, certainly struggled to find coherence in the interviews they collected, it became apparent that they were also weighing the experiences of the people in their interviews against the presumed value of creating a message that would be legible within the frame of messages about gay bullying. Despite the variety of perspectives and range of affect represented in discussions about bullying at the youth center, in their edit the group tended away from including more complex stories or a range of ways of representing the issue.

The differences between in-person discussions and their editing choices points to the constraints of working within the PSA form. The public service announcement structure, which does not typically have room for pauses, counter-narratives, and exceptions to a dominant and persuasive narrative, placed particular limitations on forms of expression and representation. These constraints were understood at every level of the production, from the administrators and staff to me and the youth. Though they were never directly articulated by anyone, they were

128   *Negotiating Expression*

reinforced through general discussions of the video's need to present a cohesive, legible narrative of queer youth experience that would resonate across different populations of San Diego youth. This pressure marks a tension between producing for an audience of the imagined public and the intimacy of the production process and relationships that were built around it within the HYC.

"This Will Make Them Cry"

The group had trouble deciding which interviews to include in their edit. Jo, who lives in The Center's housing project for 18–24-year-old homeless queer youth, had taken a camera home with her one week and returned with interviews with several of the residents. The subjects all seemed comfortable in their spaces and answered questions naturally, clearly engaged in a casual rapport with Jo. Most of Jo's interviewees spoke honestly about their experiences of being out queer youth, often touching on the ways in which their queer identities were intertwined with their ethnic, racial, religious, class, and gender identities. The interviewees spoke candidly and, using her instincts, so did Jo, who later nervously apologized to her collaborators for abandoning the interview script.

When the editing group was reviewing the over twenty interviews they had collected during the course of the project, Jo's interviews were often rejected or pushed aside to the point of being forgotten about. This had partly to do with the fact that the production values of her taped interviews (which she shot handheld while she was interviewing) were less strong than those that were filmed at the youth center by the larger crew using professional lighting and sound equipment, but primarily because they were aspects of the interviews that the teens found hard to place in their overarching narrative. A very thoughtful interview with a Latino male was initially rejected by the core producers, who felt that his accented English was unclear, as was another interview with an African–American male in his early twenties whose interview was deemed useless after they determined it lacked soundbites. Similarly with another of Jo's interviews with a Latino male who gave an account of his friend being harassed and threatened by other riders on a San Diego trolley for wearing an effeminate Halloween costume. The speaker used Mexican Spanish slang and references to San Diego gay club culture. The story took some time to tell and the teens found it difficult to cut it down so that it wasn't disproportionately long. They also considered the particularities of the story to be too much of a deviation from the narrative they were constructing and ultimately "hard to relate to."

The teen producers were especially pleased when their interviewees referred to experiences of abjection, because these moments made the harms of bullying explicit. At the same time, they rejected the performance of abjection. Interviewees who wore the signs of having lived

Negotiating Expression 129

difficult lives but were not able to articulate their experiences in ways that resonated with the explicit PSA message structure were more difficult to place. These interviews introduced a complexity to the issues at hand that we were unprepared to fully understand and incorporate into the overall story. They needed context and explanation. Interviews that told stories of experiences of overt intimidation and rejection were determined to be helpful towards shaping the overall story. Stories of incidents, such as one teen being called a "faggot" and having a milk carton thrown at her, and another being excluded from participating in after-school activities, performed an unspoken indexical reference to San Diego schools' recent anti-bullying legislation. The problem of anti-gay bullying outlined in such interviews had already been articulated within schools and the local legislature. The producers, therefore, already had a measuring stick for determining to what extent viewers might interpret the incidents as harmful and worthy of attention.

As I mentioned earlier, despite its impact on the teen producers, the group's initial interview with Michael was not included in the final cut of the video. For one, there were problems with the audio, but the reason given by the youth was that they felt that it didn't directly address the topic of bullying or fit within their narrative arc. Michael had talked directly about his humiliation and feelings of intimidation within his family but not about his experience with other teens or at school. Even though he had clearly found a place in the queer community, he chose not to focus on that aspect of his experience of being an queer teen in his interview responses. They wanted to position being "out" as an antidote to the pain of bullying. Unlike the kinds of stories the teens (including Michael) sought to include in the final PSA video, Michael's "coming out" story was not at all uplifting. His interview was long and included a lot of detail. There were no soundbites. He was directing his interview responses to the small group of intimates sitting around him, not the imagined public that the group was strategically trying to reach. Though many teens and the adults at the youth center were brought together through his story and moved to share our own painful experiences of "coming out," his video interview was ultimately deemed to have little to no value to the end product.

Ultimately, stories that overtly addressed bullying as a teen-on-teen phenomenon, occurring within the confines of school, that could be easily linked to suicidal ideation, stayed in. The teens wanted their interview subjects to articulate the phenomenon, impact, and effects of bullying, but they could not or did not seem to want to place the visible artifacts of pain, isolation, and discrimination that remained in certain interviews unless it came in the form of explicit emotionality. There seemed to be no place for subtle expressions, the banal and everyday. The teens wished to present the drama of bullying in an equally spectacular register. "I want it to be dramatic, you know?!" Michael exclaims. He was determined

130 *Negotiating Expression*

to create a soundtrack to score the video and spent the week combing through film soundtracks he had downloaded to his iPod and brought to the workshop. With his urgings, the group agreed to include an instrumental soundtrack from the films *District 9* and *127 Hours*, films about impossible obstacles, otherness, isolation, and, ultimately, triumph. Michael got the group excited about his choices by suggesting that the music would "make them [the viewers] cry." Michael's choice of music mirrored the narrative arc that the group had chosen for the piece—"I was bullied, I came out, as a result I got support, I'm happy now." While there are certainly many more ways to interpret Michael and the rest of the group's tendency towards this kind of dramatic rendering of the anti-gay-bullying experience, as I am not suggesting that their related choices were motivated solely by genre constraints, what I aim to emphasize is that the team's choices were affected by their presumption of viewers' expectations.

"She Says Exactly What We Need Her to Say!"

Another example of this is when some of the filmmakers advocated for the inclusion of a very long interview in which a 16-year-old female became visibly emotional as she spoke about her best friend's suicide attempt after he was bullied by another boy at school. The teens decided that this video should be included in its entirety because the interviewee spoke very clearly and articulately, and she specifically described an example of teen-on-teen bullying and the impact on the bullied person. In a clip that the group included in the final cut she says:

> There was a certain incident in which, um, a boy wrote on his hand "I love you" to another boy—one of my good friends. And he, of course, didn't mean it. He was just trying to mess with him. But the boy believed him. It went on like that for quite a while. And this boy developed feelings for him and it was really hard to watch because I knew, *I knew* that it wasn't true. I don't know what his intentions were, that bully, that boy, but the results ... were not good. Um [anguished sigh], there was an attempt to take his own life, which was unsuccessful, thankfully. And I've been there myself and it is a dark place. And one of the things that can bring you there is other people's discrimination. And as much as you don't want to let it affect you, it affects you. And it builds up.

The young video-makers were compelled by the potential for the audience to make visceral emotional connections to the topic of bullying through her account. The interviewee had discussed an incident of intimidation and explicitly named it as bullying, and they were so taken by this interview that they wanted to let it run in its entirety for almost three minutes of their six-minute rough cut. "This is perfect! She says exactly what we need her to say!" exclaimed one of the group members. "This is it!" Michael rejoiced. "That, right there. What she says. It could be the whole video. All we need to do is find more people who say some of these things. Can't some of us just get on camera and make the points that need to be made? That would be a lot easier." Heather, a newcomer to the group, decided to team up with Jo to see if they could get Jo to reproduce talking-points on camera. Jo, who had spoken very honestly and poignantly about her experience of coming out to her unsupportive family in one of the first interviews that had been recorded by the group but was rejected because of the poor audio and video quality, now froze in front of the camera. "You guys, just tell me what to say," she pleaded. "This is so weird. I can't talk when I'm *supposed* to say something, you know?"

Their decision to reproduce the moments of sharing and the direct quotes that they felt best conveyed their message speaks to their expectations of form and content, and perhaps their awareness of the common practice of reenactment in non-fiction production. Their approach directly challenges media literacy and empowerment models that tend to emphasize the expressive and liberatory nature of producing. Here I wish to emphasize that the PSA production process should not be conflated solely with youth expression, but instead be understood as guided by some of the same directives that motivate professional production projects.

It is clear that the production was fueled by a range of approaches to the issue of anti-gay bullying and a constant shifting, and often conflicting, group emphasis on engaging with the complexities of the topic of bullying in the space of the center and also generating coherent and appealing media. The goal of executing a PSA video incited deep engagement with the issue of bullying but, ironically, the obligation to produce the video at times placed limits on depth of expression and connection to a diversity of audiences.

Choosing not to Participate

Professional directives become most apparent when resisted. The teen who chooses to be involved in the kinds of interactions that the production process establishes in the community space, who enjoys using the digital technologies that have been brought into the space by project funding, but who is not interested in working on producing videos to be publicly circulated, calls attention to certain productive prerogatives that adults, including me, assumed of youth in this case. The story of 16-year-old Enrique, who started coming to the youth center during the media workshop time weeks after the anti-gay-bullying PSA had been wrapped up, helps to illuminate these concerns.

132 *Negotiating Expression*

Every Wednesday Enrique started off in the media workshop by giving the impression to the group that he was going to be very involved, yet whenever the group began to execute their production plans, he would typically leave the activities to use the computer to take photos or for Facebook chat. He sought opportunities in the discussion to tell stories about his week, but would change the subject when asked about his ideas for projects and acted distracted when others talked about theirs. On one particular Wednesday he ended a story about his day at school by suggesting that he would like to make a documentary. The goal of the video would be to expose how little the teachers and administrators at his school do to address the homophobia he encounters at school. "I want to make a video about bullying!" he says. A chorus of workshop participants responded in what sounded like exasperation: "We just made one!" After months of production on the PSA, no one wanted to make another video about bullying. They had begun new projects and bullying was a topic they felt they had already addressed. But the five or so youth around him engaged with his story and got into a heated discussion. The conversation included two youth who spent Wednesdays at the center but who generally chose not to participate in the media workshop.

Enrique held court as he spoke excitedly about his experience at school. His voice quivered and he talked so fast that he only half finished some of the words. His tone was at once vulnerable and angry.

ENRIQUE: We've got laws about saying things to blacks and whites. Why can't we have that for gay people too? I'm getting sick and tired of being called a faggot. This one girl called me a faggot and I said, "you're lucky I'm not getting up (cause I was sitting with my friend) and go rip your freakin' weave out strand by strand ... seriously, if you are gonna call me a faggot, I'm not going to play around." I got sent to the school counselor and I said "Wait, I get called a faggot and I get sent home but nothing is happening to her? ... if she calls me a faggot one more time, school rules or not, I'm gonna beat her ass. I'll go to county. I don't give a *damn* ... you guys want to lose more money? You want to go broke? Do you want to lose your paycheck?" ...

VERONICA: ... very few teachers actually put down the rules. That's a ...

JESSICA: ... do it Martin Luther King style!

ENRIQUE: I want to get a lot of gay people to go along with me. I want to post it on YouTube where everyone can see it. Then we'll have Ellen Degeneres call us up and say, "I love your documentary, I want to have you on our show."

The group decided that Enrique should use undercover cameras to record meetings and interactions to show that these people "really

Negotiating Expression 133

don't care" about how he is being treated by his peers. He is angry that he was called "faggot" and is incensed that the teachers and administrators don't treat the incident as hate speech and punish the other student. Enrique believes his classmate's use of the word "faggot" should be treated as equivalent to the physical threats he made in response. His idea for a video in which he confronts teachers and administrators appears to be an extension of the anger he feels towards them and implicates them in his experience of feeling targeted for being gay. Jen, who overheard the conversation, offered Enrique legal defense resources as well as information that GLSEN and other queer youth education groups have published that explain what his rights are.

His account complicates the neat story of the passive, enduring bullied gay student that is so often depicted in mainstream media representations of queer youth. His video idea and the complex portrayal of bullying is a radical departure from the PSA that the other teens in the workshop had produced. It centered on confrontation and raised more questions about oppression and blame than it provided answers. It was certainly not uplifting. Instead of raising awareness, as so many PSAs purport to do, this video's purpose was to *agitate*, and possibly even *incite* action. In some ways it speaks of the intersecting oppressions he faces, including being a person of color, learning disabled, having a police record, and occasionally finding himself living on the streets. Overlapping risk factors make it hard to see this as an instance of bullying or evidence of the kinds of experiences that other queer youth are most often reported to have killed themselves over. Enrique's experience underscores the simultaneous pressures of intersectional identity that make it challenging to discern queer bullying from the multiple forms of marginalization and discrimination that bear down upon him.

By the time the issue at hand had been resolved at school a week later, Enrique had lost interest in making his anti-bullying video. He now wanted to make a documentary in which he would interview the mother of a lesbian-identified friend of his who had killed herself. He hoped that the mother would speak out to parents who reject their queer children. The workshop participants were excited about this new idea and started strategizing with Enrique, but soon he was back on the computer with his headphones on, taking photo booth pictures and videos of himself to post online. This continued for several weeks. He would talk for a few minutes of the workshop, each time with a new idea that the group would help him develop, and then, when it came time to plan out the production, he would leave the group and start another activity or simply socialize with others. At the same time, he considered himself very much a part of the media workshop. Enrique, it turns out, wasn't so much interested in making a movie as he was in holding the adults in his life accountable for the pain he experienced when his peers used anti-gay

134 *Negotiating Expression*

slurs against him or made fun of him for being gay. His style of participation was frustrating for me as an instructor trying to help the group produce meaningful work.

Enrique was enjoying and clearly benefiting from his engagement with the workshop. He had a space and a forum to air his grievances and this helped him make new friends and form bonds. Ideas were what seemed to compel him. For Enrique, the video technology provided a means for enacting a fantasy of confronting power. It provided an apparatus and a script for confrontation. At the same time, Enrique never saw any aspect of his projects through. Even with video production and editing equipment readily available to him and a crew of friends willing to help, his interest was in the sociality of preproduction planning. The structure of planning a video required talking about important stories and, in the group, he was encouraged to talk about his life in a way that he was able to imagine would be meaningful to others outside of his everyday life.

In every way, Enrique seemed to be experiencing the benefits I had designed the workshop to provide. He was reflecting, sharing, relaxing, connecting, grieving, expressing anger, and he didn't need a finished video to achieve this. He had repurposed the means of production for his own development and gratification. He was, in fact, absolutely interested in using video technology, evident in his use of the group's iMac computer to make videos for social purposes; he was just not that interested in using them in the ways that had been designated by the workshop structure. Instead of interpreting his choices as a reluctance to participate or be productive, what if we instead value his approach as a productive form of self-making through media production?

The paradox of Enrique's enthusiasm for the idea of using video to address gay bullying (not just through the finished video, but through the act of filming) and his ultimate lack of involvement with video production towards an end video that could be circulated stands in productive tension with the final product of the anti-bullying PSA video that was produced by the other young people. Enrique's interest in using video to talk about bullying, paired with his ambivalence about seeing his project through to fruition, challenged the already-established workflow in the group. His chosen mode of participation made visible a certain imperative to produce that had been tied to my understanding of what made for a meaningful experience in the media workshop environment. Enrique's refusal to produce a video laid bare the vocational directives that the funders, staff, and I had assumed to be a natural part of the production. It raised the question: "What would have happened if the youth who had made the anti-bullying PSA had taken the same approach as Enrique and were not interested in producing or were unwilling to participate?" What if there had been no final product to show the center's administrators, or the community, or the funders? Enrique's participatory style made apparent the extent to which the PSA production had been fueled by the

Negotiating Expression   135

youth producers' professional goals and our collective sense of obligation to the community and our funders.

Enrique used the video technologies in unintended ways. He chose to stand outside of the rationale of the philanthropic economy that had led to the technologies being in that space. No visible or tangible products emerged from Enrique's involvement—no tapes or online videos—and there was probably little impact on his schooling or career opportunities. While Enrique certainly seemed to benefit from the structure of the workshop, his ultimate lack of participation in producing a video stood in contrast to the foundation's imperative to perform conspicuous concern for queer youth. Enrique's experience in the workshop suggests that perhaps where our funders and The Center's administrators had really gotten a return on their investment in the support of queer youth was in the form of benefits yielded through the *process of* making the PSA video rather than in the produced video in and of itself. Perhaps the PSA, meant to be a resource for queer youth other than those at the youth center, was most meaningful in the making.

Conclusion

It is very clear that the PSA project had several limitations. Time constraints, intuited expectations, and external pressures, paired with the hegemony of mainstream discourses regarding bullying and queer identity, seemed to over-determine the project from the start.

The production of the PSA emphasized the difficulty, perhaps even the impossibility, of making the impact of bullying visible. The video on its own could neither identify the needs of nor mobilize the necessary support for the youth who were involved in its production. What's more, the project made these teens and I complicit in the reproduction of normalizing narratives about queer experience. Examining the youth makers' discussions and negotiations about what to include in the PSA against adult assumptions about the social benefits revealed misalignments between the discourses around the social, emotional, and pedagogical benefits of youth making PSA videos and the apparent benefits for the youth producers. Considering the process of making the video also enables us to see social divisions that emerged that are indicative of larger social arrangements that made some youth more prepared to participate (behind or in front of the camera) by virtue of their background. These dynamics are also rendered invisible in the circulating video, and thereby feed the dominant discourse that media production is uniformly empowering for youth.

Yet while the extent that the finished PSA video in and of itself could improve the lives of the youth at the Hillcrest Youth Center and beyond is unclear, the *process* of making the PSA helped to open up a mode of sociality and intersubjectivity among the participants that had not been as

136 *Negotiating Expression*

available through other uses of digital media in the workshop or through other activities at the youth center.

The goal of producing together encouraged the HYC youth to engage in a level of sociality that had not formerly existed there outside of the organized discussion groups. In their off-screen discussions and nego-tiations over which content to include, the youth identified tools for imagining and working towards an understanding of what "gets better" and a resistance to the mainstream anti-gay-bullying discourse. Having the goal of creating a semi-professional quality video *product*, designed for online and DVD distribution, served the important function of giving some of the youth at the center a shared focus. But this focus should not be automatically taken as proof of the teens' investment in addressing anti-gay bullying. Nor should the PSA text itself be taken as evidence of catharsis among the youth who participated in its making. AT&T had funded The Center to promote youth expression and connection through the production of a PSA, but the PSA itself should not be mistaken for the evidence of that expression. It is important to understand the PSA pro-duction as not simply an outlet for youth expression, or as an opportunity to teach and reinforce technical skills, or even as the key framework for engaging youth in social issues; we must think of how all of these factors are intertwined and how they are impacted by external and structural factors. The making of the PSA prompted an opening to a much larger conversation among the youth about the phenomenon of bullying and the range of social factors that contribute to low self-esteem, suicidal ideation, and the other effects of humiliation, rejection, and intimidation that AT&T and The Center sought to address through their initiative. Even Enrique's choice not to engage in the production itself points to the potential personal value and political potency of ideation and process over product. Ultimately, play, imagination, performance, and commu-nication were the outcomes of the grant's investment, not the particulars that were made visible in the video.

Notes

1 All names have been changed to protect the identities of the participants.
2 Start-up support came from the Collective Voices Foundation out of Pasadena, California. The Foundation covered incidentals, such as tapes and batteries, weekly snacks, Final Cut Pro software, and a new iMac for the group. For more information about Collective Voices, see www.collectivevoices.org. The University of California, San Diego Department of Communication also provided a loaner computer and their Media Center provided loaner cameras and audio recording equipment. California State University, San Marcos also generously loaned HD camera and lighting equipment for several of the group's video shoots.
3 In the grant, The Center administrators described the program as follows: "The San Diego LGBT Community Center will seek to enhance the educational experience and involvement of LGBT high school students between the ages

of 14 and 18 working with them to design and execute proven campus-based intervention strategies, including training and education, policy mapping, modeling and the use of film and social media to produce and broadcast a Public Service Announcement which will serve as an anti-bullying resource for students."

4 Over a 4-year period (2012–2016), the video had garnered only 458 views.

5 Some of the causes of compromised video and audio quality had to do with the fact that the youth center was a less-than-ideal setting to conduct interviews. The electrical outlets needed to plug in adapters and lights were located behind heavy furniture and the giant television and it takes a person who is both brave and of slight physique to burrow behind things in order to plug in the equipment. Michael was the only one who fit these requirements, so set-up generally took twice the time it would in a location that has been set up for production. Everyone sat back and watched Michael carefully string the cords along the wall. He grimaced as he performed this specialized task on our behalf. Another challenge to production quality was our lack of ability to adjust and reposition the overhead lights or to turn them on independently of each other. There were only two choices for lighting—on or off. This left the youth with the option of shooting with a very controlled lighting set-up or in a flood of fluorescent lights that made the video appear grainy and the people on camera look jaundiced. There were also noise constraints. A security alarm beeped every time the front door was opened, and often the people entering were talking loudly to each other. And when a new teen entered the youth center for the first time, everyone stopped what they were doing to greet them.

Reference

Goodman, Steve. 2003. *Teaching Youth Media: A Critical Guide to Literacy, Video Production, & Social Change*. New York: Teachers College Press.

Conclusion
Out of the Closet and into the Tweets

"Let's all put an end to bullying, right now! ... 5, 6, 7, 8 ...!" A tracking shot moves through a school, revealing its entire student body singing, dancing, and holding signs, like one that reads "bully-free zone." At first, the ensemble video suggests a utopian collaboration in which bullies and bullied kids have come together under one auto-tuned pop anthem. But when the song reaches the chorus, the lyrics take a dark turn:

> Let's all get together and make bullying kill itself! Bullying is an ugly thing, let's shove its face in the dirt, and make bullying kill itself!
> (*South Park*, "Butterballs" episode [2012])

In describing an aggressive and violent approach to abolishing bullying, and by personifying "bullying" itself, confusion emerges over what it is, exactly, that the students are hoping to eradicate.

This video appeared in 2012, not on YouTube, but rather in an episode of the popular cartoon television comedy *South Park*. The episode pushes the popular phenomenon of youth-produced anti-bullying videos to its ironic limits, and, like all good satire, successfully identifies some of the inherent contradictions and ironies of the cultural practice it mocks—in this case, schools, community programs, and philanthropic organizations encouraging youth to produce message-oriented videos as a means to directly address experiences of intimidation and abjection. The students' video is frivolous and hypocritical, pointing to what the creators have clearly deemed an ineffective genre.

As their video gains attention and goes viral within the show's universe, it becomes the conduit for students, educators, anti-bullying organizations, and the media to perform their investment in the issue of bullying. We learn that this has much more to do with adults fulfilling administrative and funding objectives and performing a kind of image management through their public expression of concern than it does with finding the most effective way to change the circumstances of the most vulnerable kid (whose bruises prompted action in the first place). Ultimately, that student is no safer than he was at the beginning of the

Out of the Closet and into the Tweets 139

Figure C.1 Elementary students produce an anti-bullying music video in the *South Park* episode, "Butterballs", 2012

episode. If anything, the media circus around the viral video that erupts further distracts and distances the South Park community from recognizing the source of his suffering, which turns out to be domestic and not related to the school at all.

Here *South Park* throws into sharp relief the failures of the media empowerment approach. We are left to wonder about the imperative for young people to participate in media production in educational settings the first place, and to seek out the complexities and nuance binding youth media participation, voice, and power.

While bullying is not the first social issue to be associated with a generation of American youth (drunk driving and drug use, for example, dominated educational and public health discourse in the 1980s and '90s respectively), it is perhaps the first to be articulated, and in some respects experienced, through online media. In particular, producing viral video—media produced expressly for intensive online circulation through networked publics—has become a central method through which people have performed their concern and investment in the issue of bullying. Indeed, as the *South Park* episode so deftly underscores, youth-produced anti-bullying videos may ultimately function more to propel the discourse of anti-bullying then to effectively resolve the issue(s) they aim to address.

With the expansion of bullying discourse, the focus shifted away from core concerns about the needs of queer youth that initiated the movement in the first place, and towards the publicity of a *movement*, thus further abstracting and reifying their specificity. These prerogatives interfere with the emancipatory intent of the videos, ultimately advancing a type of queer visibility that threatens to sanitize or distract from the more urgent concerns of queer youth. This includes issues such as homelessness, domestic violence, depression, and forms of intimidation and humiliation

Figure C.2 "Who Do U Think U R?" Cypress Ranch High School Anti-Bully Lip Dub, YouTube video still

that are not as legible within anti-bullying discourse, which focuses primarily on in-school acts of bullying.

Throughout this book I have sought to complicate notions of *empowerment* as a viable process and a desirable social and pedagogical goal. Through digital media production, young people are often expected to produce their own conditions of freedom and develop core educational competencies through their (identity-based) expressions and connections. Support for the media empowerment approach is rooted in historically situated assumptions about the so-called *millennial* generation's comfort and ability to have meaningful interactions with and through digital technologies.

Using a feminist critical pedagogy approach to highlight the ways that calls for authentic young voices assume what Mimi Orner has called "essentialist epistemological positions," I have argued that digital youth empowerment often shifts the responsibility of acquiring a sense of power onto the youth themselves through the presumed benefits of their technology use (Orner 1992). Despite the growing number of scholars and educators critiquing the *digital natives* framework and calling for more in-depth qualitative studies of how youth use digital technology, large-scale efforts to support young people continue to foreground digital media technology use (Brown and Czerniewicz 2010; Helsper and Eynon 2010; Corrin, Bennett, and Lockyer 2013). While there is little doubt that it is common for teens to use digital technologies for creative and personal expression and connection, my study shows that when media production is prompted by adult educators, community leaders, and philanthropists with the express purpose of empowering young participants, what they produce becomes highly structured in ways that do not necessarily correspond with what might be most pleasurable, meaningful, or beneficial

Out of the Closet and into the Tweets   141

for them. We must, therefore, continually ask: where is power located in media empowerment projects? How is empowerment being defined, and by whom?

Despite the undeniable ubiquity of digital media technology use among teens, it remains highly problematic for us to automatically equate their digital media use with their empowerment. As we saw in the case study in Chapter Four, the participants' desire to create a video that would be legible to the funders and in keeping within mainstream queer rights discourse paradoxically obscured their actual lived experiences and perspectives. This made it more difficult for the adults who sought to empower them to identify their needs and determine methods of support. Hence, when we uncritically embrace the concept of media empowerment, we risk overlooking nuanced pedagogical relationships and institutional contexts that shape what youth produce and, more importantly, what the producers learn about themselves, each other, and the work they are engaged in.

The media empowerment framework becomes particularly concerning when applied to identity-based projects like the *It Gets Better Project* and the many similar online anti-gay-bullying PSA campaigns that followed suit. These projects not only interpellate queer youth into fixed, homogenous, subject positions, they also conflate video visibility with action, expression, and power. The rationale behind these viral video efforts is bolstered by what Peggy Phelan calls the "ideology of the visible," in which subjects' visibility is considered evidence of their acquisition of power. When we assume that visibility equals power, we risk "erase[ing] the power of the unmarked, unspoken, unseen" (Phelan 1993, 7). There is then the risk of the further marginalization of subjectivities and practices that do not neatly align with dominant conceptions of mainstream queer identity. Digital media therefore becomes the means by which to claim or defend identities and identity categories. Exclusions and oppressions are represented as necessarily identity-based, reinforcing the idea that young people simply need to be brave about defending those identities, rather than working to understand their places within larger histories and structures of oppression.

Truly supporting queer and other marginalized youth may require us to divest ourselves of grand media empowerment projects and campaigns in order to focus on learning about what they need in order to feel supported in their particular communities, schools, and homes. We must also take into account that when youth produce digital media as part of larger campaigns that have celebrity tie-ins or opportunities for some level of fame (even just local prominence), there are incentives in place for them to reproduce particular styles and messages. In this way, forms of *political visibility* entwine with forms of *publicity*, ultimately diluting the power of building support for marginalized subject positions and the structures and conditions that contribute to subjugation. We might

142 *Out of the Closet and into the Tweets*

imagine that any youth production made in relationship to the campaign will inevitably always be in play with the foundation's particular style, messaging strategy, and political and ideological framing. The personal is no longer (just) political; it is also good public relations.

Is it possible to encourage forms of self-expression among youth that have little to do with how they define their identities or how they are defined by others? What are the possibilities if, instead of encouraging youth to produce media along identity lines, or presuming that they will want to make videos about issues that concern them, we orient them towards open-ended forms of creativity? Might we reframe digital media empowerment as the connections, intersubjective exchange, and reflection made possible during the process of production, *regardless of what kind of media is produced*?

Up to this point, I have advocated for determining new pedagogies of youth media production in the context of marginalized youth empowerment. But what does such a pedagogical approach look like? How might we extend this idea past the pages of this book towards actionable change? I offer four concrete suggestions.

The first is on the level of theorization. While scholarship in digital media studies and education studies is increasingly concerned with studying how youth utilize digital media technologies towards civic action and self-empowerment, what scholars mean by *civic action* and *empowerment* is often unspecified, particularly in relation to broader historical and political constructs that have a bearing on the unique experiences of youth at the margins. Interdisciplinary research is especially needed to best understand contemporary youth media use and its effects. As José Van Dijck has argued, agency in the age of digital media "can no longer be assessed from one exclusive disciplinary angle as the social, cultural, economic, technological and legal aspects of UGC [user-generated content] sites are inextricably intertwined" (Van Dijck 2009, 55). We must come prepared with complex and appropriate methodologies that "combine empirical research of users' activities, motivations, status and intentions with contextual analyses charting techno-economic aspects of media use" (Van Dijck 2009, 55). Only then can we fully attend to the complexities of youth media production at this point in our media history, including the possibilities for networked publics, personal empowerment, and new political and social formations. A good place to start is by supporting interdisciplinary collaborative research directed towards the study and practice of digital media pedagogy that actively recruits and incorporates practitioners and theorists at the margins. One strong example of this is The Digital Pedagogy Lab, which offers a host of scholarly and practical tools and financial support to people whose "voices are not always heard in education … perspectives not always visible at other education and technology conferences" (www.digitalpedagogylab.com/join-digital-pedagogy-lab-2018-fellow/).

"Media production pedagogy" has long been synonymous with video and film production and often becomes standard fare for educational programming both within schools and in out-of-school contexts. Yet the creation of memes, vlogs, blogs, vines, Twitch videos, selfies, and other habitual media have become integral to youth culture and foundational to new forms of involvement in social, political, and economic life (Chun 2016; Kahne, Middaugh, and Allen 2015; Jenkins et al. 2016). As Jonathan Alexander (2002) argues, it is important to look to these media as important sites of queer youth connection and expression to account for the multiple forms of everyday media production through which young people may actually be experiencing forms of personal liberation—perhaps in ways that are difficult to make visible or articulate. As Avery Dame (2016), Maggie MacAuley and Marcos Moldes (2016), and Parisa Zamanian (2014) have illustrated, the affordances of forms of social media are integral to how queer youth utilize contemporary media, not just for self-representation but as platforms for debating and determining the lexicon and imagery with which to represent diverse experiences and identities, or, as Dame calls it, "ontological practice." It has also provided queer youth with the opportunity to follow more mainstream queer and trans celebrities and identify—and even sometimes *become*—queer microcelebrities themselves (Hogan 2015), such as underground filmmaker Samuel Shanahoy (@teeveedinner).

As Wendy Chun warns, communicating through any networks involves risks through unintended exposure to people outside of the media producer's intended audience. Networks are leaky, and acting privately in public often leads to getting "caught." She explains that this is symptomatic of networks which work "by exposing YOU, by making YOU vulnerable, so that there can be a 'we,' again however inoperative, however YOUs, to begin with" (2016, 164). Alexander Cho (2015) has also shown how social media like Facebook can have devastating consequences for queer youth, particularly youth of color, due to the "design bias of default publicness." For this reason, queer youth have gravitated to platforms like Tumblr for expression, self-care, and political engagement. But Tumblr is not necessarily a queer utopia either. Parisa Zamanian's (2014) ethnography describes the phenomenon of "Tumblr queers," a term that is used to identify a collective counter-public, but is also a title "thrust upon others" who are "radical, more sensitive, more argumentative" and perceived as annoying and overly involved on the site. In a similar vein, Dame, MacAuley, and Moldos warn of the ways in which being open and legible online makes non-normative identities more visible to the state and the market, but they also see opportunities for resistance to the ways in which the media structures queer users within systems of meaning—for instance, debating the ways in which transgender tags appear on Tumblr in posts that are offensive (Dame 2016) or by making non-normative identities more legible through the

144 *Out of the Closet and into the Tweets*

existing affordances of the site, such as engaging with Facebook's "real names" policy (MacAuley and Moldos 2016). This extends to using "the site against itself and surveillance culture generally, demonstrating possibilities for resistance" (Shaw and Sender 2016).

A related mode of queer youth media production that is useful, but possibly harder to study, is queer youth contributions to online video memes. Participation in video memes is a way in which queer youth creatively reimagine existing videos, and in doing so identify both stereotypes and shared perspectives and experiences. According to Limor Shifman, "mimetic videos invite participants to creatively respond to existing videos through innovation of existing features of the original video," a structure of participation that "lures extensive creative user engagement in the form of parody, pastiche, mash-ups or other derivative work." Shifman has described mimetic videos as "the building blocks of complex cultures, intertwining and interacting with each other" (Shifman 2012). For example, a meme that became popular in early 2012 emerged from a video called "Shit Girls Say" (Hyland and Shepherd 2011) in which a white woman played by a male actor is shown in micro-scenes performing stereotypical white female behaviors and speech. This was followed by such videos as "Shit White Girls say ... to Black Girls," (chescaleigh 2012), in which a black woman performs a variety of white women making racist remarks to her. This meme was picked up across many queer youth communities, who subsequently made videos that creatively innovated and personalized the clip. Some of the videos that are part of this meme include the queer-youth-produced "Shit Straight Girls say to Lesbians" (Scarcella 2012) or "Sh!t People ask Trans Guys" (shabbamitsnoah 2015).

Taking selfies is another form that involves an active "grabbing" of media in a tactical and segmented fashion that allows even more opportunity to examine where agency is and is not happening for both producers and viewers (Senft 2008; 2013). The selfie is a gestural image that shows the "self enacting itself" and which, therefore, is helpful in revealing the inherent fragmentation of selves in the first instance (Frosh 2015). Unlike the PSAs and viral videos examined in this book, selfies make visible their constructedness, and, as Senft and Baym have illustrated, just as selfies rose to popularity, philanthropic organizations and other institutions began utilizing them as a method for engaging youth voices and networks (2015). These dynamics allow us to study the interplay between the production of "self" and authenticity in relation to the production of institutional brands and messages. Ephemeral media production enables new modes of queer relations which form the groundwork for identity-based reflection and activism (Wargo 2015). Through taking and sharing selfies and other forms of social media interaction through sites like Instagram and Snapchat, selfies can enable queer youth to design social futures by mapping their own embodied experiences onto space and provide a means for a strategic performance of identity that can address intersectionality and the fragmented nature of the self. Yet as Senft and Baym, and Losh, have cautioned, it is critical to understand how selfie producers might be politically, socially, or economically disempowered by their circulation (Senft and Baym 2015; Losh 2015). Because selfies can be a powerful way to locate oneself in spatial and affective landscapes through framing the photographs, sharing, and tactical geolocation, studying their circulation can both reveal and produce new political formations and understandings (Zimanyi 2017; Wargo, 2015). As the Selfies Research Network elucidates in their online open-sourced pedagogical tools, selfies can be used to invite youth to reflect on the production of discourse, evidence, affect, ethics, visibility/invisibility, and the presentation of the self (www.selfieresearchers.com).

A second recommendation is for more research on the part of funding organizations into the specific needs of the communities and individuals they hope to serve. It is imperative that philanthropic foundations that wish to support youth at community centers like the Hillcrest Youth Center first speak to the youth and adults in the community to determine what their needs (and wants) actually are, involving media teachers in the project design and evaluation process from the beginning. Participatory action research methods can be useful to this end), enabling participants to engage in collective goal-setting and reflection. Inquiry should be collaborative and grounded in local and larger socio-political histories (McIntyre 2000a; 2000b; 2008)

It may surprise funders and administrators to learn that providing digital media production equipment or incentives to produce may in fact be more of an imposition than a blessing for the community, who must then find the institutional support to sustain media-making practice and maintain the equipment. In the case of the Hillcrest Youth Center's production of a corporate-sponsored anti-bullying PSA, discussed in Chapter Four, there were fewer participants in the video production than there were at crafts nights and movie nights that the center put on during the same period of time. With the $20,000 that the sponsor spent to support the production of what turned out to be a marginally circulated public service announcement that only a fraction of the youth at the center were invested in making, they could have housed and fed one of the homeless youth for a year, provided college scholarships, or paid a therapist to be on call.[1]

Needs often do not become apparent until our attention is called to the lack of services in place. This is why formative program evaluation is essential. Media educators are rarely in the room when budgeting and programmatic assessments are made; they are more likely called into the process after budgets and objectives have been set. While they may bring a host of media and pedagogical skills to bear on their work, it is the rare

146　*Out of the Closet and into the Tweets*

media practitioner or educator who has been trained in program evaluation. Community psychologist Lauren Lichty has expressed concern about what she calls "adultist language" and framing that is imposed on youth participants by well-meaning administrators. All contributors to a project, she argues, need to be attentive to their own goals and values rather than seeking particular outcomes that they believe will please funders and other constituents. Empowerment, she argues, "is not pre-defined" and thus we must get creative with how we define and gather data. (Losh 2014). Having media instructors and makers involved in the planning will help determine where media belongs in an approach, if at all. Then, together, all constituents can determine the most appropriate course of action to meet community objectives that will most benefit the youth.

Third, if the goal is to promote expression, we must put aside rubrics, formulas, guidelines, and talking points that impart particular frameworks onto what and how youth produce. Empowerment through digital media may come in unanticipated forms, at unexpected moments. It may be in the outtakes, or in the small victories during the editing process that will only ever be recognized by the youth themselves. Media content may not even remotely resemble the makers' initial goal or be legible as being made by queer youth. A gathering of queer youth might result in a camera being passed around, filming spontaneous interactions. There is no explicit agenda or message, only a clear aim towards social cohesion.

This leads to the final, and perhaps most vital claim of this study, which is that teachers, administrators, and funding organizations must emphasize the *process* of making media as more valuable and important than the final products. One of the major concerns I have raised is the widespread emphasis on finished media products within youth media production pedagogy. I have advocated instead for media practices that highlight intersubjective exchange during the production process as a priority over the creation of specific types of content thought to be empowering for its producers. A completed video, such as an anti-bullying PSA, can be used to *prompt* the production process, but if we truly wish to provide youth with opportunities to experiment, express, and reflect on what they are making, we must be willing to let go of the idea of a glossy (or even just finished) video as the ultimate marker of a given project's success. In the case of the anti-bullying PSA production at the Hillcrest Youth Center, I outlined how the goal of making a video that could cohere with the funders' philanthropic goals to circulate to people outside of the organization placed certain constraints on what could be produced. Examining the production process has enabled me to identify some of the limitations inherent within the liberatory model of video production and the PSA model in particular, while also recognizing the importance of a program development and evaluation process that understands "success" as emerging from meaningful involvement, rather than particular mastery, execution, or reach.

When we look back at media pedagogy practices that were common prior to the introduction of digital media technologies, we can identify valuable approaches to production that may be worth resurrecting. As Alexandra Juhasz's research on the production of community video as AIDS activism has shown, community-based media authorship helped to link queer video-makers to the politics of AIDS in enduring ways that may have ultimately superceded the circulation of the videos themselves (Juhasz and Gund 1995; 2006). We might begin by thinking of the emphasis on final media products as a by-product of the digital age, where in just a few clicks students and teachers can upload and circulate their material. When producing with digital media, there is always an audience online (no matter how small). Prior to digital media, media teachers needed to actively *seek out* audiences and contend with the reality that there were few venues showcasing youth media work. With few people beyond the filmmakers ever seeing the final films, teachers had little choice but to de-emphasize the value of the final media product. "Process, sure," writes media activist and educator Dee Dee Halleck in a 1976 essay about teaching film to teens. "But what about the product? I've got closets full of it. And so do all other film teachers I know. What do we do with it?" (Halleck 2002, 55). Halleck describes the value of the process, which resonates strongly with the connection and pleasure that occurred during the PSA process at the Hillcrest Youth Center:

> The film that came back from the lab never quite captured the brilliance and group energy of those moments. Or even in the editing: it was watching those kids with film draped around their necks, hanging from their knees to grab that close-up shot off the clothespinned improvised trim barrel, and shouting with glee when it fit perfectly. Those were the moments we worked for—the actual film was only a by-product.
> (Dee Dee Halleck, Hand-Held Visions: The Impossible
> Possibilities of Community Media [New York:
> Fordham University Press, 2002], 55)

Halleck's account underscores the potential pedagogical and social value of the production experience. For the community of youth and adults at the Hillcrest Youth Center, and for the funders and administrators involved in the anti-gay-bullying PSA video they made, the value was discussed as being located in the final video. But, as my research indicates, the process helped to open up a mode of sociality and intersubjectivity among the participants in the workshop. What might it look like to shift the emphasis to the *process*?

While digital video contains the capacity for broad circulation, its power lies most potently in its ability to serve as a mirror, an archive,

148   *Out of the Closet and into the Tweets*

and a lens for youth at the margins to see and contend with themselves and each other. Goals must shift to being fully present in the production process, looking together for ways to strengthen bonds and learning experiences more than searching for ways to align with popular issues. It is useful to think of media technology as a catalyst for conversation and reflection rather than as a means to an end. It is an excuse to perform oneself for oneself and to imagine queer possibilities and futures together. But we must also take that last sentence with a grain of salt. Most of the time, it won't feel like radical or reflective work is occurring. In fact, the times that may be most process-oriented will probably be the days that will, in the moment, feel the least meaningful. Take the time to talk about your lives. Consider the stages of production, such as editing sound clips from interviews, as a key opportunity for connecting with the interview's content and the makers' feelings about it. This flipped approach makes way for participants to begin linking personal experiences with the broader, systemic issues that have a bearing on their lives. Centering discovery, joy, making mistakes, and experimentation should be the goal. Yes, those participants who are invested in building their professional portfolios may feel frustrated when your program design clearly diverts from having a finished product, and that is why it is helpful to provide handles and guidance to those people so that they can develop the media product if they choose.

I am not advocating that we should all abandon completed media products in youth media programming. On the contrary, I believe that having goals helps to orient and anchor the process. What is key here is that the project itself should not be the most prominent marker of the success of a program; the weight of the pedagogy should tip towards critical reflection occurring at many intervals in the process. Of course, focusing on the process rather than the product will be frustrating to some administrators, and possibly even the media educator at the heart of the project, if they have been accustomed to relying on the gravitational pull of a premiere screening or other occasions to motivate and inspire youth makers towards an end point. This potential tension can be mitigated by building moments of group meta-cognitive reflection into the schedule, during which participants take account of what they have accomplished and what they are learning together. These are moments to assess the motivations of the different participants, and might lead to the development of different production tracks that meet their interests and level of commitment to seeing a project through to fruition. In other words, there may be a group of youth devoted to working diligently on a project, a group that wants to experiment, and a group that is unsure of their involvement in the first place and just wants to hang out. In identity-related media production these goals should be considered equally worthy. It will never be apparent at the outset which one might lead to a meaningful experience for those involved.

Out of the Closet and into the Tweets   149

If the participants are those who are also hoping to learn or enhance their technical skills in the process, or who are seeking to use the media they produce as an artifact for their professional portfolios, you can still help them to get there by creating standards for technical components or other metrics that you determine together, but these must be carefully separated from whether or not the video's content and message is legible to an external audience. These reflective moments can happen in a large group, but can also take the shape of smaller discussions that result in sharing out to the larger group, or a hands-on session where participants record each other or themselves reflecting on their experiences to date. For example, at the Hillcrest Youth Center we recorded a "behind-the-scenes" video that enabled us to check in with ourselves and each other about how we were feeling about the use of our time together, our project decisions, and our hopes for what was to come in the following weeks. Nothing ever became of the footage—it lives on a wildly-obsolete hard drive that collects dust in my drawer—but the act of shooting created an opportunity for thinking about what we were doing, rather than simply doing it and thinking (or not thinking) about it later.

This is similar to what visual anthropologist Richard Chalfen calls the *home mode* of communication (Chalfen 1987). For Chalfen, home mode artifacts have an important cultural function in the retention of details of people, places, and events; the depiction of kinship and gen-erational continuity; and connections to geographies, goods, and other material signifiers. Home mode media have autobiographical functions—to represent the events of one's own life, and to observe one's image in action, as well as rites of passage functions for seeing one's place in rela-tion to others in the family. These functions are used as performances of membership, identity, and lifestyle, and they enable individuals to produce and circulate their own images, measure them against other images, and to negotiate their place in a mediated culture (Chalfen 1987, 8). Chalfen argues that home movies tend to resemble each other in that they are most often produced without any voiceover, establishing shots, or inten-tional character development. As a result, viewers who are not already connected to the diegetic world of the home movie are less able to draw on its contextual, intertextual, and indexical references. The symbolic world is, therefore, a relatively bound one. For this reason, queer youth videos shot in the home mode are unlikely to be of wide interest unless they include keyword tags that connect them to popular videos. And often concerns about privacy and identifying information prevent teens from overtly identifying their videos as related to queer issues. They may be recorded in queer community centers and Gay/Straight Alliance clubs at school, where youth record events and everyday conversations that they circulate to each other through the site, or the participants may choose not to upload and circulate at all. In home mode videos, life appears to be captured unaware, with little to no context provided for the viewer.

150 *Out of the Closet and into the Tweets*

A video from a youth dance or another organized entertainment event, in which a roving camera records people interacting, is one such example.

Home mode videos are extremely important in the formation of offline queer youth community, as they can serve as a form of symbolic communication that both reflects and coheres invested spectators as integral to the depicted community. Home mode videos, made by and featuring queer youth, provide representations that, like other types of performative videos discussed in this chapter, expands the terrain of queer youth representation on YouTube in ways that indirectly challenge the representation of queer youth as fundamentally affected and overwhelmed by violence and suffering. Rather than didactically speaking about their experiences with bullying, self-harm, and suicidal ideation to an imagined audience, the home mode video seeks to serve and appeal to the individuals and communities who are featured.

The dominant narrative about queer youth describes this demographic as being especially vulnerable to violence (particularly bullying) and suicidal ideation, in part due to the ubiquity and reach of queer youth pedagogical videos like the *It Gets Better Project*. These videos eclipse other types of videos that achieve less visibility online. Yet thousands of YouTube videos created by and for queer youth actively refute this discourse. This is not to say that queer youth contributors to YouTube always produce videos with the explicit intention of providing counternarratives, but rather that the sheer range of content produced, in aggregate, provides a multiplicity of narratives and representations that in effect contradict any attempts to homogenize queer youth experience. We must encourage youth to carefully consider the equation of video spreadability and popularity with expression and empowerment, and invest in the power of video as a form of self and peer communication.

To begin, rather than thinking of the video, like a PSA, as an end in itself, we might instead re-imagine the *process* of making the video as the center of the pedagogical exercise. A process-oriented approach encourages criticality and forms of liveness that can help develop individuals who can be habituated into forming critical communities. Hence, there is an opportunity to capitalize on the fact that youth already "get" the structure of the PSA and that it therefore presents a relatively simple task that anyone, regardless of media experience, can be involved with. One might use the process as an opportunity to work with youth to deconstruct hegemonic discourse and representation. In the case of the anti-bullying PSA at the Hillcrest Youth Center, that would have meant investing more time in discussing the goals of the project and coming to understand where we saw it situated within other circulating discourses. My research leads me to recommend that the PSA production process be leveraged as an opportunity for dialogical exchange and reflection. If we are serious about empowerment, then the first order of business should be reflection, with an eye towards transformation. Encouraging youth to reflect on their

Out of the Closet and into the Tweets 151

media-making choices is a goal that has potentially wide-reaching effects both on youth practice and on their overall critical thinking.

Centering the process of media-making may be most powerfully accomplished by moving away from traditional forms of media production and encouraging youth to reflect on the social media practices they engage with in their everyday lives in tactical and habitual ways, such as taking selfies, sharing status updates, and using memes. As we invent new pedagogies for media production, it remains imperative that we support youth, particular those at the margins, in their delicate movement between public and intimate spheres. We might consider what Chun refers to as "a wary embrace of the vulnerability and leakiness that is networking" rather than a wholesale indictment of networks and desires for intimacy and contact (2015, 106). Youth empowerment, therefore, may be possible if adults help youth to acquire the necessary digital media literacies to enable them to interpret and navigate friendship, desire, intimacy, conflict, transparency, collaboration, and safety in networked online media so as to transform networks into "latent publics" that enhance the potential for participatory politics (Chun 2015). And, perhaps more radically, consider the limits of technology to provide the connections we seek (Turkle 2015) as well as the ways in which youth civic engagement and social life entangles with their "volatile" economic roles as consumers, producers, and data providers (Van Dijck 2009, 55).

Re-thinking youth media empowerment has significant implications for the future of education and activism. Can we cast aside the idea of young people as inherently equipped to benefit from engagement with digital media technologies while recognizing the centrality of those technologies as a method of their communication? If we are able to successfully evacuate the place of *empowerment* as the de facto objective, what other criteria for reflection or analysis might then enter the equation? What if joy or connection or self-awareness was placed at the center? As institutions of higher learning are increasingly turning to online education as a lower-cost alternative to in-person instruction, it is vital that educators and students alike consider the value of the space of pedagogy and the value of learning and communication that happens when students and teachers have the opportunity to experiment, dialogue, and deconstruct materials and ideas together. Indeed, we must think about what we are doing and making. And this is best accomplished through dialogue, reflection, and critical reckonings with the media processes we engage in and promote.

Note

1 One year after the PSA "Finding Strength: LGBT Teens Talk about Bullying" it had been viewed on YouTube only 163 times. Also, contrary to the original plan, it had not been circulated to more than a handful of Gay/Straight Alliance clubs. This had mostly to do with a change in leadership at the youth center.

152 *Out of the Closet and into the Tweets*

References

Alexander, Jonathan. 2002. "Homo-Pages and Queer Sites: Studying the Construction and Representation of Queer Identities on the World Wide Web." *International Journal of Sexuality and Gender Studies* 7 (2–3):85–106.

Brown, Cheryl, and L. Czerniewicz. 2010. "Debunking the 'Digital Native': Beyond Digital Apartheid, Towards Digital Democracy." *Journal of Computer Assisted Learning* 25 (5):357–69. Doi: 10.1111/j.1365-2729.2010.00369.x.

Chalfen, Richard. 1987. *Snapshot Versions of Life.* Bowling Green: Bowling Green State University Popular Press.

Cho, Alexander. 2015. "Queer Reverb: Tumblr, Affect, Time." In *Networked Affect.* Cambridge, MA: MIT Press, 43–57.

Chun, Wendy Hui Kyong. 2015. "The Dangers of Transparent Friends: Crossing the Public and Intimate Spheres." In *From Voice to Influence: Understanding Citizenship in a Digital Age,* edited by Daneille Allen and Jennifer S. Light. Chicago: The University of Chicago Press.

———. 2016. *Updating to Remain the Same: Habitual New Media.* Boston, MA: MIT Press.

Corrin, Linda, Sue Bennett, and Lori Lockyer. 2013. "Digital Natives: Exploring the Diversity of Young People's Experience with Technology." In *Reshaping Learning: Frontiers of Learning Technology in a Global Context,* edited by Ronghuai Huang, Kinshuk, and J. Michael Spector, 113–38. Berlin: Springer-Verlag.

Dame, Avery. 2016. "Making a Name for Yourself: Tagging as Transgender Ontological Practice on Tumblr." *Critical Studies in Media Communication* 33 (1)23–37.

Digital Pedagogy Lab. Last accessed June 15, 2007. www.digitalpedagogylab. com/.

Frosh, Paul. 2015. "The Gestural Image: the Selfie, Photography Theory, and Kinesthetic Sociability." *International Journal of Communication* 9:22. http://ijoc.org/index.php/ijoc/article/view/3146/1388.

Halleck, DeeDee. 2002. *Hand-Held Visions: The Impossible Possibilities of Community Media.* New York: Fordham University Press.

Helsper, Ellen Johanna, and Rebecca Eynon. 2010. "Digital Natives: Where is the Evidence?" *British Educational Research Journal* 36 (3):503–20. Doi: 10.1080/01411920902989227.

Hogan, Healther. 2015. "100+ Queer and Trans Women to Follow on Instagram." Autostraddle, September 11. www.autostraddle.com/100-queer-and-trans-women-to-follow-on-instagram303834/3/.

Humphrey, Kyle, and Graydon Sheppard. 2011. "Shit Girls Say." December 11. www.youtube.com/watch?v=u-yLGIH7W9Y.

Jean, Aymar Christian. 2010. "Camp 2.0: A Queer Performance of the Personal." *Communication, Culture & Critique* 3 (3).

Jenkins, Henry, Sangita Shresthova, Liana Gamber-Thompson, Neta Kligler-Vilenchik, and Arely Zimmerman. 2016. *By Any Media Necessary: The New Youth Activism.* New York: New York University Press.

Juhasz, Alexandra. 2006. "Video Remains: Nostalgia, Technology, and Queer Archive Activism." *GLQ: A Journal of Lesbian and Gay Studies* 12 (2):319–28. www.Muse.jhu.edu/article/193874.

Out of the Closet and into the Tweets 153

Juhasz, Alexandra, and Catherine Gund. 1995. *AIDS TV: Identity, Community, and Alternative Video.* Durham: Duke University Press.

Kahne, Joseph, Ellen Middaugh, and Daneille Allen. 2015. "Youth, New Media, and the Rise of Participatory Politics." In *From Voice to Influence: Understanding Citizenship in a Digital Age,* edited by Daneille Allen and Jennifer S. Light. Chicago: The University of Chicago Press.

Klein, Jessie. 2012. *The Bully Society: School Shootings and the Crisis of Bullying in America's Schools.* New York: NYU Press.

Losh, Elizabeth. 2014. "Recasting the Bullying Narrative," DML Central, September 25. https://dmlcentral.net/recasting-the-bullying-narrative/.

———. 2015. "Feminism Reads Big Data: 'Social Physics,' Atomism, and Selfiecity." *International Journal of Communication* 9:1647–59. http://ijoc.org/index.php/ijoc/article/view/3152/1390.

MacAulay, Maggie, and Moldes, Marcos. 2016. "Queens Don't Compute: Reading and Casting Shade on Facebook's Real Names Policy." *Critical Studies in Media Communication* 33 (1):6–22.

McIntyre, Alice. 2000(a). *Inner-City Kids: Adolescents Confront Life and Violence in an Urban Community.* New York: New York University Press.

———. 2000(b). "Constructing Meaning about Violence, School and Community: Participatory Action Research with Urban Youth." *The Urban Review,* 32 (2)123–50), 2 (2):123–54.

———. 2008. *Participatory action research.* Vol. 52. SAGE Publications, Incorporated.

Orner, Mimi. 1992. "Interrupting the Calls for Student Voice in 'Liberatory' Education: A Feminist Poststructuralist Perspective." In *Feminisms and Critical Pedagogy,* edited by Carmen Luke and Jennifer Gore, 74–89. New York: Routledge.

Phelan, Peggy. 1993. *Unmarked: The Politics of Performance.* New York: Routledge.

Powell, Nicholas. 2011. "LGBT Youth Empowered by Victories." Liberation News, June 21. www.liberationnews.org/lgbt-youth-empowered-html/.

Reid, Roddey. 2009. "The American Culture of Public Bullying." *Black Renaissance* 9 (2/3):174–87.

Scarcella, Arielle. 2012. "Shit Straight Girls say to Lesbians." January 5. www.youtube.com/watch?v=lgHiKx5l1ZA&t=1s.

Senft, Theresa M. 2008. *Camgirls: Celebrity and Community in the Age of Social Networks.* New York: Peter Lang.

———. 2013. "Microcelebrity and the Branded Self." In *A Companion to New Media Dynamics,* edited by John Hartley, Jean Burgess, and Axel Bruns, 346–54. Malden: Blackwell Publishing Ltd.

Senft, Theresa M., and Nancy K. Baym. 2015. "What Does the Selfie Say? Investigating a Global Phenomenon: Introduction." *International Journal of Communication* 9:1588–606. http://ijoc.org/index.php/ijoc/article/view/4067/1387.

Shabbamitsnoah. 2015. "Sh!t People ask Trans Guys." April 15. www.youtube.com/watch?v=J5wwFXamzkk.

Shaw, Adrienne and Katherine Sender. 2016. "Queer Technologies: Affordances, Affect, Ambivalence." *Critical Studies in Communication* 33.

Shifman, Limor. 2012. "An Anatomy of a YouTube Meme." *New Media & Society* 14 (2):187–203. Doi: 10.1177/1461444811412160.

154 *Out of the Closet and into the Tweets*

South Park. 2012. Episode 5, April 11, by Comedy Central. Directed and written by Trey Parker.

Turkle, Sherry. 2015. *Reclaiming Conversation: The Power of Talk in a Digital Age.* New York: Penguin Press.

Van Dijck, José. 2009. "Users Like You? Theorizing Agency in User-Generated Content." *Media, Culture & Society* 31 (1):41–58. Doi: 10.1177/ 0163443708098245.

Wargo, Jon M. 2015. "Spatial Stories with Nomadic Narrators: Affect, Snapchat, and Feeling Embodiement in Youth Mobile Composing." *Journal of Language and Literacy Education* 11 (1):47–64. Doi: files.eric.ed.gov/fulltext/ EJ1061110.pdf.

Zamanian, Parisa. 2014. *Queer Lives: The Construction of Queer Self and Community on Tumblr.* Master's thesis, Sarah Lawrence College.

Zimanyi, Eszter. 2017. "Digital Transience: Emplacement and Authorship in Refugee Selfies." *Media Fields Journal* 12. www.mediafieldsjournal.org/ digital-transience.

Index

7 Questions (video chain), 77–79

access 5–6, 25–26, 28–31, 39; *see also* digital native discourse
Ad Council 90, 92–93, 95–96, 113n8
Adair, John 40
advertising effectiveness 11n4, 95, 96–98
Alexander, Jonathan 37, 143
Alper, Meryl 33
Anna and Amanda (vloggers), 71–72
anti-bullying discourse: use of term, 18n10; pedagogical videos *vs.* performative videos, 79; queer youth suicide and, 1–2, 16nn1–3, 17n4, 79–80n1; spreadability of videos, 14, 18n15, 56, 61–63, 70, 80n2; viral video production, 56; youth empowerment and, 138–40; *see also It Gets Better Project* campaign
anti-drug campaigns 92–93, 95
anti-smoking campaigns 85–87, 91–95, 113nn9–12
authenticity 6, 31, 37–40, 93, 97, 110, 140, 144–45
authoritative voice 41, 85–87, 99, 100, 111, 111n2; *see also* "youth voices" discourse

Baddash, David 137n5
Bakhtin, Mikhail 39
Banet-Weiser, Sarah 4, 34, 49n8
Barnhurst, Kevin G. 7, 26–27
Baym, Nancy K. 144–45
Belonging 24, 48n4, 66, 68
Benkler, Yochai 44
boyd, danah 26, 27, 44
"Boyfriend Tag, The" (LGBTeens) 78, 80n11

Briggs, Charles and Daniel C. Hallin 99
Brynner, Yul 85–87, 92, 111n1
Bryson, Mary K. 35
Buckingham, David 28, 49n8
Burgess, Jean 6
"Butterballs" episode *(South Park, 2012)* 138–39

Castells, Manuel 3, 67
Chalfen, Richard 40–41, 149
Cho, Alexander 143
Chun, Wendy 143, 151
civic engagement: media praxis and, 5, 7, 17n6; participatory media culture and, 42–46; performative video and, 71–72; performative video projects and, 71–72; PSAs and, 58, 73, 75, 136; public voice as civic engagement, 3–4, 42–46, 69; self-expression and, 42–46, 69; social difference and, 3–4; youth empowerment discourse and, 42–46, 69
collaborative practices 5–6, 25–26, 28–31, 37–40, 70–72, 72–79
community formation 70–75, 149–50; *see also* identity formation
Confronting the Challenges of Participatory Culture (Jenkins, et al, 2009) 27–29
Connolly Greg, 93–94
Couldry Nick, 39–40
critical media pedagogy: use of term, 17n7; digital native discourse and, 27–31, 43–44; intersubjective exchange and, 38–46, 146–51; listening-centered models, 39–42; media literacy education, 27–31; media praxis, 5, 7, 17n6;

156 Index

non-professional production and, 111n4; participatory media culture and, 5, 27–31; process-oriented approach and, 16, 125–27, 136, 146–51; reflection, 9–10, 145; social media creation, 61–62, 70–79, 124–25, 143; student-centered media pedagogy, 46–47; Video Intervention/Prevention Assessment (VIA) method, 40–42

Dahya, Negin 34
Dame, Avery 143
Dawkins, Richard 61, 77–79, 124–25, 144
digital native discourse 3–4, 24–27, 27–31, 39, 43, 140–41; *see also* generational relationships
Digital Pedagogy Lab 142–45
distribution *see* online distribution
Driver, Susan 10, 68
Duggan, Lisa 7, 37
Duncan, Arne 1–2
Dussel, Inés 34

Ellsworth, Elizabeth 33
expression *see* self-expression

Federal Communications Commission (FCC) 90–91
feminist critical pedagogy 5–6, 13, 30, 32–38, 44–46, 140–41
Fiercee, Sascha 103–4, 106–10
Fleetwood, Nicole 38
Ford, Sam 18n15, 56, 61–63
Foucault, Michel 32, 36, 80n9
Freire, Paolo 17n7

generational relationships 24–27, 43, 47, 48n4, 66, 70, 72–77, 140–41; *see also* digital natives discourse
Ginsburg, Faye 40, 49n7
"Girlfriend Tag, The" (LGBTeens), 78, 80n11
Girls' Voice Contest (Canadian Women's Creative Foundation) 23
Giroux, Henry A. 80n9
Glee (television show) 27, 63
Global Action Project 75–77
Goldfarb, Brian 17n8, 30
Goltz, Dustin Bradley 66
"goodbye, scale!" (YouTube video) 103–4, 106–10
Goodwill Communications 111n3

Google 11–12, 18n13, 31, 104–5; *see also* YouTube
Gore, Jennifer 30, 32
Gore Commission 112n6
Gray, Herman 33
Gray, Mary L. 10, 12–13, 65
Green, Joshua 18n15, 56, 61–63
Grefe, Lynn 102
Gross, Larry 27, 68, 80n8

"H1N1 Rap by Dr. Clarke" 100–102, 109
Habermas, Jürgen 44
Halberstam, J. Jack 17n9
Halleck, Dee Dee 147
Hauge, Chelsey 35
Hearn, Alison 34
Herring, Susan C. 25–26
Hillcrest Youth Center (HYC): administrative priorities, 4, 122–25; behind-the-scenes video, 149; bullying discourse and, 15, 136; *Changing Reels* workshop overview, 119–22; civic engagement and, 136; distribution of PSA, 137n4; editorial choices, 127–31; empowerment discourse and, 15–16, 135; financial support for, 136nn2–3; normalizing narratives, 123, 125–27; overview of project, 136n3; participation preparation, 135; process-oriented approach and, 9, 125–27, 136, 150–51; sociality, 68, 69–70, 135–36; youth participation, 131–35, 136; youth sexual self-identification, 10–11, 18nn11–12
Hilmes, Michelle 90
Hirota, Janice M. 89
Hobbs, Renee 29–31

"I Can't Breathe" (Laffin campaign) 93–94
identity formation: Black and Muslim girls, 35; home mode of communication and, 149–50; intimate relationship modeling, 79; as knowledge creation, 77; mass self-communication and, 3, 67–68; normalization of, 62–63, 65–69, 123, 125–27; as priority, 146–51; process-oriented approach and, 16, 125–27, 136, 146–51; queer visibility and, 12–13, 35, 65–69;

rural youth, 12–13, 35, 65; self-expression, 15, 38–42, 41, 42–46, 69, 136; self-staging and, 3, 68; spreadability and, 14, 18n15, 56, 61–63, 70, 80n2; strategic essentialism, 13; technical skill *vs.*, 147–49; trans youth and, 77–79; youth narrowcasting, 95

identity management: digital freedom and, 26–27; legibility, 56, 61–63, 63–65, 67, 141; liberation discourse and, 37; normalization of, 66–67; online participation and, 26–27, 48n5; participatory media culture and, 26–27; performativity and, 34; privacy/personal narratives, 35; public sphere and, 143–44; queer scholarship on, 37; safety and, 26–27; selfie production, 144–45; sociality and, 67–68, 69–70, 135–36; survival and, 66–67; transgender identities and, 143–44

Ira, Stephen, 77–78

It Gets Better Project campaign: aesthetic framing and style, 62–63; anti-gay bullying and, 56–57, 59; civic engagement and, 58; corporate support for, 59–60, 64–65; development of, 56–58; identity management and, 63–65, 67–68; legibility and, 63–65; *Make It Better Project* and, 17n5, 80n6; marketing and, 30, 63–65; nonprofit industrial complex and, 56, 59–60, 80n4; normalization and, 62–63; online circulation of, 58, 60–61; participatory culture and, 56, 59–61; production process, 60; queer youth suicide and, 56, 66–67; Jamey Rodemeyer and, 54–55, 65; San Francisco 49ers and, 64–65, 81n7; sociality and, 67–68; viral video approach, 59–61

"It's Time to Talk About It" campaign 102–4

Jackall, Robert 89
Jenkins, Henry 18n15, 25, 27–29, 56, 61, 62, 68
Jensen, Amy 29–31
Jordan, Sid 72–75
Juhasz, Alexandra 37, 105, 147

Kearney, Mary Celeste 8
Kelman, Herbert C. 96
Kennedy, Megan 72–75

Laffin, Pam 93–95, 96, 110
Lange, Patricia 46
legibility 56, 61–63, 63–65, 67, 141
Lessig, Lawrence 104
Levine, Peter 69
LGBTeens (YouTube channel) 71, 78
Lichty, Lauren 146
Luke, Carmen 30

MacAuley, Maggie 143
Make It Better Project 17n5, 47n2, 80n6
Malcolm, Beth 22
Marchessault, Janine 38
marketization 22–24, 30–31, 33, 92–97, 104; *see also* online distribution
Masterman, Len 30–31
McCarthy, Anna 90, 112n5
McPherson, Tara 69
media empowerment framework 2–3, 8–10, 14, 16, 23–24, 31–35, 138–42, 151
media literacy education 27–31, 48n6
media praxis 5, 7, 17n6
memes 14, 61, 70, 77–79, 144
messaging tactics: aesthetic framing and style, 62–63; amateur aesthetics, 31, 100–102, 109–10; amateurism and, 30–31; authoritative voice and, 85–87, 98–102, 110–11, 111n2; nonprofessional production, 96–98; normalization, 62–63, 65–69, 123, 125–27; professionalism, 7, 30–31; public relations, 35, 63–65, 88–95, 102–3, 141–42; resemblance/perceived similarity approach, 86–87, 95; similarities, 96–98; skepticism about, 112n7; testimonial style, 2, 54–58, 92, 105, 108–10, 114n16; vernacular voices, 15, 85–86, 92, 93–95, 102–11; vernacular voices and, 15, 85–86, 92, 93–95, 102–11; viral video strategies, 99–100
methodology: feminist critical pedagogy, 5–6, 13, 30, 32–38, 44–46, 140–41; participatory action research, 8–10; use of sexual identity terms, 10–13

158   *Index*

millennials *see* digital native discourse
Miller, Terry 2, 56–59, 62; *see also It Gets Better Project* campaign
Mills, Geoffrey 9
Moldes, Marcos 143

National Eating Disorders Association PSA Video Competition 102–104, 114n15
Navajo Film Themselves project 40, 49n7
non-profit organizations 2, 22, 60, 92–93, 109–10, 122

online distribution: decentralization/peer-to-peer networks, 34; identity management and, 36; non-market economy sharing, 104; public relations, 35, 63–65, 88–95, 102–3, 141–42; spreadability of videos, 14, 18n15, 56, 61–63, 69–70, 80n2; vernacular voices and, 99–100; viral video, 61, 99–100; YouTube search infrastructure and, 104–5
Orner, Mimi 32–33, 34–37, 45, 140

Paek, Hye-Jun 96–97
Papert, Seymour 48n4
participatory action research 9–10, 145–46; *see also* Hillcrest Youth Center (HYC)
participatory media culture: alternative media production pedagogy and, 16; civic engagement and, 42–46; communities of practice and, 16; context management, 27; critical media pedagogy and, 5, 27–31; empowerment discourse and, 3–8, 27–31; mass self-communication and, 3, 67–69; media praxis and, 5, 7, 17n6; online identity management and, 26–27; process-oriented production and, 16, 125–27, 136, 146–51; sociality and, 67–69
Partnership for a Drug Free America 92–93
pedagogical videos 69–70, 79; *see also It Gets Better Project* campaign
pedagogical *vs.* performative videos 79
performative video 69–72, 75–77, 79, 150
Perloff, Richard M. 100

persuasiveness 11n4, 96–98
Peters, Kathrin 3, 68
Phelan, Peggy 141
Phillips, David J. 27, 48n5, 49n9
Postman, Neil 48n6
power dynamics 4–6, 16, 32–39, 43–45, 48n4, 48n6, 65, 141
Prensky, Marc 25, 48n4
process-oriented approach: critical media pedagogy and, 16, 125–27, 136, 146–51; identity formation and, 146–51; intergenerational alliances, 72–79
PSAs (public service announcements): use of term, 90–91; anti-smoking campaigns, 85–87, 91–95, 113nn9–12; business models, 88–95; civic engagement and, 73, 75; as community collaborations, 73–75; corporate sponsorship of, 47n3; drunk driving campaigns, 47n1, 57, 89, 96, 139; eating disorder campaign, 102–3; Federal Communications Commission and, 90–91, 112n6; flu prevention campaign, 98–102; "Fried Egg" ad, 93; "I Can't Breathe" Laffin campaign, 93–95; limitations of PSA form, 15, 96–102, 127–28, 135–36, 146–51; *Make It Better Project*, 17n5, 47n2, 80n6; non-profit organizations and, 2, 22, 60, 92–93, 109–10, 122; Partnership for a Drug Free America and, 92–93; "ReTeaching Gender and Sexuality," 73–75; YouTube and, 92–93; *see also It Gets Better Project* campaign; messaging tactics
public relations 35, 63–65, 88–95, 102–3, 141–42
public service announcements *see* PSAs (public service announcements)
public sphere: critiques of, 44–45; identity management and, 143–44; latent publics, 151; local publics, 14, 66, 69–70; public voice as civic engagement, 42–46, 69; queer youth vulnerability and, 26–27
Pullen, Christopher 66–67

queer youth suicide: anti-bullying discourse and, 1–2, 16nn1–3, 17n4; *It Gets Better Project* campaign and, 2, 17n5, 56, 66–67; statistics on, 16n1

Rangan, Pooja 33
Reid, Roddey 79–80n1
ReTeaching Gender and Sexuality
  (PSA) 73–75
Rheingold, Howard 42–46, 69
Rich, Michael 40–41
Rodemeyer, Jamey 54–55, 65
Rose, Nikolas 8

Savage, Dan 2, 56–61, 64–65, 80n3,
  80n5, 80n6; *see also It Gets Better
  Project* campaign
Sebelius, Kathleen 98, 102
Seier, Andrea 3, 68
Selfe, Richard J. and Cynthia L. 111n4
selfies 144–45
Senft, Theresa M. 144–45
Shade, Leslie Regan, 4
Sherman, Laura 40–41
Shifman, Limor 144–45
"Shit Girls Say" (mimetic video) 144
Snickars, Pelle 104
social interaction: intersubjective
  exchange and, 38–46, 146–51;
  mass self-communication and, 3,
  67; participatory media culture
  and, 67–69; sociality, 67–68,
  69–70, 135–36
social media 24, 48n4, 66, 68, 144–45
Soep, Elizabeth 37–40
Somervile, Siobhan 10
South Park (television show) 138–39
Spade, Dean 37
Spivak, Gayatri 13, 18n14
spreadability 14, 18n15, 56, 61–63,
  69–70, 80n2
Sternecker, Sascha 103–4, 105–9
Stoddard, Rick 93
SupaFriends 75–77
suicide *see* queer youth suicide

Thompson, Pat 41
tobacco advertising 91–93, 95,
  113nn9–11
trans youth 12–13, 16n1, 77–79,
  143–44

Vaidhyanathan, Siva 104–5
Van Dijck, José 105, 142
vernacular voices 15, 85–86, 92,
  93–95, 102–11; *see also* "youth
  voices" discourse
Video Intervention/Prevention
  Assessment (VIA) method, 40–42

viral video 18n15, 61–63, 65–69,
  79, 80n2
visibility 6, 7–8, 33–34,
  65–69, 141–42
vlogs (video blogs) 70–72

WeHappyTrans project 77–79
Weingartner, Charles 48n6
Worth, Sol 40, 48n6

youth empowerment discourse: use of
  term, 31–32; access to digital video/
  internet and, 2–3; administrative
  impositions on, 146; belonging and,
  24, 48n4, 66, 68; civic engagement
  and, 42–46, 69; conspicuous
  concern, 14, 64, 135; critiques of,
  44–46, 79; limitations of PSA form
  as, 15, 96–102, 127–28, 135–36,
  146–51; listening-centered models,
  39–42; media literacy and, 5–6,
  29–31, 37–39, 38, 48n6, 111n4;
  media praxis, 5, 7, 17n6; Navajo
  Film Themselves project, 40, 49n7;
  power dynamics and, 4–6, 16,
  32–39, 43–44, 48n4, 48n6, 65,
  141; Video Intervention/Prevention
  Assessment (VIA) method, 40–42;
  see also media empowerment
  framework; "youth voices"
  discourse
"youth voices" discourse: audience
  and, 40–42; authenticity, 31, 37–40,
  93, 97, 110, 140, 144–45; black
  and Muslim media producers, 35;
  civic engagement and, 42–46, 69;
  collaboration and, 38–39; digital
  native discourse and, 43–44;
  empowerment discourse and,
  22–24, 33–35; liberatory
  educational discourse and, 17n7,
  18n12, 32–33, 35–37, 47, 124, 134,
  146; Nicaraguan media makers, 35;
  public participation and, 42–46, 69
YouTube platform: bullying/
  suicide ideation and, 71–72;
  business model, 31, 102, 103,
  104–6; democratic nonprofessional
  engagement and, 87, 97–103;
  It Gets Better Project channel,
  2, 54, 57–59, 66, 80n7, 150;
  LGBTeens channel, 71–72, 78;
  as mass self-communication
  platform, 3, 27, 31, 65, 66, 67–68,

87, 110–11, 113n13; National Eating Disorders Association PSA Video Competition, 102–4, 114n15; performative queer youth publics and, 66, 67–68, 69–72, 80n10, 150; *ReTeaching Gender and Sexuality* campaign, 73–75; search engine, 102, 103, 104–6, 105–6; "SupaFriends," 75–77; user-generated content dissemination, 70, 95, 97, 102–3, 104, 105–6; youth-produced PSA contests, 47n3

Zamanian, Parisa 143